90 DAYS TO SUCCESS AS A PROJECT MANAGER

Paul Sanghera, Ph.D.

Course Technology PTR
A part of Cengage Learning

COURSE TECHNOLOGY
CENGAGE Learning™

Australia, Brazil, Japan, Korea, Mexico, Singapore, Spain, United Kingdom, United States

COURSE TECHNOLOGY
CENGAGE Learning™

90 Days to Success as a Project Manager
Paul Sanghera, Ph.D.

Publisher and General Manager, Course Technology PTR:
Stacy L. Hiquet

Associate Director of Marketing:
Sarah Panella

Manager of Editorial Services:
Heather Talbot

Marketing Manager:
Mark Hughes

Acquisitions Editor:
Mitzi Koontz

Project Editor/Copy Editor:
Cathleen D. Small

Editorial Services Coordinator:
Jen Blaney

Interior Layout Tech:
Bill Hartman

Cover Designer:
Luke Fletcher

Indexer:
Sharon Shock

Proofreader:
Melba Hopper

For product information and technology assistance, contact us at **Cengage Learning Customer & Sales Support, 1-800-354-9706**

For permission to use material from this text or product, submit all requests online at **cengage.com/permissions** Further permissions questions can be e-mailed to **permissionrequest@cengage.com**.

All trademarks are the property of their respective owners.

Library of Congress Control Number: 2008935222

ISBN-13: 978-1-59863-869-1

ISBN-10: 1-59863-869-6

Course Technology, a part of Cengage Learning
20 Channel Center Street
Boston, MA 02210
USA

Cengage Learning is a leading provider of customized learning solutions with office locations around the globe, including Singapore, the United Kingdom, Australia, Mexico, Brazil, and Japan. Locate your local office at: **international.cengage.com/region**.

Cengage Learning products are represented in Canada by Nelson Education, Ltd.

For your lifelong learning solutions, visit **courseptr.com**.

Visit our corporate Web site at **cengage.com**.

Printed in Canada
1 2 3 4 5 6 7 11 10 09

To
Each stakeholder of
The Human Genome Project
Who contributed to its success

Acknowledgments

Each time I get a book published, I re-learn a lesson that transforming an idea into a finished book takes a project: It produces a unique product—the book—it has a beginning and an end, and it needs a project team. As they say—well, if they don't say it anymore, they should—first things first. Let me begin by thanking Mitzi Koontz for initiating this project. With two thumbs up, thanks to Cathleen Small for managing this project from the planning stage through the executing stage, the monitoring/controlling stage, and all the way to the closing stage, in addition to her editorial responsibilities.

It's my pleasure to acknowledge the hard work of other members of the team as well: Bill Hartman for layout, Melba Hopper for proofreading, and Sharon Shock for indexing.

In some ways, writing this book is an expression of the project manager and educator inside me. I thank some great minds from whom I directly or indirectly learned about management during my journey in the computer industry, from Novell to Netscape to Dream Logic: Chuck Castleton at Novell, Delon Dotson at Netscape and MP3.com, Kate Peterson at Weborder, and Dr. John Serri at Dream Logic. I also thank my colleagues and seniors in the field of education for helping me in so many ways to become a better educator. Here are a few to mention: Professor David Hayes (San Jose State University), Professor Michael Burke (San Jose State University), Dr. John Serri (University of Phoenix), and Dr. Gerald Pauler (Brooks College).

Last but not least, my appreciation (along with my heart) goes to my wife, Renee, and my son, Adam, for not only peacefully coexisting with my projects but also supporting them.

About the Author

One of the world's leading experts in project management, **Dr. Paul Sanghera** is a manager, educator, technologist, and entrepreneur. He has more than 15 years of diverse project management experience in the computer industry, from Netscape to MP3 and at research labs from Cornell to CERN. Having worked in various roles including director of project management, director of software development, software developer, trainer, and scientist, he has a broad view of project management. Expertise in multiple application areas, including physics, computer science, RFID, biotechnology, and nanotechnology, enabled him to climb the mountain of project management. Paul has several industry certifications, including PMP, CAPM, Project+, Network+, Linux+, SCJP, and SCBCD, and has contributed to building world-class technologies such as Netscape Communicator and Novell's NDS. As an engineering manager, he has been at the ground floor of several startups and has been a lecturer at San Jose State University and Brooks College. He has authored or co-authored more than 100 technical papers published in well-respected European and American research journals. Paul is the bestselling author of several books on science, technology, and project management, including *PMP In Depth* (Course Technology PTR, 2006). He has a master's degree in computer science from Cornell University and a Ph.D. in physics from Carleton University. He currently lives in Silicon Valley, where he runs an information company, Infonential Inc., that specializes in project management and emerging technologies.

Contents

Part I: Starting a Project

Chapter 1
Welcome to the Brave New World of Project
Management 3

Chapter 2
Rollercoaster Ride to Project Management:
Buckle Up 13

Chapter 3
So You Want to Be a Project Manager. 35

Chapter 4
Initiating a Project 61

Part II: Planning the Project

Chapter 5
Scoping the Project 85

Chapter 6
Scheduling the Project 105

Chapter 7
Planning for Project Resources 137

Chapter 8
Planning for Project Communication. 161

Chapter 9
Planning for Quality and Risk Management. . . . 183

Part III: Executing the Project

Part IV: Monitoring and Controlling the Project

Chapter 13
Monitoring and Controlling the Project Work . . . 277

Chapter 14
Monitoring and Controlling the Golden
Triangle. 297

Chapter 15
Monitoring and Controlling Reporting
and Risks **315**

Part V: Finishing the Project

Chapter 16
Closing the Project: Reaching the Finish Line. . . **329**

Chapter 17
Project Management for Success **343**

Index. **349**

Introduction

> "Begin at the beginning, and go on till you come to the end: then stop."
>
> —*Alice in Wonderland* by Lewis Carroll

90 Days to Success as a Project Manager will help first-time project managers hit the ground running with any project during the critical first 90 days on the job. The book introduces readers to and is organized around the five keys to successful project management: initiating, planning, executing, monitoring and controlling, and closing. It covers all nine knowledge areas of project management: integration management, scope management, time management, cost management, quality management, human resource management, communication management, risk management, and procurement management.

All this information could be very overwhelming for a beginner. However, this book makes it interesting by explaining all concepts from scratch, exploring their needs and their connections to one another and presenting the big picture in a cohesive way.

No previous knowledge of project management is required to read this book. All the concepts are explained from scratch when they first appear. The book presents a cohesive, concise, yet comprehensive introduction to project management.

Project management is both an art and a science. This book has been written with a scientific spirit: Every concept and topic has a reason to be there and is logically connected to its neighbor concepts and topics. Whether your project duration is a few weeks, a few months, or a few years, and whether your project is in construction, biotechnology, or any other field, this guide will help you ensure that you manage the project effectively, efficiently, and successfully, and it will lay down the foundations for your success as a project manager during the first 90 days on the job!

Who This Book Is For

With an ever-increasing need for leadership in business and increasing competition among executives for fewer and fewer positions, developing one's project management skills is a must for survival and success in today's business environment. This book is designed to serve the following audiences:

• Professionals who want to kick-start their career in project management.

• Professionals who are not project managers, but who deal with the projects—such as project team members, project administrators, and functional managers.

• Experienced project managers with very limited formal education in project management or those who need a refresher course in project management.

• Senior managers at corporations, vocational institutes, and other organizations who want to improve their understanding of running successful projects or who just want to add project management to their body of knowledge and skill set.

• Although this book is a self-learning tool, instructors can use this book as a resource for an introductory course in project management.

The book is applicable to any project manager in any industry and will appeal to corporations as a training tool, individuals as a self-help tool, and seasoned project managers as a tool for further development.

How the Book Is Organized

90 Days to Success as a Project Manager tells the story of project management in a cohesive, concise, yet comprehensive fashion. It explains each concept from scratch, logically connects all concepts together into a big picture, connects project management knowledge to real-world experience, and presents the material in a perfect logical flow that makes it easier to understand. It is compatible with the Fourth Edition of *A Guide to the Project Management Body of Knowledge (PMBOK)* by PMI. The discipline of project management, according to PMBOK, contains nine knowledge areas, such as cost management and quality management, and five process groups: initiating, planning, executing, controlling, and closing. Almost all project management books are organized along the knowledge areas and put the emphasis on the theoretical side of project management, at least in presentation. This poses a problem for a beginner in project management who wants to quickly ramp up a career in project management in practical terms and who does not want to get lost in a body of theoretical-sounding knowledge. After all, in the real world, projects are run more along the line of process groups: initiate, plan, execute, monitor and control, and close. *90 Days to Success as a Project Manager* solves this problem by presenting the material in the order of the process groups: initiating, planning, executing, monitoring and controlling, and closing. Because this order of presentation is also consistent with the lifecycle of a project, it therefore facilitates natural learning by connecting to real-world experience.

The book is organized in the following five parts:

- **Part I, "Starting a Project."** Chapters in this Part introduce you to project management, and you also learn in detail how to initiate a project, which includes defining the project and the project success.

- **Part II, "Planning the Project."** Chapters in this Part explain project planning, which includes further refining the project definition and developing the project management plan and the project performance baseline.

- **Part III, "Executing the Project."** Chapters in this Part describe how to execute (or implement) the project management plan.

- **Part IV, "Monitoring and Controlling the Project."** Chapters in this Part describe how to monitor and control the project work to ensure that the project stays on the right track as defined by the project management plan.

- **Part V, "Finishing the Project."** Chapters in this Part explain how to properly close the project, regardless of whether the project was completed or was terminated without completion. This Part also puts the material covered in the book in a nutshell and summarizes what makes projects successful.

How Each Chapter Is Organized

In the first section of each chapter, we establish three underlying concepts or topics that will be explored in the chapter. Each chapter also begins with a list of learning objectives on which the chapter is focused. Most of the chapters start with a big picture, in which I introduce how the topics discussed in the chapter are related to each other. The rest of the chapter delves into the details of the components of the big picture. Furthermore, each chapter has the following features and conventions:

- **Standardize This.** This section summarizes the material covered in the chapter in terms of the project management standard by the PMI.

- **Quick Success Mantras.** This last section in each chapter highlights the key points in the chapter.

- **Marginal notes.** Marginal notes present additional helpful material related to the topic being described or offer additional real-world insight, based on the author's experience, into the topic being discussed. They also highlight points that are crucial and may not fit into the commonsense framework of the section.

- **Success Shot.** These emphasize points that are particularly important for the successful implementation of effective project management.

- *Italics* are used to emphasize terms.

Thank you for your interest in this book. May it help you to advance your career in project management.

With best wishes,
Paul Sanghera, PhD, PMP, CAPM, Project+
Silicon Valley, California, U.S.A.

PART I

Starting a Project

Welcome to the brave new world of project management. Here is project management for you in six words: initiate, plan, execute, monitor and control, and close. The rest is the detail. In order to optimize your learning about initiating a project, you will want to know what a project is and have an overview of the field of project management. You will also want to know what it takes to be a project manager. While covering these issues in this part, I will also define the basic terms and concepts so that we will be on the same page throughout the book.

Chapter 1

Welcome to the Brave New World of Project Management

- Projects Are Everywhere
- Where There Is a Project, There Is Project Management
- Project Management Is Made of Processes
- Standardize This
- Quick Success Mantras

Although project management as a controlled discipline is a relatively new field, the concepts of project and management in one or another form are as old as the struggle of humankind for survival and progress on this planet. Efforts that went into minor and major human achievements, ranging from control of fire by early humans to building modern power plants, may be looked upon as projects. All of us in our personal, family, and corporate lives are always involved in what I would call projects, regardless of whether we name them so. Building the Leaning Tower of Pisa was a project, and so was building a tree house in your backyard for your child. The Human Genome Project was (obviously) a project, but so is writing and publishing an article in a newspaper. Human history on this planet is full of projects, and so is your own life. A secret of success is to recognize the projects in your personal, family, and corporate lives and manage them. It turns out that project management is largely performed by using a set of processes. In this chapter, I welcome you to the brave new world of project management by breaking the ice with three concepts: project, project management, and process.

In this chapter, you'll learn:

- Why you should learn project management
- Project management in terms of timely implementation of knowledge
- Process definition
- The relationship between processes and project management
- The evolution of project management as a discipline

Projects Are Everywhere

What do the Taj Mahal, the Internet, the Human Genome Project, and this book have in common? Projects! All these are products of projects. Even given all the required material and the knowledge, how do people really build such immense and complex structures or systems as the Taj Mahal of Agra, the Eiffel Tower of Paris, and the World Wide Web of the Information Age? How do they determine the sequence of billions of molecules in the human genome? The answer is, again, projects. Through projects, it is possible to build small and big and simple and complex things, and to solve simple and complex problems in an effective and efficient manner.

The good news is that what you may think is your first project is not your first project. All of us have been doing projects, whether we named them so or not. Whenever you accomplished something in your life, you went through some effort that can be called a project. For example, think of the last time you took a course or you threw and managed a party at your home. And how about the efforts that you made to clean your backyard? And to renovate your house? The rule of thumb: Any set of efforts made to produce a specific output can be considered as a project.

See, now you know that your past is full of projects (if only you had known before now!), and currently you are in the middle of several projects. A secret of success? Identify them and manage them.

While trying to sort out project management concepts, always distinguish between a project and project management; they are related but different concepts. For example, the project management efforts are a subset of the overall project work, which also includes activities directly focused on creating the product of the project.

A PROJECT-BASED APPROACH TO YOUR LIFE

Stating the obvious, the simplest and the highest-level definition of project management is *management of projects*. It can be a great intellectual and stimulating exercise to look at your life as a set of projects. Consider each set of efforts that had a beginning and an end with certain results as a project. It could be as short as writing a term paper or as long as completing a few years' long degree program. Then think of some management efforts you put into those "projects" consciously or unconsciously. As you go through this book and learn about project management, rethink the important things that you have done in your life, and think how you could have done them differently to produce more effective results. This way, you will also be able to relate the knowledge in this book to your experience, and therefore optimize your learning.

Where There Is a Project, There Is Project Management

Now that you know that you have been doing projects all your life, and that you are, as we speak, amidst several projects, think about the management side of the projects. All projects need to be managed, and they are managed consciously or unconsciously. If you did not formally manage your projects, it means—with all due respect—that those were poorly managed projects. Yes, a so-called unmanaged project is simply a poorly managed project,

All projects need to be managed—either consciously or unconsciously.

and it is destined to fail or produce poor results. Therefore, the importance of project management cannot be overstated.

In essence, project management is not new. Building of structures such as the Taj Mahal and the pyramids required project management skills, such as planning and coordination, and went through the project management challenges, such as limited resources and incomplete specifications, if not in so many words. This is true even though it's only in the second half of the 20th century that the modern terminology and titles of project management started appearing. Starting from the major defense projects and programs during the Cold War in the 1950s, the discipline first grew within the research labs (think of the Internet project that originated from the U.S. Department of Defense) and defense and aerospace industries. Like the Internet, during the 1990s, project management started spreading out to all industries. It is now generally recognized as a valuable skill set across a spectrum of fields from software to health care, from research to manufacturing, and from genomics to economics.

Don't think that all projects are huge and run by large teams. A project may last for a few days or a few years, and may be run by an organization or by an individual, by one person or by many.

Even though through the whole history of humankind on this planet, we (knowingly or unknowingly) have always been involved in projects, the development and acceptance of project management as a discipline, like any other discipline (such as physics, biology, or engineering), is a relatively new phenomenon. Project management as a discipline has made great strides in the last decade or so; it's rapidly establishing itself as a business practice to implement the business strategy, a profession, and an academic discipline. Training seminars, classes, certifications, and books focused on project management have been mushrooming. Universities are increasingly offering master's degrees in project management, and a few have already started offering doctorates.

As organizations continue to adopt project-based management as an effective and efficient way of implementing the business strategy, the demand for effective project managers continues to grow, and ever more individuals are finding themselves in the situation to manage projects for the first time. The goal of this book is to help those individuals turn this situation into an opportunity.

Project management is such an important and useful skill that it is being accepted and adopted across nearly all business fields and industries. However, it is still true that often project managers are assigned tasks based on subject knowledge or peer relationships, without proper guidelines or training. To add to this challenge, often project managers have little or no managerial authority over the project team members. After all, projects are run in the real world. In this challenging environment, successful execution of projects and professional development and career advancement often hinge on successful mastery of project management skills. Without proper project management knowledge and skills, it will be impossible to strike a proper balance of dealing with people, processes, deadlines, and technology in a cohesive manner to create a high-performance environment.

Like any other discipline, project management also has two sides to it, theory and practice, and you need to master both to become a successful project manager. It's equivalent to learning a skill and then using that skill to accomplish your goals and objectives. When you are learning the rules of a business or a profession, you are acquiring knowledge, and when you are performing business and professional activities, you are doing implementation. Neither knowledge without implementation nor implementation without knowledge can produce effective and efficient results. As illustrated in Figure 1.1, the timely implementation of knowledge generates effectiveness.

> You need to master both the theory and the practice of project management to become a successful project manager.

Figure 1.1 *Timely implementation of knowledge generates effectiveness.*

Project management is all about implementing the relevant management knowledge in a timely fashion. The knowledge required to attain the project management skill needs to be learned before it can be implemented to produce effective results.

So, you have been doing projects and project management in an unconscious way, and this book will put you on the path to doing the same in a conscious way. I'm sure you will agree that doing things in a conscious way generates more effective results. This underlines the importance of learning project management.

The building block of project management is a process.

Project Management Is Made of Processes

As stated in the previous section, project management is all about implementing the relevant management knowledge in a timely fashion. As illustrated in Figure 1.2, the triplet of knowledge, implementation, and timeliness makes a process, and project management is performed through processes: Project management largely boils down to performing a number of processes. A process is the implementation of certain management knowledge at a certain time during the project.

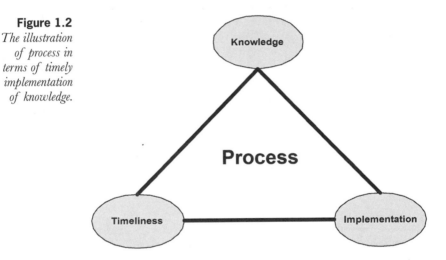

Figure 1.2
The illustration of process in terms of timely implementation of knowledge.

Project management is essentially performing a number of processes. We will derive and explore the more formal definitions of project management and process in the next chapter. For now, think of a process as a set of related tasks with a specific output. Look around, and you will see processes everywhere, not only in project management. For example, when you make coffee in the morning, you go through a process, and the output is a hot, refreshing cup of coffee. If you ever cook in your kitchen, you go through a process, and if you don't cook in your kitchen, you still go through a process to eat out. If you keep looking at your life and the world around you from this angle, it won't take long to see that your days and nights are full of processes.

> **PROCESS**
> In science and engineering, a process is a method that transforms specific input elements into specific output elements. For example, a chemical reaction is a process in which the reactants are the input elements and the products are the output elements.

Standardize This

A *standard* refers to the way something should be done, such as manufacturing a product or performing a set of tasks. Standards are guideline documentations or specifications that reflect agreements on products, practices, or operations by nationally or internationally recognized industrial, professional, or trade associations or governmental bodies. All mature (or maturing) industries and fields have their regulations and standards, and the field of project management has its own.

Standards have several advantages, including the following:

- Standards are necessary to bring some order and interoperability within a specific industry or a field.

- Without agreed-upon standards, all vendors will manufacture or develop products and devices by following their own rules, and there will be chaos instead of interoperability.

- Using the same standards, different organizations in the same field can share their experience in a more consistent and beneficial way by comparing oranges to oranges.

- Standards create a sense of community in a field by creating a common language and processes and ease the way for developing the field smoothly.

An internationally recognized standard for project management developed by the Project Management Institute (PMI) is presented in the Project Management Body of Knowledge (PMBOK) Guide.

Regulations and standards are not the same thing. A standard is a guideline document, whereas a regulation is a legal restriction promulgated by a government administrative agency through rulemaking and is typically supported by a threat of consequences, such as a fine for not following it.

PROJECT MANAGEMENT INSTITUTE

With more than 265,000 members from more than 170 countries, PMI is the professional organization in the field of project management. Founded in 1965, the PMI develops standards and offers certifications in the fields of project management and program management. Its most popular standard is the Project Management Body of Knowledge (PMBOK) Guide, and the most popular certification is the Project Management Professional (PMP) credential. You can learn more about PMI from its website: www.pmi.org.

The project management standard presents project management knowledge at such a level so that it can be implemented in any industry and field. The standard recognizes the subset of the project management knowledge and practices that are generally recognized as a good practice. This means that this knowledge and these practices are applied to most of the projects most of the time, and it is widely accepted that their application can increase the probability of success for a wide range of projects. Of course, the rigor and the details of implementation can vary not only from one field to another, but also from organization to organization and from one project (and project manager) to another project (and project manager).

There are always some best practices—or right things to do—in order to succeed in anything you do. For example, clearly define the problem before attempting to solve it, plan a task before doing it, monitor and control the execution of task, and so on. Project management puts these best practices in action in the form of rules, principles, or processes.

Quick Success Mantras

- A high-level definition of a project: Any finite amount of effort made with a specific output in mind is a project. That means you have been performing projects all your life.

- A project may last for a few days or a few years and may be run by an organization or by an individual, by one person or by many.

- Where there is a project, there is project management. A so-called unmanaged project is only an ill-managed project.

- Project management is all about implementing the relevant management knowledge in a timely fashion. Relevant means needed for the given project.

- Project management is largely run through performing a set of processes.

- A process is the implementation of certain management knowledge at certain times during the project.

- Project management is independent of any specific application area and is applicable to all application areas and industries.

- The biggest advantage of project management is that you get best practices as a built-in feature.

Chapter 2

Rollercoaster Ride to Project Management: Buckle Up

- What Are Projects?
- What Is Project Management?
- The Life of a Project
- Understanding the Project Management Knowledge Areas
- Standardize This
- Quick Success Mantras

What is project management? Because project management is such a vast field, your view and perception of it will vary depending upon area of education, work experience, industry, application area, and roles. However, before you begin your journey to learn how to hit the ground running as a successful project manager, we must be on the same page in our view of project management. The good news here is that project management has by now established a standard that we can discuss independent of any specific industry and apply to any industry. This standard functions as the common ground for all industries, backgrounds, and experiences. To create a common ground for the readers of this book and to make your learning ride smooth, I will briefly define and describe important terms and concepts in this chapter in light of this standard. This will be done in a cohesive fashion so that you can explore the relationship between different concepts and also get a bird's-eye view of the project management landscape.

Project management is largely performed by running a set of processes. Processes are grouped into process groups and knowledge areas. Depending on what task is performed by using a process, when during the project the process is performed, and what management knowledge is used, each process maps to a process group and a knowledge area. So, the story in this chapter is woven around three major characters: project, process group, and knowledge area.

In this chapter, you'll learn to:

- Identify the difference between a project and an operation
- View project management from different perspectives
- Compare project management to management by projects
- Understand the relationships among processes, process groups, knowledge areas, and project management
- Identify the need and motivation for project management
- List the standard project management processes

What Are Projects?

In our individual and organizational lives, we do our work in the form of tasks, assignments, and activities. Which of these can be performed as a project? In other words, where do projects fit into our work? To answer these questions, we need to define a project.

The bottom line is that all the activities at your organization can be classified into two categories: projects and operations.

Defining Projects

A project is a work effort made over a finite period of time with a start and a finish to create a unique product, result, or capability to offer a service. Because a project has a start and a finish, it is also called a *temporary effort or endeavor*. So, a project has two defining characteristics: It is temporary, and it creates a unique product. Let's explore further these two defining concepts: temporary and unique.

STANDARDIZE THIS

A project is a temporary endeavor undertaken to create a unique product, service, or result. The temporary nature of projects indicates a definite beginning and end.

—PMBOK Guide, Fourth Edition

Temporary. The temporary nature of projects refers to the fact that each project has a definite beginning and a definite end. A project can reach its end in one of the two possible ways:

- The project has met its objectives—that is, the planned unique product has been created.

- The project has been terminated before its successful completion for whatever reason.

The temporary nature of projects can also apply to two other aspects:

- The opportunity to market the product that the project will produce is temporary—that is, the product needs to be produced in a limited timeframe; otherwise, it will be too late.

- A project team is temporary—that is, the project team is disbanded after the project ends, and the team members may be individually assigned to other projects.

The temporary characteristic of a project does not mean that the project is short-lived or that it creates a temporary product.

However, remember that the temporary nature of a project does not refer to the product it creates. Projects can create lasting products, such as the Taj Mahal, the Eiffel Tower, or the Internet. The second defining characteristic of a project is that it must create a unique product.

Unique product. The outcome of a project must be a unique product, service, or result. How do a product, service, and result differ from each other?

- **Product.** This is a tangible, quantifiable artifact that is either the end item or a component of it. The big-screen television set in your living room, the Swiss watch on your wrist, and the wine bottle on your table are some examples of products.

- **Service.** Actually, when we say a project can create a service, we really mean the capability to perform a service. For example, a project that creates a website for a bank to offer online banking has created the capability to offer the online banking service.

- **Result.** This is usually the knowledge-related outcome of a project—for example, the results of an analysis performed in a research project.

> If certain work meets the definition of a project, it can be performed as a project. The goal here is to achieve the set of business objectives at which the work is aimed more effectively and efficiently.

Quite often we will refer to a product, service, or result as just "product" for brevity.

Projects are organized to execute a set of activities that cannot be addressed within the limits of the organization's normal ongoing operations. To clearly identify whether an undertaking is a project, you must understand the difference between a project and an operation.

Projects are not operations: If it's not a project, it must be an operation.

Defining Operations

An organization executes a multitude of activities as part of the overall work directly or indirectly aimed at achieving objectives. Some of these activities are to support projects and others are to support what are called *operations*. An operation is a set of tasks that does not qualify as a project. In other words, an operation is a function that performs ongoing tasks: It does not produce a unique (new) product, or it does not have a beginning and an end—or both. For example, to put a data center together is a project, but after you put it together, keeping it up and running is an operation. Building a house is a project, whereas keeping it clean and ordered is an operation.

OBJECTIVES

A project objective is a planned outcome of the project. Objectives must be defined in a way that makes them specific, measurable, and verifiable. For example, growth in revenue is not a good objective, whereas 20 percent annual growth in revenue is. The project objectives must also be realistic, and you must define the methods to measure them.

It is important to understand that projects and operations share some characteristics, such as the following:

- Both require resources, including human resources (people).

- Both are constrained to limited, as opposed to unlimited, resources.

- Both are managed—that is, planned, executed, and controlled.

- Both have objectives.

An operation performs ongoing tasks. It does not produce a new product.

The distinctions between projects and operations can be made by sticking to the definition of a project—that it is temporary and unique. Operations are generally ongoing and repetitive. Although both projects and operations have objectives, a project ends when its objectives are met, whereas an operation continues toward attaining a new set of objectives when the current set of objectives has been attained.

STUDY CHECKPOINT 2.1

Question: A set of activities has a beginning and an end, but it does not create a unique product. Does it qualify as an operation or a project?

Answer: An operation. An operation does the same thing over and over again and does not create a unique product. But you can always define (or redefine) an operation in a limited time so that a set of activities has a beginning and an end—for example, a day of work for a bank teller.

Projects can be performed at various levels of an organization; they vary in size, and accordingly can involve just one person or a team. Table 2.1 presents some examples of projects and operations.

Table 2.1 Examples of Projects and Operations

Work Effort	Project or Operation?	Outcome
Constructing Taj Mahal	Project	Product
Running presidential election campaign	Project	Results: Win or lose; Products: Documents
Developing a website to offer online education	Project	Service
Restaurant employees serving breakfast to customers every day	Operation	Customers served
Setting up a computer network in one building	Project	Service
A bookseller processing customer orders	Operation	Orders processed
Moving a computer network from one building to another	Project	Result: The network has been moved
Studying the genes of members of Congress	Project	Results (of the research); Product: Research paper

A project can result in a product (or service) that is sustained by an operation. For example, constructing Taj Mahal was a project, whereas managing it for the tourists visiting it every day is an operation.

Just like operations, projects need to be managed.

What Is Project Management?

Although project management is industry independent, project managers may not be. They may be required to have a certain level of technical skills in the application area of the project.

The practice of managing projects is called *project management*. To be more specific, project management is the usage of knowledge, skills, and tools to manage a project from start to finish with the goal of meeting the project requirements. The standard project management explored in this book is independent of any specific industry and applicable to all industries.

Project management is not a fashion or a belief system; in order to be adopted, it must offer a solution to some problem. In today's fast-paced global economy, organizations must adapt to a more global, competitive, demanding, and constantly changing business environment. That means organizations must continually innovate, respond quickly and effectively to the changes, and focus their work directly toward the organization's strategy and business objectives. Project management is gaining popularity because it offers the promise to help organizations do just that. Following are some of the advantages of doing work through projects and hence project management. It:

- Optimizes project results by striking the right balance among scope, cost, schedule, and quality.

- Focuses projects on the business objectives and strategy of the organization.

- Makes optimal use of resources, including expertise.

- Responds to the internal changes in the organization and the project, changes in the market, and availability of new opportunities in an effective way.

- Provides useful information for making timely decisions.

- Promotes creativity and innovation by creating an environment of openness and visibility underlined by the importance of communication.

- Helps create healthy relationships with stakeholders through stakeholder management.

These advantages are built into the design of project management and can be harnessed through effective project management. This is because by design, project management is the implementation of management knowledge about areas such as project scope, project cost, project risk, and human resources at the right time during the lifecycle of the project, such as initiating, planning, executing, monitoring and controlling, or closing. In other words, as shown in Figure 2.1, project management occurs in a two-dimensional space, with one dimension being the management knowledge in various areas, and the other being the project lifecycle.

PROJECT MANAGEMENT AND FUNCTIONAL MANAGEMENT
Traditional management, also called *functional management,* focuses on ongoing activities and operations. This view of management looks at an organization as a set of ongoing activities. So, functional management is focused on operations, whereas project management is aimed at projects, and both are relevant for a 21st-century organization.

Figure 2.1
Illustration of project management as a two-dimensional field.

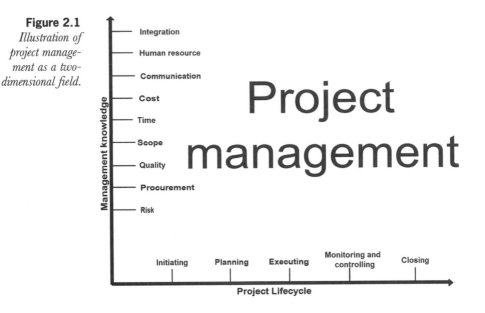

Management knowledge

— Integration
— Human resource
— Communication
— Cost
— Time
— Scope
— Quality
— Procurement
— Risk

Project management

Initiating   Planning   Executing   Monitoring and controlling   Closing

Project Lifecycle

MANAGEMENT BY PROJECTS

To reap the benefits of project management, organizations are applying project management to manage some of their ongoing operations in addition to managing their projects. Such an approach is called *management by projects*. Before you can bring an operation under project management, it must be redefined so that it satisfies the definition of a project. Some operations will lend themselves to project management, others won't.

Project management occurs in two dimensions—the management knowledge in various areas and the project lifecycle.

The two-dimensional characteristic of project management is realized in the form of a process, which is an implementation of project management knowledge in a specific area, such as scope during a specific stage in the lifecycle of a project (such as executing). Figure 2.2 illustrates the relationship between project, project management, process, project lifecycle, and management knowledge. For example, you use your human resource management skills in the process to manage the project team during the execution of the project.

In a nutshell, a project, by definition, has a finite life with a beginning and an end, which is managed by using various knowledge areas.

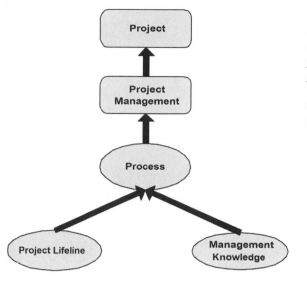

Figure 2.2
Relationship between project, project management, process, project lifetime, and management knowledge.

The Life of a Project

From authorization to completion, a project goes through a whole lifecycle or lifetime that includes defining the project objectives, planning the work to achieve those objectives, performing the work, monitoring and controlling various aspects of the project (such as the progress), and closing the project after receiving product acceptance. The different stages of the project life are shown in Figure 2.3, where the arrows indicate the flow of information. For example, an arrow from planning to executing means the project is executed as it is planned. The back-and-forth arrows between executing and monitoring and controlling mean that both stages can use info from each other—that is, they can overlap.

As illustrated in Figure 2.3, all project activities happen during one of the five stages of the project: initiating, planning, executing, monitoring and controlling, or closing.

Note that what we refer to as *stages* are called *process groups* in the project management standard. Also, as illustrated in Figure 2.3, these stages do not occur in a perfect sequential manner. There is an overlap between various stages. For example, monitoring and controlling overlaps with planning, executing, and closing.

Initiating a Project

This stage defines and authorizes the project. The project manager is named, and the project is officially launched through a signed document called the *project charter*, which contains items such as the purpose of the project, a high-level product description, assumptions and constraints, a summary of the milestone schedule, and a business case for the project. The processes used to perform this stage fall into a group called the *initiating process group*.

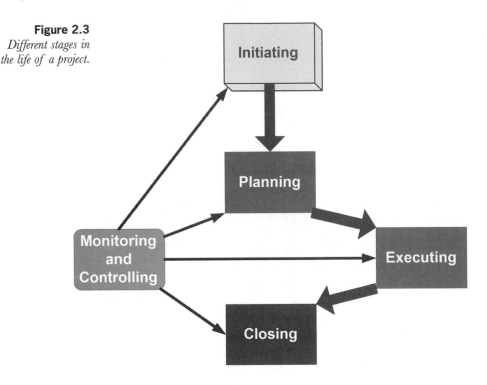

Figure 2.3
Different stages in the life of a project.

Planning the Project

Do not confuse project lifecycle with the product lifecycle. A project's life is from initiating to closing. A project may produce more than one product, and a product's lifecycle may contain more than one project— for example, a project to produce a product and a project to market and sell the product, and so on.

In this stage, you, the project manger, along with the project management team, refine the project objectives and requirements and develop the project management plan, which is a collection of several plans that constitute a course of action required to achieve the objectives and meet the requirements of the project. The project scope is finalized with the project scope statement. The project management plan, the outcome of this stage, contains subsidiary plans, such as a project scope management plan, a schedule management plan, and a quality management plan. The processes used to perform this stage fall into a group called the *planning process group*.

Executing the Project

In this stage you implement the management plan, and the project team performs the work scheduled in the planning stage. You coordinate all the activities being performed to achieve the project objectives and meet the project requirements. Of course, the main output of this project is the project deliverables. Approved changes, recommendations, and defect repairs are also implemented in this stage. But where do these changes and recommendations come from? They arise from monitoring and controlling the project. The stakeholders can also suggest changes, which must go through an approval process before implementation. The project execution is performed using the processes that fall into a group called the *executing process group*.

Monitoring and Controlling the Project

You monitor and control the project through its lifecycle, including the executing stage. Monitoring and controlling includes defending the project against scope creep (unapproved changes to the project scope), monitoring the project progress and performance to identify variance from the plan, and recommending preventive and corrective actions to bring the project in line with the planned expectations. Requests for changes, such as a change to the project scope, are also included in this stage; they can come from you or from any other project stakeholder. The changes must go through an approval process, and only the approved changes are implemented. The processes used in this stage fall into a group called the *monitoring and controlling process group*.

SUCCESS SHOT

If not checked, scope creep can kill a project. Scope creep refers to unapproved changes that change the scope of the project; it usually means more work and cost than planned. You are not against the change, but you must be against unapproved changes because they went into the project without you determining what effect they would have on various aspects of the project, such as scope, cost, and schedule.

Closing the Project

In this stage, you manage the formal acceptance of the project product, close any contracts involved, and bring the project to an end by disbanding the project team. Closing the project includes conducting a project review for lessons learned, and possibly turning over the outcome of the project to another group, such as the maintenance or operations group. Don't forget the last, but not the least, task of the closing stage: celebration.

What we refer to as *project stages* here are not actually the project phases. A project phase is part of the whole project in which certain milestones or project deliverables are completed. All these stages can be applied to any phase of a project that is divided into multiple phases.

All projects, whether terminated or completed, must go through the closing process.

Terminated projects (that is, projects cancelled before completion) may pass on celebration, but they must go through the closing stage. The processes used to perform the closing stage fall into the group called the *closing process group*.

Table 2.2 presents a summary of the project lifecycle. The initiating stage authorizes a project by naming the project manager, the planning stage further defines the project objectives and plans the work to meet the objectives, the execution stage executes the work, monitoring and controlling monitors the progress of the project and controls it to keep it in line with the plan, and the closing stage formally closes the project by obtaining the product acceptance. Each of these stages is performed by using a group of processes. Therefore, these stages are called *process groups*.

The stages of a project lifecycle determine when a process is executed, whereas the processes themselves belong to certain knowledge areas of project management.

Table 2.2 The Stages of a Project Lifecycle: The Project Process Groups

Project Stage (Process Group)	Major Goal	Major Outcome
Initiating	Authorize the project	Project charter, project scope statement
Planning	Plan and schedule the work to perform the project	Project management plan that contains subsidiary plans, such as scope management plan and schedule management plan
Executing	Perform the project work	Project deliverables: product, service, results
Monitoring and controlling	Monitor the progress of the project to identify the variance from the plan and to correct it	Change requests and recommendations for preventive and corrective actions
Closing	Close the project formally	Product acceptance and contract closure

Understanding the Project Management Knowledge Areas

As you must have figured out by now, managing projects is applying management knowledge and skills to project activities at the right time during the project time in order to meet the project objectives. It boils down to performing some processes at various stages of the project discussed in the previous section. This also means processes are part of the knowledge required to manage projects. Each aspect of a project is managed by using the corresponding knowledge area. For example, each project has a scope that need to be managed, and the knowledge required to manage scope is in the knowledge area called *project scope management*. To perform the project work within the project scope, you need human resources, which need to be managed, and the knowledge used to manage human resources is called *human resource management*. You get the idea. Just like each process belongs to a process group, it also belongs to one of the nine knowledge areas discussed in the following sections.

STANDARDIZE THIS

Project management is the application of knowledge, skills, tools, and techniques to project activities to meet project requirements.

—PMBOK Guide, Fourth Edition

Managing Project Scope

The processes used to manage the project scope belong to the management knowledge area called *project scope management*. The primary purpose of project scope management is to ensure that all the required work and only the required work is performed to complete the project successfully. This is accomplished by defining and controlling what is included in the project and what is not.

The project scope management, in part, defines the work required to complete the project. It's a finite amount of work and will need a finite amount of time, which needs to be managed as well.

Project scope management ensures that all the required work is performed to successfully complete the project.

Managing Project Time

The processes used to manage the project time belong to the management knowledge area called *project time management*. The primary purpose of project time management is to develop and control the project schedule. You perform these tasks by using the corresponding processes. It will cost you to get the activities in the schedule completed, and the cost needs to be managed, too.

Managing Project Cost

The processes used to manage the project cost belong to the management knowledge area called *project cost management*. The primary goal of project cost management is to estimate the cost and to complete the project within the approved budget. You will perform the appropriate processes to accomplish the tasks of managing the project cost. The resources needed to complete the project activities include human resources, which need to be managed as well.

Managing Human Resources

The processes used to manage human resources working on the project belong to the management knowledge area called *project human resource management*. The primary purpose of project human resource management is to obtain, develop, and manage the project team that will perform the project work.

There will be situations when your organization does not have the expertise to perform certain schedule activities in house. For this or other reasons, you might want to outsource some of the project work, called *procurement*, which needs to be managed.

Managing Project Procurement

If your organization does not have the expertise to perform certain schedule activities in house, you must manage project procurements.

The processes used to manage project procurements belong to the management knowledge area called *project procurement management*. The primary purpose of the procurement management is to manage acquiring products (that is products, services, or results) from outside the project team in order to complete the project. The external vendor that offers the service is called the *seller*. Procurement management includes planning acquisitions, planning contracts with the sellers, selecting sellers, administering contracts with the sellers, and closing contracts. You use the corresponding processes to accomplish these tasks.

Be it the procured or the in-house work, there are always some uncertainties, which give rise to project risks, which need to be managed as well.

Managing Project Risk

The processes used to manage project risks belong to the management knowledge area called *project risk management*. A project risk is an event that has a positive or negative effect on meeting the project objectives if it occurs. The primary purpose of project risk management is to identify the risks and respond to them should they occur. To be specific, project risk management includes the following:

- Planning the risk management—that is, determining how to plan and execute the risk management tasks
- Identifying risks
- Performing risk analysis
- Developing a risk response plan—that is, what action to take should a risk occur
- Monitoring and controlling risks—that is, tracking the identified risks, identifying new risks, and implementing the risk response plan

These tasks related to risk management are performed by using the corresponding processes. The goal of risk management is to help meet the project objectives. The degree to which the project objectives and requirements are met is called *quality*, which needs to be managed.

Managing Project Quality

The processes used to manage project quality belong to the management knowledge area called *project quality management*. Project quality is defined as the degree to which a project satisfies its objectives and requirements. For example, a high-quality project is a project that is completed on time and with all the work in the project scope completed within the planned budget. Project quality management includes the following:

- Performing quality planning—that is, determining which quality standards are relevant to the project at hand and how to apply them

- Performing quality assurance—that is, ensuring the planned quality standards are applied
- Performing quality control—that is, monitoring specific project results to ensure they comply with the planned quality standards and recommending actions to eliminate the causes of unsatisfactory progress

These tasks of project quality management are performed by using the corresponding processes. In order to unify different pieces into a whole project, the different project management activities need to be integrated.

Managing Project Integration

Communication is the most important aspect of a project.

The processes used to manage project integration belong to the management knowledge area called *project integration management*. The project is planned and executed in pieces, and all those pieces are related to each other and need to come together. That is where integration management comes in. For example, integrating different subsidiary plans into a project management plan needs to be managed. Project integration management includes developing the project management plan, directing and managing project execution, monitoring and controlling the project work, and closing the project.

So, while managing all the aspects of the project, you, the project manager, will need to coordinate among different activities and groups, and for that you need to communicate.

Managing Project Communication

The processes used to manage project communication belong to the management knowledge area called *project communication management*. It is absolutely imperative for the success of the project that the project information is generated and distributed in a timely fashion. Many will agree that communication is the most important aspect of a project and the most important skill for a project manger to have. Communication management includes the following:

- Planning communication—that is, determining the information and communication needs of the project at hand

- Distributing needed information to the project stakeholders in a timely fashion
- Reporting this project performance, including the project status
- Communicating to resolve issues among the stakeholders

Standardize This

As you have seen, managing a project largely means performing a set of processes at various stages of the project, such as initiating and planning. Accordingly, processes are grouped corresponding to these stages, and the groups are called *process groups*. Processes are part of the knowledge required to manage projects. So, each of these processes belong to one of the nine knowledge areas identified in the PMBOK Guide.

Process Mapping

A process has a dual membership: one in a process group indicating at which stage of the project the process is performed, and the other in a knowledge area indicating which aspect of the project is managed by using the process. Table 2.3 shows this membership for all the processes identified in the PMBOK Guide, Fourth Edition. The names of the processes are self-explanatory—for example, develop project charter describes the processes used to develop the project charter.

Now that we are at it, let's develop the definition and concept of a process.

SUCCESS SHOT

Not all the processes are used in all the projects. You, the project manager, along with the project management team, decide which processes need to be used in a given project. It depends on the need of the given project determined by its characteristics, such as the size and scope. The goal here is to improve the efficiency and effectiveness of the project to maximize the benefits and minimize the cost. Remember: Processes are for the project, and not the other way around.

Table 2.3 Mapping of the Project Management Processes to Process Groups and Knowledge Areas

Process Groups => Knowledge Areas ‖ V	Initiating Process Group	Planning Process Group	Executing Process Group	Monitoring and Controlling Process Group	Closing Process Group
Communications Management	Identify stakeholders	Plan communications	Distribute information Manage stakeholder expectations	Report performance	—
Cost Management	—	1. Estimate costs 2. Determine budget		Control costs	—
Human Resource Management	—	Develop human resource plan	1. Acquire project team 2. Develop project team 3. Manage project team	—	
Integration Management	Develop project charter	Develop project management plan	Direct and manage project execution	1. Monitor and control project work 2. Perform integrated change control	Close project or phase
Procurement Management	—	Plan procurements	Conduct procurements	Administer procurements	Close procurements

Process Groups => Knowledge Areas ‖ ∨	Initiating Process Group	Planning Process Group	Executing Process Group	Monitoring and Controlling Process Group	Closing Process Group
Quality Management	—	Plan quality	Perform quality assurance	Perform quality control	—

Risk Management	—	1. Plan risk
		   management
		2. Identify risks
		3. Perform qualitative
		   risk analysis
		4. Perform quantitative
		   risk analysis
		5. Plan risk responses
			—	Monitor and
				control risks
					—

Scope Management	—	1. Collect requirements 2. Define scope 3. Create work breakdown structure	—	1. Verify scope 2. Control scope	

Time Management	—	1. Define activities
		2. Sequence activities
		3. Estimate activity
		   resources
		4. Estimate activity
		   durations
		5. Develop schedule
			—	Control schedule	

Understanding a Process

To think like a project management professional, think in terms of processes.

Processes are the heart of project management. If you want to think of project management like a project management professional, think in terms of processes. Almost everything in the world of project management is done through processes.

In the previous chapter we defined a process as a set of interrelated activities performed to obtain a specified set of products, results, or services. If project management is made of processes, what are processes made of? To be more specific, a process, as illustrated in Figure 2.4, is made of three elements: input, tools and techniques, and output.

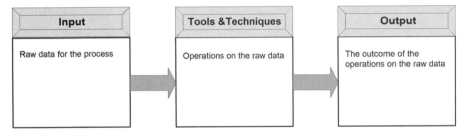

Input	Tools &Techniques	Output
Raw data for the process	Operations on the raw data	The outcome of the operations on the raw data

Figure 2.4 *Three elements of a process.*

This picture of a process is very general and can be used outside of project management as well. In project management, you use processes to accomplish things, such as developing a project schedule, directing and managing the project execution, and developing and managing the project team.

Each process consists of three elements:

- **Input.** The input to a process consists of the raw data that is needed to start the process. For example, the list of activities that need to be scheduled is one of several input items to the process that will be used to develop the schedule of a project.
- **Tools and techniques.** Tools and techniques are the methods used to operate on the input to transform it into output. For example, project management software that helps to develop a schedule is a tool used in the schedule development process.
- **Output.** The output is the outcome or the result of a process. Each process contains at least one output item; otherwise, there would be no point in performing a process. For example, an output item of the schedule development process is, well, the project schedule.

STUDY CHECKPOINT 2.2

To really grasp and understand an involved concept, you must
be able to look at it from different perspectives and define it at
different levels.

Exercise 1:

 A. Based on what you learned in this chapter and the previ-
    ous chapter, present multiple definitions of project man-
    agement.
 B. Argue how these definitions are consistent with each other.

Exercise 2:

Repeat Exercise 1 for process.

Solution:

Exercise 1:

 1. Project management is management of projects.
 2. Project management is implementation of relevant man-
    agement knowledge in a timely fashion.
 3. Project management is a set of processes performed to
    manage a project.
 4. Project management is an application of management
    knowledge to perform project activities in order to
    achieve project objectives.

Exercise 2:

 1. A process is a method that transforms specific input ele-
    ments into specific output elements.
 2. A process is the implementation of certain management
    knowledge at a certain time during the project.
 3. A process is a method that applies tools and techniques
    to input elements to produce output elements.

In this book, I address only one kind of project process, called *project management processes*. However, there is a second kind of project
process, called *product-oriented processes*, used to create the project's
product. These processes obviously depend on the product and
hence the application area of the project. The project team members who will do the product-related work will select these
processes. However, the project manager should not ignore these
processes because there may be an overlap of these processes with
the project management processes. For example, it's not possible
to define the scope of the project without some basic understanding of how the product will be created.

Quick Success Mantras

- Every project has a beginning and an end.

- Every project is performed to create a unique product, service, or result.

- An operation is a function that performs ongoing tasks: It is different from a project because it does not produce a unique (new) product or it does not have a beginning and an end—or both.

- Project management is the application of management knowledge, skills, and tools and techniques to project activities in order to obtain the project objectives and requirements.

- Project management is implemented through processes in a two-dimensional space: project management knowledge areas and project lifetime.

- There are nine standard project management knowledge areas: scope, time, cost, quality, risk, human resource, procurement, communication, and integration.

- There are five stages, which may have overlaps, in the life of a project: initiating, planning, executing, monitoring and controlling, and closing. These stages are called *process groups* in the project management standard.

- Project management is implemented in two-dimensional space, meaning each process maps to a knowledge area and a process group (that is a stage in the life of a project).

- Not all the processes in standard project management are implemented in all projects.

- There are two types of project processes: project management processes and product-oriented processes. The project as a whole uses both of these processes, but the project management team is responsible for implementing the project management processes.

- To successfully implement the project management processes, the project manager (or the project management team) should have some basic understanding of the processes used to create the project's product.

Chapter 3

So You Want to Be a Project Manager

- The Role of a Project Manager: Big Picture
- Playing the Role of a Project Manager
- Onc Head, Many Hats
- Management Skills of a Project Manager
- Interpersonal Skills of a Project Manager
- Expectations and Success
- Know Your Stakeholders
- Excelling in the Project Environment
- Standardize This
- Quick Success Mantras

By their very nature, projects, in general, do not lend themselves to management by a team. There can be and usually is a project team, but there must be one person in the driver's seat: the project manager. If people have any questions about the project, they go to the project manager. Let's start with the simplest definition of a project manager: a person who manages the project. The apparent scope of the role of project manager suddenly expands and becomes clearer if you spin this definition a little bit: A project manager is a person who is responsible for implementing project management for the projects.

What does it take to be a project manager? Everything you've got to offer: management skills, interpersonal skills and qualities, and any level of expertise in any number of application areas. Remember, project management spans all application areas, whereas a given project is usually run in one application area, but it may involve more than one application area. This makes project management more challenging and useful, and it's a field where you can use almost all of your skills to the fullest and grow while doing so. Don't be discouraged if you think you do not have all the skills, qualities, and expertise listed in this chapter; you start from what you have and develop the rest on the job. You use your skills and experience to navigate through the organizational culture, organizational structure, and global environment factors in order to lead the project to success.

So, the three underlying themes of this chapter are: the role of a project manager, the skills and qualities of a successful project manager, and coping with the project environment constituted by organizational culture, organizational structure, and global environmental factors.

In this chapter, you'll learn:

- The role of a project manager
- Management skills required to be a successful project manager
- Interpersonal skills required to be a successful project manager
- How to cope with the organizational culture, organizational structure, and global environmental factors in which your projects are being run
- Organizational environmental factors and process assets
- How to understand project stakeholders

The Role of a Project Manager: Big Picture

If I had to use only one word to describe the role of a project manager, I would say *challenging*. The major responsibility of a project manager is to ensure that the project objectives and requirements are accomplished on time and within the budget. Managing a project means applying project management to the project at hand, which includes initiating, planning, executing, monitoring and controlling, and closing the project. While managing this big picture, you will find yourself involved in tasks such as identifying requirements; developing plans, approaches, and specifications; adapting plans to a whole spectrum of concerns and expectations coming from a multitude of stakeholders; and balancing the often competing requirements of cost, scope, time, and quality.

You will be doing different things at different stages of a project. But the needs of certain activities can emerge at any stage of a project, or you might be performing them all through the project. Those activities include the following:

The most important word in the profile (and life) of a project manager is *challenge*. If you like—love could even be a better word—meeting challenges head on, project management is the field for you. If you don't, this is the time to begin developing a healthy relationship with the concept called *challenge* because you will be living and dealing with challenges. Develop this attitude: The path to success passes through challenges.

- **Optimizing requirements.** The essence of your job is to deliver the planned output of the project while balancing the opposing requirements of several areas, such as cost, scope, schedule, and quality. For example, extending the scope of a project will affect cost, schedule, or both. It may also affect quality. Your job is to balance these requirements in order to optimize the project output.
- **Managing expectations.** Throughout the project, you will need to manage the expectations of the project stakeholders to ensure that those are in line with the project plan.
- **Managing priorities.** Different stakeholders will often have different views of what the most important aspects of the project are. The most important factor of the project to one stakeholder may not be that important to another. So one of the challenges you will face is keeping the project priorities straight while managing the demands and expectations toward the success of the project.
- **Managing changes.** From day one of the project, the changes will begin creeping in. Changes often change the scope of the project. Some of your continuing job tasks will be to guard against scope creep, channel the incoming change suggestions to the proper process, and implement only the approved changes.

> **SUCCESS SHOT**
>
> One of the major challenges of managing a project is to balance the opposing requirements, demands, and priorities coming from different stakeholders. The goal here is to create a balance in order to optimize the project output. Creating balance does not always mean to compromise. The key here is to stick to the project plan, implement changes only after they have been approved through the proper process, and manage stakeholder expectations. The ball that you and your team want to keep your eyes on is the success of the project by delivering the planned output.

As a project manager, you will be optimizing requirements and managing expectations, priorities, and changes, as well as performing various other duties.

Guarding against scope creep does not necessarily mean to oppose the change. It means to ensure that only approved changes are implemented. You do not want to be looked upon as a person who always opposes changes. Rather, you should build your reputation as a *change manager* or even a *change agent*. Assess the impact of a proposed change on all aspects of the project and put it through the proper process to evaluate and approve or reject the proposed changes.

In a nutshell, the ultimate big-picture responsibility of a project manager is to deliver the planned project output, such as products, within the planned scope, schedule, cost, and quality. In order to perform this critical responsibility, you must understand your role as a project manager.

> **STUDY CHECKPOINT 3.1**
>
> You have just determined the scope, schedule, and cost of your project. A stakeholder is suggesting that you extend the scope of the project by adding one more deliverable that will require a few more activities. State how this change to the scope could possibly change the schedule, cost, or quality of the project.
>
> **Solution:**
>
> These new activities will need to be scheduled, so the schedule will change.
>
> These new activities will most likely cost you, which will change the cost determination. Otherwise, you might have to cut corners on the cost, which will compromise the quality.

Playing the Role of a Project Manager

An organization assigns a project manager charged with the responsibility of achieving the project goals and objectives. As a project manager, you manage the details of a project from the perspective of the big picture: Manage the big picture and the details at the same time. For example, if a change in one aspect of the project has been suggested, you must evaluate the effects of this change on other aspects of the project, should it be implemented. Also, you are the go-to person for the project—that is, the point person who interfaces with all the stakeholders of the project. You are in charge of all the aspects of the project, including developing plans for the project, executing the plans, monitoring and controlling the project to keep it on track as planned, communicating with the stakeholders, managing risks, and closing the project properly at the right time.

> Make sure you can distinguish between objectives and requirements. An *objective* is an outcome of the project, whereas a *requirement* is a characteristic of the outcome. For example, building a house is an objective of a construction project, and the characteristic that the house will withstand an earthquake is a requirement.

The core general job responsibilities of a project manager overlap with the project lifecycle and include the following:

1. **Initiating.** Defining the project by determining its objectives, requirements, and constraints. These elements lay out the foundation of the project and are necessary to set the right track for the project.

2. **Planning.** Developing plans to meet the objectives and requirements. This sets the track for the project.

3. **Executing.** Executing the plans—that is, managing the execution of the project work according to the project plan, which includes developing and managing the project team, and while doing so, managing stakeholders' expectations.

4. **Monitoring and controlling.** Monitoring and controlling the project to keep it on the planned track, which includes monitoring and controlling the project progress, risks, and changes. Changes to the plan must be approved before implementations. While doing so, make sure you manage the golden triangle properly—that is, balance opposing requirements from scope, schedule, and cost.

5. **Closing.** Regardless of whether the project is terminated or completed, closing the project properly according to the plan, which includes handing over the project outcome to proper groups, recording lessons learned, and releasing resources in a timely fashion.

The core job responsibilities of a project manager include initiating, planning, executing, monitoring and controlling, and closing the project.

An important key to performing all these responsibilities successfully is communication, a common thread that runs through the whole project lifecycle. This is exactly where you will need to wear different communication hats.

One Head, Many Hats

As a project manager, you might be dealing with a wide functional variety of individuals, ranging from executives, to marketing personnel, to technologists. You should be able to wear different communication hats depending upon whom you are communicating with. For example, you will not be using technical jargon to talk to executives or marketing folks, and you will not speak marketing lingo to the software developers. You will be speaking to different stakeholders in their language, while filling the language gap between different functional groups and eliminating misunderstandings due to miscommunication. The key point is that you put on the appropriate communication hat depending on which individual you are communicating with. Be able to switch communication hats quickly and avoid technical jargon and acronyms that are not understood by the person or group with whom you are communicating. The goal is clarity of the language to convey the message accurately.

As a project manager, you will be facilitator, point person, organizer and planner, resource manager, leader, and coach and mentor.

Furthermore, here are some of the sub-roles you will be playing in the role of a project manager:

- **Facilitator.** You will use different communication hats to facilitate the progress of the project by ensuring that stakeholders, including the team members from different backgrounds and groups, work together toward the success of the project.

- **Point person.** You will be the point of contact for all the project stakeholders.

- **Organizer and planner.** You organize your team to plan for the project and then organize the activities to implement the plans.

- **Resource manager.** You develop and manage the project team. You also determine the need for other resources, acquire them, and manage them.

- **Leader.** You develop a vision and strategy for the project and motivate the project team to achieve that vision. The implementation of the project management processes is not enough to bring a project to success; you must lead the project to success. In other words, as a project manager, it is your responsibility to lead all the stakeholders.

- **Coach and mentor.** While developing your team, you may be coaching the project management team members to effectively perform the project management activities. You may also act as a mentor to the team members and help them gear their career in the right direction.

STANDARDIZE THIS

According to the PMI standard, effective project management requires that the project management team as a whole must have the following three-dimensional competency:

1. Project management knowledge
2. Ability to successfully apply the knowledge to the project at hand
3. Right behavior during the project activities, including attitudes and core personality characteristics

In a nutshell, the three dimensions of the required competency are knowledge, performance, and personality. This is in addition to any skills specific to the application area of the project that the team is required to have.

To play these multiple roles successfully, you need to have (or develop) a multitude of management and interpersonal skills.

Management Skills of a Project Manager

Managing projects effectively takes a multitude of skills. Some of these skills you may already have, and others you will develop as you go. The major management-related skills needed in project management are discussed in the following paragraphs.

Accounting and financial management. You will need to do some accounting and financial management while performing project management. If you do not already have these skills, you can learn as you go. We will explore some cost-, schedule-, and performance-related calculations in this book.

Attention to details. As an old saying goes, *the devil is in the details*. The importance of this skill—paying attention to details—cannot be overemphasized. Attention to details provides you with a microscopic headlight that helps you to foresee troubles ahead, identify risks in a timely fashion, develop effective plans, execute those plans efficiently, and monitor and control the project toward success. To develop this skill, you need to have the curiosity of a child, the analytical mind of a scientist, and the focus of a laser beam. You must also be a good listener.

SUCCESS SHOT

The ability and practice of paying attention to details is a key to success in project management (and in almost any other field, for that matter). With everything else equal, this may make the difference between success and failure. It's an especially important skill to have in order to succeed in the complex field of project management. This ability has two dimensions to it: to see the details that are already there, and to break a complex problem (or task) down to enough detail that you can handle it better.

Information technology. A successful project manager meets or exceeds the minimum IT skills required for the job. For example, you will be using project management software tools, such as Microsoft Project and Microsoft Excel, web communication tools, and so on. IT skills are useful and helpful in almost all fields these days.

Negotiation and conflict management. A negotiation is give and take, with the goal of generating a win-win outcome for both parties. You might need to negotiate at any stage of the project lifecycle. Here are some examples of negotiations:

- Negotiating with the stakeholders regarding the expectations during the project planning. For example, the suggested deadline for the project schedule might not be practical, or you might need a certain type or quantity of resources to make it happen.
- Negotiating with the functional managers for obtaining human resources, such as software developers.

- Negotiating with the team members for specific job assignments and possibly during conflict resolution among the team members.

- Negotiating the changes to the project schedule, budget, or both because a stakeholder proposed changes to the project objectives.

- Negotiating with the external vendors in procurement. However, in contract negotiations, representatives from the legal department might be involved.

There will be conflicts among stakeholders during the project lifecycle. You will need to have or develop conflict management skills. We will explore this issue further in another chapter.

Sometimes you will use your negotiating skills to solve a problem.

Problem-solving. Project-related problems might occur among the stakeholders—team members included—or with the projects. Either way, they are there to damage the project. Your task is twofold: Identify the problem early enough and solve it. Here is the general technique for accomplishing this:

- Look for early warning signs by paying close attention to the formal progress reports and to what the team members say and do regarding the project.

- Once you identify a potential problem, do your homework. Understand and identify the problem clearly by collecting more information without passing judgment.

- Once the problem and its causes are clearly identified, work with the appropriate stakeholders, such as project team members, to explore multiple (alternative) solutions.

- Evaluate the multiple solutions and choose the one you will implement.

The key point throughout the problem-solving process is to focus on the problem, not on the individuals, with the goal of finding the solution in order to help the project succeed. There should be no finger-pointing.

Sales and marketing. A successful project manager is a customer-oriented manager who has developed good sales and marketing skills. You will be selling the project vision and objectives to the team members and inspiring and motivating them to achieve that vision.

> As a project manager, you need to have or develop skills in accounting and finance management, in attention to detail, in information technology, in negotiation and conflict management, in problem-solving, and in sales and marketing.

> **SUCCESS SHOT**
>
> If you have a background in the application area of the projects being run in your company, such as information technology or biotechnology, you can better understand the details of the project and lead it to success. If you happen to have a diverse background in multiple application areas, project management is one of very few fields that will truly benefit from your expertise. Needless to say that it will help you become a successful project manager. After all, project management runs through almost all application areas, and a given project is run in one or more application areas.

You will be dealing with a wide spectrum of people and leading the project stakeholders, so you must have excellent interpersonal skills.

Interpersonal Skills of a Project Manager

The project manager must know who the decision makers are in the organization and work with them to ensure the success of the project. Besides that, you will be interacting with all the project stakeholders. To lead your team to success, you must have excellent interpersonal skills, including those discussed in the following paragraphs.

Communication. Many will agree with me that communication is the most important aspect of managing a project. You will be communicating throughout the project to do almost anything: exchange information, resolve conflicts, manage expectations, and lead. For a given project, you must have the skills to develop a communication strategy that addresses the following issues:

- What needs to be communicated?
- With whom do you want to communicate? You might need to communicate different items to different individuals or groups.
- How do you want to communicate—that is, what is the medium of communication? Again, this might differ depending on whom you are communicating with.
- What is the outcome of your communication? You need to monitor your communication and its results to see what works and what does not, so you can improve communication.

You must have the skills to implement this strategy successfully. Communication is an ingredient for many other skills, such as negotiation, problem-solving, and influencing.

Influencing. Influencing means getting individuals or groups to do what you want them to do without necessarily having a formal authority to mandate an outcome from them. This is increasingly becoming an essential management skill in today's information economy. To exercise influence, you must understand the formal and informal structure of your organization. Again, you might need to use influencing when you are dealing with any aspect of the project—for example, controlling the changes to the project, negotiating schedule or resource assignments, resolving conflicts, and the like.

Leadership. In the traditional organizational structure, the functional structure, project managers do not have formal authority over the project team members who perform the team work. So you have no other choice than managing by leadership and not by authority (power). The good news is that managing by leadership is overall more effective and productive than managing by authority anyway; of course, it's more challenging. A project team is generally a group of individuals coming together for the lifetime of the project from different functional groups with different skills and experience. They need a leader to show them the vision and to excite, inspire, and motivate them toward the goals and the objectives of the project. You, the project manager, are that leader.

Networking. Burn it in your head: Networking is one of the golden secrets you have for succeeding as a project manager, especially in an organization in which functional managers hold all the power (hiring, firing, bonuses), and the project managers are running around with nothing in their hands other than the project schedules and status reports. To network effectively, you should understand the influence of political and interpersonal factors in your organization that might impact various staffing management options. Some of the essential networking happens at the beginning of each project, and you must make full use of it. However, networking is a regular practice, and you should be using all the human resource network activities, such as proactive correspondence, informal conversations, luncheon meetings, and trade conferences.

A project manager must have excellent interpersonal skills, including communication, influencing, leadership, networking, and savvy navigation.

Savvy navigation. In dealing with people, a successful project manager is a savvy navigator through troubled waters. That means you take initiative, responsibility, and accountability for the project; bring energy and excitement into the project; understand the organization's dynamics and players; and quickly identify and diffuse emotionally charged situations. You flourish on ambiguity, you take the heat from project stakeholders with a smile on your face, you are calm and confident while dealing with stressful situations, and you navigate through the tricky politics of the organization to take your project to success.

You can use all these skills to lead your project to success, but you may still be looked upon as a failure if you did not manage the expectations of the stakeholders.

Expectations and Success

You must define success in order to achieve it.

Expectations and success are highly correlated concepts. First thing first: Define success, because you may never achieve it if you don't define it. The general and most obvious definition of success for any project is to deliver its planned outcome with full scope and quality, within budget, and on time. Scope, budget, and time (schedule) are easier to measure and monitor than quality, which is generally measured by usability of the product and conformance to requirements. For example, if a software tool is difficult and clumsy to use, it's of low quality; if the promised feature (requirement) is not in the tool, it did not meet that quality requirement.

Quality is one area where you need to manage the stakeholder expectations; otherwise, you may deliver a project with high quality, on time, and within budget, but it may still not be seen as successful by some stakeholders. This is because your definition of quality may differ from that of stakeholders, and that will lead to different expectations from the project and hence different views of what will make the project successful.

Therefore, it is crucial that the success of a specific project is defined in the beginning of the project. In the beginning of the project, you ensure that all the project stakeholders agree on how the success is defined for the project and how it will be measured.

You ensure the success of the project by the following three-prong formula:

1. Develop a realistic definition of success for a project by setting realistic expectations.
2. Manage those expectations throughout the project.
3. Deliver the project outcome with planned scope and quality, on time, and within the budget.

Because you will be managing the stakeholder expectations throughout the project, you should identify the stakeholders and know them in the beginning of the project. Who are they?

STUDY CHECKPOINT 3.2

Describe how project scope, cost, and schedule are essential measures of project success.

Solution:

If the project is not delivered with full scope, that means it did not deliver what was planned, hence it is a failure.

If the project overruns the cost, it will affect the benefits, and you may lose money instead of benefiting from the project.

If the project is not completed according to the schedule, it may delay the revenue that would come from the project product, or the window of opportunity for which the project is being run may close by the time project is completed.

Know Your Stakeholders

Right from the day you assume responsibility for managing a project, you start meeting a very special class of people called *project stakeholders*. It is very important for the success of the project that you identify these individuals and organizations and communicate with them effectively throughout the project.

Project stakeholders are individuals and organizations whose interests are affected—positively or negatively—by the project execution and completion. In other words, a project stakeholder has something to gain from the project or lose to the project. Accordingly, the stakeholders fall into two categories—positive stakeholders, who will normally benefit from the success of the project, and negative stakeholders, who see some kind of disadvantage coming from the project. The implications obviously are that the positive stakeholders would like to see the project succeed, and the negative stakeholders' interests would be better served if the project was delayed or cancelled all together. For example, your city mayor might be a positive stakeholder in a project to open a Walmart store in your neighborhood because it brings business to the city, whereas some local business leaders might look at it as a threat to the local small businesses and thereby may act as negative stakeholders.

Identify positive and negative stakeholders early on in the project.

Negative stakeholders are often overlooked by the project manager and the project team, which increases the project risk. Ignoring positive or negative project stakeholders will have a damaging impact on the project. Therefore, it's important that you, the project manager, start identifying the project stakeholders early on in the project. The different project stakeholders can have different and conflicting expectations, which you need to analyze and manage.

In addition to some obvious stakeholders, such as you, the project sponsor, and project team members, who are easy to identify, there can be a number of other stakeholders inside and outside of your organization who might be more difficult to identify. Depending upon the project, these might include investors, sellers, contractors, family members of the project team members, government agencies, media outlets, lobbying organizations, individual citizens, and society at large. Have I left anyone out?

So, the stakeholders not only are affected positively and negatively by the project, but the project can also be impacted positively or negatively by them. It is critical for the success of the project that you identify positive and negative stakeholders early on in the project, understand and analyze their varying and conflicting expectations, and manage those expectations throughout the project.

The project manager must identify those aspects of the culture and structure of the organization that will influence project management and thereby the success of the project.

Excelling in the Project Environment

A secret of success: You use all your skills and qualities to lead the project to success by navigating through the project environment, constituted by realities inside and outside of the performing organizations. A project is typically performed inside an organization called the *performing organization*. Therefore, projects are influenced by many characteristics of the performing organizations, such as culture, style, organizational structure, and maturity of the organization.

From the perspective of a project, there are two kinds of organizations: project-based and non-project-based. The project-based organizations fall into two subcategories—those that derive their revenue primarily from performing projects for others, and those that do in-house projects to deliver products or services for customers. Project-based organizations are well aware of the importance of project management and generally have tools and systems to support project management. Non-project-based organizations generally have a low appreciation and understanding of the importance of project management and often lack tools and systems to support project management.

So, the project environment that will affect your job as a project manager is constituted by three major elements: organizational culture, organizational structure, and global environmental factors internal and external to the organization. You must understand these elements in order to navigate successfully through the project environment.

Understanding the Organizational Culture

Each organization often develops its own unique culture, which depends on many factors, such as the application area of the organization and the general management philosophy implemented in the organization. The organizational culture includes the following elements:

Organizational culture includes work environment, management style, policies, and values.

- **Work environment.** The organizational culture reflects from work ethics and work hours. For example, do the employees work strictly from 8:00 a.m. to 5:00 p.m., or do they work late nights and on weekends?

- **Management style.** Do the managers manage by authority or by leadership? How much feedback is taken from the employees in making management decisions? How do the employees view the authority of the management?

- **Policies.** The organizational policies and procedures also reflect the organizational culture.

- **Values.** A significant part of organizational culture lives in the set of values, norms, beliefs, and expectations shared within the organization. For example, a non-profit organization will have different values than a for-profit organization. Furthermore, one organization may encourage an entrepreneurial approach, while another organization may be rigidly hierarchical and may take an authoritarian approach in making decisions on what to do and what not to do.

Organizational culture influences multiple aspects of a project, including the following:

- **Project selection.** The organizational culture will creep into the selection criteria for projects and programs. For example, a rigidly hierarchical and authoritarian organization may not be very adaptive to programs and projects with high risk.

- **Project management style.** The project manager should adapt the management style to the organizational culture. For example, an authoritarian style may run into problems in an entrepreneurial organization with a participative culture.

- **Team performance assessments.** While making the team performance assessment, the project manager should keep in mind the established norms and expectations within the organization.

- **Project policies and procedures.** The project policies and procedures will be influenced by the organizational policies and procedures because both should be consistent with each other.

The culture of an organization is greatly influenced by its structure.

Understanding the Organizational Structure

To do your job efficiently and effectively, you must figure out what kind of organizational structure you are in. From the perspective of structure, organizations fall into three categories—functional organizations, projectized organizations, and matrix organizations.

Functional Organization

A functional organization has a traditional organizational structure in which each functional department, such as engineering, marketing, and sales, is a separate entity. The members of each department (staff) report to the functional manager of that department, and the functional manager in turn reports to an executive, such as the chief executive officer (CEO). Depending on the size of the organization, there could be a hierarchy within the functional managers—for example, directors of engineering, QA, and IT operations reporting to the vice president (VP) of engineering, who in turn reports to the CEO.

The scope of a project in a functional organization is usually limited to the boundaries of the functional department. Therefore, each department runs its projects largely independent of other departments. When a communication needs to occur between two departments, it is carried through the hierarchy of functional managers.

All the managerial power (authority) in a functional organization is vested in the functional managers, who control the team members' performance evaluations, salaries, bonuses, hiring, and firing. Project managers are held responsible for the project results even though they have little say over resource assignments and holding team members accountable for their work. As a result, project managers in a functional organization are often frustrated. Their work is, at best, challenging. You, as a project manager in a functional organization, can benefit greatly from your good relationships with functional managers and team members. Networking and leadership are the key points to your success in a functional organization.

In functional organizations, project management might be performed under other titles, such as project coordinator, team leader, or project leader.

A project manager in a functional organization has the following attributes:

- The project manager's role and project team are part-time.
- The project manager has little or no authority over anything: resource assignments, team members, and the like.
- The project manager reports directly to a functional manager.
- There is little or no administrative staff to help with the project.

On the other end of the spectrum is the projectized organization.

Projectized Organization

A projectized organization's structure is organized around projects. Most of the organization's resources are devoted to the projects. The project team members report directly to the project manager, who has a great deal of independence and authority. Along with responsibility comes the high level of autonomy over the projects. The project managers are happy campers in a projectized organization. A functional organization and a projectized organization are on the opposite ends of the spectrum of a project manager's authority.

A project manager in a projectized organization has the following attributes:

• The project manager is full-time.
• The project manager has full authority over the project team.
• There is full-time administrative staff to help with the project.

In the middle of the spectrum are the matrix organizations.

Matrix Organization

A matrix organization is organized into functional departments, but a project is run by a project team, with members coming from different functional departments. On the spectrum of a project manager's authority, matrix organizations are in the middle of two extremes: functional and projectized organizations. Matrix organizations are generally categorized into a strong matrix, which is closer to a projectized structure; a weak matrix, which is closer to functional structure; and a balanced matrix, which is in the middle of strong and weak.

Table 3.1 summarizes the influences of the different organizational structures on the projects.

The organizational culture and structure contribute significantly to the overall project environment. In addition, there are some global environmental factors that can contribute to or impact the project environment from inside and outside of the performing organization.

Table 3.1 Influences of the Organizational Structures on Projects

Project Characteristic	Organization Structure		
	Functional	Matrix	Projectized
Project manager's authority	None to low	Low to high	High to full
Project manager's role	Part-time	Part-time to full-time	Full-time
Project management administrative staff	None to part-time	Part-time to full-time	Full-time
Project budget controlled by	Functional manager	Functional manager, project manager, or both	Project manager
Resource availability	Low	Limited to high	High to full

STUDY CHECKPOINT 3.3

Questions:

1. In which organizational structure does the project manager have the maximum authority?
2. In which organization can the project budget be controlled by the project manager, the functional manager, or both?
3. In which organization is a project manager usually employed part-time?

Answers:

1. Projectized
2. Matrix
3. Functional

Understanding the Global Environmental Factors

The global environmental factors can be broadly classified into three interrelated categories: physical, social, and international.

Physical environment. You must take into consideration the aspects of the project that may affect its physical surroundings, such as ecology and geography. There may be some factors in the physical environment that might affect the project.

Social environment. You must know how the project will affect the people not only inside the organization but also outside the organization, and also how people may affect the project. For example, there may be some special-interest organizations that are against or for your project because it affects their interest in a negative or positive way.

Depending on the project, you may not have all the required knowledge and information about the global environment. However, according to your need, you take two steps: 1. Collect the required information. 2. Make sure the team as a whole has the capability to handle and deal with these issues effectively.

International environment. In this information age, you should think globally even when you act locally. There may be people with different cultural backgrounds right in your organization and even on your project team. Think what factors of local, regional, national, and international customs, laws, and political environment can interact with your project. Here are some obvious ones: time-zone differences, cultural diversity, national and regional holidays, and travel requirements. For example, the time-zone differences will be important in setting up a teleconference. A note on dealing with cultural diversity: Recognize and respect cultural differences. If managed properly, the differences originating from cultural diversity may help you reach a better solution for an issue or a problem.

Identifying Environmental Factors and Process Assets

While exploring the environment of the performing organization, you should also identify the environmental factors and the process assets that will influence your project. Some of these assets and factors can be used to help the project; others may have a negative influence.

Enterprise Environmental Factors

The enterprise environmental factors are related to the environment internal or external to the performing organizations and can potentially impact the project. They may originate from within the performing organization or any external organization participating in the project or both. These factors may have a positive or negative influence on the project, and some of these factors may give rise to constraints for the projects.

Organizational environmental factors include the following:

- The culture and structure of the performing organization

- Government and industry standards, such as legal requirements, product standards, and quality standards relevant to the project

- Infrastructure, such as facilities and equipment to do the project

- Human resources currently available in the organization, such as skills and expertise

- Personnel administration information, such as guidelines for hiring, firing, and performance reviews

- Project management information systems, such as software tools for scheduling tasks and meetings

- Commercial databases, such as standardized cost estimating data and risk databases

- Risk tolerances of the project stakeholders

- Work authorization system of the organization, because the project needs to be authorized

- Marketplace conditions relevant to the project

Enterprise environmental factors may originate from within or be external to the performing organization.

Note that the environmental factors can be internal to the performing organization, such as the organization's culture, or external to the organization, such as market conditions.

Organizational Process Assets

Organizational process assets are the organization's processes that act as assets for the project or assets that support the various processes. Organizational process assets refer to the process assets of any participating organization that can be used to move the project toward success.

The organizational process assets are typically grouped into two categories: processes and procedures for conducting work, and a corporate knowledge base for storing and retrieving information. For example, the performing organization might have its own guidelines, policies, and procedures, whose effect on the project must be considered while developing the project charter and other project documents that will follow. Other examples of an organization's process assets are the knowledge and learning base acquired from the previous projects. The following paragraphs list some items from both categories: processes and procedures and knowledge database.

Processes and procedures. This category includes processes, procedures, guidelines, and requirements as described in the following:

- **Standardized guidelines and criteria.** Examples are project closure guidelines, project acceptance criteria, proposal evaluation criteria, performance measurement criteria, and so on.

55

- **Templates.** Examples are the templates to support some project management tasks, such as risk, project schedule network diagrams, and work breakdown structure.
- **Standardized procedures.** Examples are the procedures for defect management; procedures for controlling changes, finance, and risks; and procedures for issuing work authorizations.
- **Requirements.** Examples are communication requirements, hiring requirements, and safety and security requirements.

Knowledge base. This category includes databases that allow you to store information and to retrieve the stored information when needed. Here are some items in this category:

- **Project files.** The documents and files related to the project, such as the project charter and scope statement.
- **Measurement database.** Examples are the performance measurements.
- **Historical information and lessons learned.** Archives of the files from previous projects and lessons learned from them.
- **Issue and defect management.** Database that allows managing issues and defects such as to log, control, and resolve an issue or defect. You can also find the status of the issue or the defect from this database.
- **Financial database.** The financial information related to the project, such as budget, work hours, and cost overruns.

Standardize This

Identifying all the project stakeholders might be a difficult task, but the following are the obvious stakeholders listed in the PMI standard.

- **Project manager.** Include yourself, the project manager, in the list of the stakeholders to start with. You are responsible for achieving the project objectives.
- **Project management office (PMO).** If your organization has a PMO and it is directly or indirectly responsible for the outcome of a project, then the PMO is a stakeholder in that project. You might be managing one project at a time, whereas

a PMO oversees all the projects within the organization to provide a uniform approach, logistics, and support regardless of the department in which the project is being run.

- **Project management team.** These are the members of the project team involved in the project management tasks.

- **Project team.** This team consists of the project manager, the project management team, and the individuals who perform the work of the project to produce the project outcome. The project management team is composed of those members of the project team who are involved in the project management tasks.

- **Program manager**. If your project is part of a program, then the program manager is certainly a stakeholder in your project.

- **Portfolio managers**. A portfolio manager is an individual who performs high-level management (governance) of a set of projects or programs and interfaces between the projects/programs and the business strategy of the organization from which the projects and programs are being run.

- **Portfolio review board**. This is a committee that is usually composed of the organization's executives, who act as a selection panel for the projects and evaluate the projects for their progress, return on investment, and overall value from time to time.

- **Customer/user.** In general, customers are the entity that will acquire the project's outcome, such as product, and users are the entity that will use the product. In some cases the customers and users may be the same entity, and in other cases there may be a whole chain of customers and users. For example, a textbook produced by a project run by a publisher is recommended by the instructors, bought by the bookstores, and used by the students.

- **Project sponsor.** This is the individual or group that provides financial resources for the project. A sponsor has a major stake in the project and may perform an active role in the project team from time to time.

- **Functional managers.** These are the individuals who play the management roles within administrative or functional areas of the organization. For example, the VP of marketing is a functional manager and so is the director of engineering.

The level of authority depends on their position in the hierarchy and also the organizational structure. If you are using resources that are under a functional manager, that functional manager is a stakeholder in your project.

- **Operational managers**. These are the individuals who are performing management roles in the operational areas of the organization—for example, the director of IT, who is responsible for maintaining the computer network that your team is using is a stakeholder in your project. Depending on your project, you might be handing over the product of the project to an operations group that will be responsible for providing the long-term support for it.

- **Vendors and business partners**. Vendors are entities external to the performing organization, such as contractors and suppliers who enter into a contractual agreement with the performing organization to provide certain components for the project. These components are the products, services, or results that you procure. Business partners are the external organizations that fill a specific role for the project, such as installing the product of the project, providing training and support for the product, or providing a specialized expertise for the project. Business partners are different from vendors in that they have a special ongoing relationship with the organization, which is often attained by satisfying some requirements, such as a certification.

PROGRESSIVE ELABORATION

You will develop the plans for the project from the needs, objectives, and requirements that you will gather. You will see that in some, if not most, cases, the requirements do not come all at once in one nice bundle. Depending on the complexity of the project, they come from different stakeholders at different times. A requirement may be in, but the related estimate may not be that precise. However, you do not need to wait until all the requirements are in. When a sufficient number of requirements are in, you can begin to develop plans. These plans will be improved and detailed further as more requirements come in. The continual process of improving and detailing plans as new and more precise requirement information comes in is called *progressive elaboration*. To some degree, progressive elaboration may continue throughout the project's lifetime.

Quick Success Mantras

- Project manager is a role in which you apply project management to the project at hand.
- Build your reputation as a change manager or a change agent and not a change opponent.
- The ultimate responsibility of a project manager is to deliver the planned project output, such as products, within the planned scope, schedule, cost, and quality.
- You use all your skills and qualities to lead the project to success by navigating through the project environment.
- In order to lead the project stakeholders, you will be wearing different communication hats at different times, communicating with different individuals and groups.
- An effective project manager has a multitude of management and interpersonal skills.
- The project environment is constituted by organizational culture, organizational structure, and global environmental factors.
- The general definition of success of a project is delivering the project outcome with full scope, on time, and within the budget.
- To ensure that a successful project will be seen as successful by all the stakeholders, you must manage stakeholder expectations throughout the project.

Chapter 4

Initiating a Project

The foundations for the success of a project are laid in the project definition: A poorly defined project is destined to fail. Before the project can be defined, it has to originate from somewhere. It may originate from inside the performing organization or from outside of it. In either case, it is based on a business need that is linked to the business strategy of the performing organization. It is crucial to the success of the project that the definition of the project is agreed upon by all parties and preserved in a document such as project charter. Based on this definition, you will need to identify and analyze the project stakeholders and develop a strategy to manage them. All these tasks are performed under one umbrella: initiating the project.

So, the central question in this chapter is: How is a project initiated? In search of the answer, you will explore three avenues with me: origins of projects, project definition, and identification and analysis of project stakeholders.

In this chapter, you will learn about:

- What constitutes the project initiation
- Origins of projects
- What constitutes the project definition
- The impact of the project definition and the stakeholders on the project success
- How to identify and analyze project stakeholders and develop a strategy to manage them
- How different elements of initiating a project, such as origin, definition, and stakeholder identification, are related to each other
- How projects are selected and approved

Initiating a Project: Big Picture

Initiating a project means defining the project, getting approval to start it, and identifying and analyzing the project stakeholders. During this stage, the initial scope of the project is defined. Accordingly, initial resources are determined and allocated, a project manager with the appropriate authority level is assigned, and project stakeholders are identified. Defining the project includes the following:

- Developing project objectives and describing how they are related to the organization's business objectives and strategy.

- Specifying the project deliverables, such as products, services, or results that will meet the objectives. In some cases, a deliverable and an objective may be the same.

- Based on the objectives and deliverables, defining the initial scope of the project by explaining what will be done and drawing boundaries around what will be done. Where necessary, this means stating what will not be included.

- Based on the initial scope, estimating project duration and the resources needed. More accurate estimates will be made during planning.

- Assigning the initial project resources. For example, some initial resources are needed just to define and plan the project before even beginning to execute it.

- Assigning a project manager.

- Authorizing the project. While different organizations may have different procedures to approve the processes, the standard way to do it is to approve the document that holds the definition of the project, such as the project charter.

Based on the project definition, you will identify the stakeholders. Figure 4.1 presents the big picture of initiating a project by illustrating the relationship between major elements of this stage.

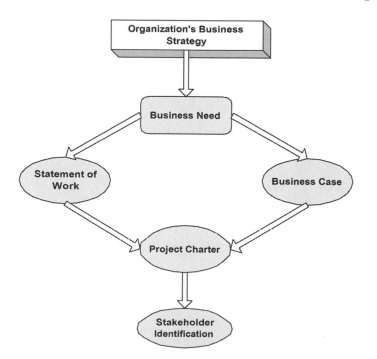

Figure 4.1
Illustration of the relationship among the major building blocks of the big picture of initiating a project.

If your project is divided into different phases, you will be going through the initiation stage at the beginning of each phase to check whether the decisions and plans made during the initiation of the project are still relevant to this phase. It helps to ensure the project is still focused on the business need for which it was started.

The business need to be met by the project emerges from the organization's business strategy, and based on the business need, somebody writes the statement of work and makes the business case. The business case and statement of work are the starting points to develop the initial project scope and thereby determine the initial resources. All this information is captured in the project charter, which will help in identifying the stakeholders.

We will explore all these elements in detail further on in this chapter. However, before you can begin the project initiation process, someone must request the project. So let's back up a little and ask a fundamental question: Where do the projects originally come from?

Where Projects Come From

Projects are often originated from sources external to the project management office—for example, internally, by some department of the company, or externally, by an enterprise or a government agency. A project may originate as a result of one or more of the following categories of reasons.

Business and legal requirements. This category includes projects based on a business need or a legal requirement. For example, a web design company authorizes a project to automate certain aspects of maintaining websites to increase its efficiency and revenue. As another example, consider a building owner authorizing a project to make the building accessible to physically disabled persons in order to meet the legal requirements for using the building for a specific business.

Opportunities. The projects that fall into this category might include those based on a customer request, a market demand, or a breakthrough in technology. For example, several electronics companies authorized projects to manufacture MP3 players following the invention and popularity of MP3 technology. The performing organization takes on these opportunities to satisfy its business needs.

Problems. Projects are also authorized to offer solutions to certain problems in a company, a country, or a society. For example, the government might start a project to help the victims of a natural disaster, such as a hurricane. A company might authorize a project to analyze the problem of low employee productivity and to design a solution for this problem. In a direct or an indirect way, addressing these problems serves the business needs of the performing organization.

Social needs. Governmental or non-governmental organizations initiate projects to satisfy some social needs, such as a project to provide access to the Internet in an underprivileged community or a project to set up a latrine and sewer system in a remote community. These kinds of projects based on social needs are often run by nonprofit organizations. Even if not for profit, the projects in such organizations are also linked to the business needs of the organization because in order to perform the projects the organization must survive, and in order to survive the organization must work according to its strategic business plan.

A project may originate due to business and legal requirements, opportunities, problems, and/or social needs.

The sources of the project requests can vary widely in different organizations. Depending upon your organization, the origins of projects might be inside the organization, outside the organization, or both. In any case, there is a business need driving the project.

STUDY CHECKPOINT 4.1

The goal of the nonprofit organization *Mind the Gap* is to eliminate the digital gap between the rich and the poor. The organization has started a project that will help underprivileged communities get access to the Internet. Explain how this project is based on a business need of the organization.

Solution:

Obviously, the strategic business plan of this organization includes the goal of eliminating the digital gap. To achieve that goal, one of the business needs of the organization is to get the underprivileged communities onto the Internet. This project is based on that business need.

Once the idea of a project has been offered, entertained, and discussed, it comes down to the following two questions:

1. **Should we do it?** The answer to this question is determined by the benefits expected to be obtained from the project as compared to the effort and the cost.

2. **Can we do it?** The answer to this question is determined by whether the project is technically and financially feasible.

These questions are explored in more detail during the project selection process. But if the answer to these two questions obtained just by expert judgment at this stage is yes, you can begin defining the project.

Defining the Project

Defining the project means specifying certain aspects of the project at a high level, such as project objectives and product, project scope, project budget, and success criteria. Defining the project effectively may make the difference between a failed project and a successful project. The seeds of success are sowed into the definition of the project.

Laying Down the Foundations for Success

You may have heard phrases like this: In order to succeed, keep your eyes on the ball. Well, it's certainly not going to help if you don't exactly know where the ball is to begin with or if you keep your eyes on the wrong ball. Not only you, but the whole team and all the other project stakeholders should agree on which ball you are talking about. In this analogy, defining the project is identifying the right ball. This is how critical defining the project is to the success of the project.

Following are the three cornerstones for the foundation of the project success:

1. Define the project clearly and effectively.
2. Define the project success and make it part of the project definition.
3. Get agreement on this project definition from all the participating stakeholders.

A clear and effective project definition answers the following ten questions.

1. Why are we doing this project? What's the purpose?
2. What are the objectives of this project?
3. What are the project deliverables and the requirements for the deliverables?
4. How are the project objectives related to the organization's business objectives? That is, what are the benefits of the project? This will help make the business case for the project and define the project success.

5. How are we going to accomplish the project objectives? This will lead to defining the project scope.

6. What resources are needed and how much is it going to cost us?

7. How long is it going to take to complete the project?

8. Who are the individuals and organizations that are going to be impacted by this project? This will help identify the stakeholders.

9. How is this project related to other projects in the organization? This will put the project in the right context of the big picture and also will expose the dependencies and needed coordination.

10. How will we know whether the project was successful? This question will lead to the definition of success.

It is critical that all the participating stakeholders, such as the project team, sponsor, involved executive management, and customer, agree on these defining components. You must listen to and consider the different views of different stakeholders. Balancing different expectations and requirements by give and take may take some time, but it's worth it: If they can't agree now, it will be that much harder to bring them to an agreement after the project begins. Any unresolved disagreements during the initiating stage will keep getting wider during the course of the project.

How do you actually get agreement from all stakeholders on the project definition? You put the definition in a document and get the stakeholders to sign off on this document. You can call it the *project definition document*. Documentation is an integral component of project management, and it starts right from the beginning: the initiation stage.

Documenting the Project Definition

The project definition is the basis on which the project planning and thereby the project execution will depend. This is also an agreement among the stakeholders. Therefore, it's important to preserve it in a document. In practice, the document will be developed as you are developing the definition and getting the agreement of all the stakeholders.

The standard name for the project definition document is the *project charter.*

Different organizations have different names for the project definition document, such as project charter, statement of work, scope statement, preliminary scope statement, and so on. Some organizations may be using more than one document to contain the definition.

Project Charter

The project charter is more than just a project definition document. When approved, it becomes a declaration for launching the project. The project charter, in general, includes the items discussed in the following list.

- **Purpose and justification.** The project justification includes the purpose of the project and the business case for the project, which in turn may include return on investment. This section should describe what problem is being solved and what business need is being met by this project.

- **Project objectives.** This section is derived from the purpose section. It explains what exactly is going to be accomplished to meet the purpose—that is, the outcome of the project. Each objective should be measurable and should have a success criterion assigned to it.

- **High-level requirements.** This section specifies the requirements for the project and the project outcome, such as project deadline or product characteristics. These requirements are derived from the needs of the customer, the sponsor, and other stakeholders.

- **High-level project description.** This project description includes the business needs that the project addresses and the high-level deliverables, such as products and product requirements. It may also include items such as the following:

  - A list of participating functional departments of the organization and their roles in the project.

  - Organizational, environmental, and external assumptions and constraints.

- **Project scope.** A high-level scope of the project—that is, determination of the work that needs to be done to produce the project objectives and deliverables. The scope will be worked out in more detail during the planning stage.

- **Schedule.** A summary of the high-level schedule, including milestones.

- **A budget summary.** This will include the resources required for the project and the cost/budget to ensure those resources.

- **Project acceptance requirements and criteria:**
  - What constitutes the project success?
  - Who decides whether the project is successful?
  - Who signs off on the project completion?
- **Project manager.** An assigned project manager and a specified responsibility and authority level for that project manager.
- **Approval.** The name and responsibility of the person or committee that will approve the charter.

SUCCESS SHOT

In the field of project management, there is a general agreement that each project objective should be SMART: specific, measurable, achievable, realistic, and timely. If an objective is not specific and not measurable, it will mean different things to different stakeholders, resulting in different expectations. If the objective is not achievable and realistic, you are setting up the project for failure. The objective must be achieved in a timely manner because an achievable objective can always be obtained if there is no time limit, and it does not mean success if the deadline was not met.

ASSUMPTIONS AND CONSTRAINTS

An *assumption* is a factor that you consider to be true without any proof or verification. For example, an obvious assumption that you might make during planning for an in-house project could be the availability of the required skill set to perform the project.

It's important to document assumptions clearly and validate them at various stages of the project because assumptions carry a certain degree of uncertainty with them, and uncertainty means risk. Assumptions can appear in both the input and the output of various processes.

A *constraint* is a restriction (or a limitation) that can affect the performance of the project. It can appear in both the input and the output of various processes. For example, there could be a schedule constraint that the project must be completed by a predetermined date. Similarly, a cost constraint would limit the budget available for the project.

You may ask: From where do I get all this information that goes into the project charter? You get this information from documents that contain the business case for the project and the project statement of work. Depending on the project, you may even have participated in writing these documents and gathering information from the sources, such as the customer and the sponsor.

Business Case

The origins of the business case are pretty much the same as the origins of a project, discussed earlier in this chapter. The business case is built on the business need addressed by the project that justifies the project. This will determine whether the project is worth the effort and the investment. The business case may contain the cost benefit analysis described further on in this chapter. The business case is written either by the person or group within the performing organization that is proposing the project or by an external organization or the customer who is requesting the project or the product that will be produced by the project.

If the organization that is requesting the project is a separate legal entity than the organization that is performing the project, each may have its own business case. In this scenario, the business case that goes into the project is the business case of the performing organization. The business case of the requesting organization will make its way to the project through the contract or the statement of work.

Project Statement of Work

The statement of work (SOW) describes the products or services that will be delivered by the project. For an internal project, the SOW is provided by the project initiator or the project sponsor, whereas for an external project the SOW is received from the customer as part of a bid document, such as a request for proposals or a request for bids, or it can be derived from a contract. The SOW at minimum should include the following items:

- **Business need.** Describes the business need addressed by the project.
- **Product scope.** Describes the product and the scope of the product to be produced by the project. Product scope means what characteristics and features are included and what are not.
- **Strategic plan.** Describes how the project and its product are related to the organization's business strategy.

Do not confuse the *product* scope with the *project* scope—these are related though different concepts. Product scope is defined as features and functions that characterize a product, service, or result to be delivered by the project, whereas the project scope is the scope of the whole project and is defined as the entire work required to create the project deliverables.

Some organizations might perform a feasibility study or its equivalent to justify the project before developing the project charter and initiating the project. The feasibility study may itself become a project.

At minimum, the statement of work should include the business need, the product scope, and the strategic plan.

STANDARDIZE THIS

In the PMI standard, the document that contains the project definition is called the *project charter*. Once this document is signed by the proper individuals, the project is said to be *chartered*. That means the project has been authorized and a project manager has been assigned with appropriate authority to use the resources for the project.

You know by now that a project can originate from multiple possible sources. Understanding the origin of a specific project helps you to develop the project definition. However, not all requested and well-defined projects are authorized. How does an organization decide which projects to select?

Understanding Project Selection

Depending on your organization and your place in it, you may or may not be involved in selecting projects, but in order to be a savvy project manager, you must know how projects are generally selected. A project can be selected by using one or more project selection methods that fall into three categories: benefit measurement methods, constrained optimization methods, and expert judgment.

Benefit Measurement Methods

These methods use comparative approaches to compare the benefits obtained from the candidate projects so that the project with the maximum benefit will be selected. These methods fall into three subcategories: scoring models, benefit contributions, and economic models.

Scoring Models

A scoring model evaluates projects by using a set of criteria with a weight (score) assigned to each criterion. You can assign different weights to different criteria to represent the varied degree of importance given to various criteria. All projects are evaluated (scored) against this set of criteria, and the project with the maximum score is selected. The set of criteria can include both objective and subjective criteria, such as financial data, organizational expertise, market value, innovation, and fit with the corporate culture. The advantage of a scoring model is that you have the freedom to assign different weights to different criteria in order to select projects consistent with the goals, mission, and vision of your corporation. This freedom, however, is also a disadvantage because your selection is only as good as the criteria with larger weights. Furthermore, developing a good scoring model is a difficult task that requires unbiased cross-departmental feedback from different levels of the organization.

> A scoring model assigns a weight to each criterion to evaluate projects based on the final score the project receives.

Benefit Contributions

These methods are based on comparing the benefit contributions from different projects. These contributions can be estimated by performing a cost benefit analysis, which typically calculates the projected cost, revenue, and savings of a project. This method favors the projects that create profit in the shortest time and ignores the long-term benefits of projects that might not be tangible at the current time, such as innovation and strategic values.

Economic Models

An economic model is used to estimate the economic efficiency of a project, and it involves a set of calculations to provide overall financial data about the project. The common terms involved in economic models are explained in the following list.

- **Benefit Cost Ratio (BCR).** This is the value obtained by dividing the benefit by the cost. The greater the value, the more attractive the project is. For example, if the projected cost of producing a product is $20,000, and you expect to sell it for $60,000, then the BCR is equal to $60,000/$20,000, which is equal to 3. For the benefit to exceed cost, the BCR must be greater than 1.

- **Cash flow.** Whereas cash refers to money, cash flow refers to both the money coming in and the money going out of an organization. Positive cash flow means more money coming in than going out. Cash inflow is benefit (income), and cash outflow is cost (expenses).

- **Internal Return Rate (IRR).** This is just another way of interpreting the benefit from the project. It looks at the cost of the project as the capital investment and translates the profit into the interest rate over the life of that investment. Calculations for IRR are outside the scope of this book. Just understand that the greater the value for IRR, the more beneficial the project is.

- **Present Value (PV) and Net Present Value (NPV).** To understand these two concepts, understand that one dollar today can buy you more than what one dollar next year can buy. (Think about inflation and return.) The issue arises because it takes time to complete a project, and even when a project is completed, its benefits are reaped over a period of time, not immediately. In other words, the project is costing you today but will benefit you tomorrow. So, to make an accurate calculation for the profit, the cost and benefits must be converted to the same point in time. The NPV of a project is the present value of the future cash inflow (benefits) minus the present value of the current and future cash outflow (cost). For a project to be worthwhile economically, the NPV must be positive. As an example, assume you invest $600,000 today to build a house, which will be completed and sold after three years for $900,000. Also assume that real estate that is worth $700,000 today will be worth $900,000 after three years. So the present value of the cash inflow on your house is $700,000, and hence the NPV is the present value of the cash inflow minus the present value of the cash outflow, which equals $700,000–$600,000, which equals $100,000.

- **Opportunity cost.** This refers to selecting a project over another due to the scarcity of resources. In other words, by spending this dollar on this project, you are passing on the opportunity to spend this dollar on another project. How big an opportunity are you missing? The smaller the opportunity cost, the better it is.

- **Discounted Cash Flow (DCF).** The discounted cash flow refers to the amount that someone is willing to pay today in anticipation of receiving the cash flow in the future. DCF is calculated by taking the amount that you anticipate to receive in the future and discounting (converting) it back to today on the time scale. This conversion factors in the interest rate and opportunity cost between now (when you are spending cash) and the time when you will receive the cash back.

- **Return on Investment (ROI).** The ROI is the percentage profit from the project. For example, if you spend $400,000 on the project, and the benefit for the first year is $500,000, then ROI equals ($500,000–$400,000)/$400,000, which equals 25%.

The details and calculations for these quantities are outside the scope of this book. Just understand the basic concepts and whether a larger or a smaller value for a given quantity favors the project selection.

STUDY CHECKPOINT 4.2

You have been offered a Project B that will earn you a profit of $20,000 in three months. You already have an offer of a Project A that will earn you a profit of $25,000 in three months. You can only do one project during these three months, and the project requesters are unable to move the project durations.

1. What is the opportunity cost of Project A?
2. What is the opportunity cost of Project B?
3. Just based on the opportunity cost, which project will you select?
4. Describe what can change your decision based just on the opportunity cost.

Answers:

1. **$20,000** because this is the opportunity that you are missing when you take on Project A.
2. **$25,000** because this is the opportunity that you are missing when you take on Project B.
3. **Project A** will be selected because it has a smaller opportunity cost.
4. Opportunity cost is only one of several criteria that are used to select projects. Perhaps some other criteria, such as scoring model, may produce different results. You have to see which method is more relevant for your case.

As the name suggests, all the benefit measurement methods are based on calculating some kind of benefit from the given project. However, the benefit will never be realized if the project fails. This concern has given rise to methods based on calculating the success of the projects; these methods are called *constrained optimization methods.*

Constrained Optimization Methods

Constrained optimization methods are concerned with predicting the success of the project. These methods are based on complex mathematical models that use formulae and algorithms to predict the success of a project. These models use the following kinds of algorithms:

- Linear
- Nonlinear
- Dynamic
- Integer
- Multiple objective programming

The details of these models are outside the scope of this book.

Either in conjunction with other methods or in absence of them, organizations often rely on expert judgment in making selection decisions.

Expert Judgment

Expert judgment is one of the techniques used in project management to accomplish various tasks, including project selection. It refers to making a decision by relying on expert advice from one or more of the following sources:

- An appropriate unit within the organization
- The project stakeholders, including customers and sponsors
- Consultants
- Professional and technical associations
- Industry groups

Keep in mind that expert judgment can be very subjective at times and might include political influence. An excellent salesperson or an executive with great influence can exploit this method successfully.

The use of expert judgment is not limited to the project selection; it can be used in many processes, such as developing a project charter.

An organization might use multiple selection methods to make a decision. If the project is selected, it must be properly authorized.

Getting Project Authorization

The single most important outcome of the project initiating stage is the project authorization. The standard way of authorizing a project is through an approval of the project charter by an appropriate person in the performing organization. Who this person is depends on the organization and the project. This person, for example, could be the CEO of the company, the project sponsor, or a representative of the project selection committee.

With the approval of the project charter, the project is officially authorized, the project manager is officially assigned, and the authority level of the project manager is determined. In practice, it does happen that the (future) project manager participates in developing the project charter, but project approval and resource assignments, such as funding, generally happen outside the boundaries of project management.

Approval of the project charter officially authorizes the project. Before reaching this point in time, you will already know some of the project stakeholders. But it is time that you begin identifying and analyzing the project stakeholders in more detail.

Identifying the Project Stakeholders

Actively involving the project stakeholders during the initiating stage improves the sense of ownership among the stakeholders, helps you manage stakeholder expectations throughout the project lifecycle, gets the stakeholders on the same page, helps deliver stakeholder satisfaction, and thereby contributes to the project success.

Identifying stakeholders includes the following:

- Identifying individuals and organizations that will influence and be impacted by the project
- Documenting relevant information about the individuals and organizations and about their interests and involvement in the project
- Documenting how these individuals and organizations can influence the project and how they can be impacted by the project
- Determining their levels of importance

As said earlier, stakeholder identification is necessary in order to manage stakeholder expectations and to manage their influence on the project. They can influence various aspects of the project, such as definition, changes, execution, deliverables, and ultimately success. They may come from inside the organization, with different levels of authority, or from outside the organization.

Identifying stakeholders is an iterative process—that is, you might have to perform the identification over and over again because some old stakeholders may become irrelevant and some new stakeholders may appear during the life of the project. Because identifying and analyzing the stakeholders and managing their expectations and influence is so critical to the success of the project, you should start this task early on in the project.

The two major components of the stakeholder identification process are stakeholder analysis and stakeholder management strategy.

Stakeholder Analysis

Stakeholder analysis is an activity to gather and analyze information about the stakeholders. Following are some major steps in this process:

1. Identify all potential stakeholders.
2. Identify the following characteristics of each potential stakeholder:
   a. **Name, department, and role.** For example, Dr. John Serri, Vice President, Research and Development.
   b. **Interest in the project.** Why should the stakeholder be interested in the project—is the stakeholder seeking to benefit or being threatened?
   c. **Knowledge level.** What is the knowledge level of the stakeholder, especially about the project and in the application area of the project?
   d. **Expectations.** What are the stakeholder's expectations from the project?
   e. **Kind and level of influence.** In what way and how much can the stakeholder influence the project?
3. Depending on their level of interest, influence, and participation, group the stakeholders into two categories: key stakeholders and other stakeholders.
4. Depending on whether they will benefit from the project or feel threatened by the project, group the stakeholders into two categories: positive stakeholders and negative stakeholders.

5. For each stakeholder, determine the level of impact the project can exert on the stakeholder and the level of influence the stakeholder can exert on the project.

6. Make an assessment of how a stakeholder is going to react to various situations in the project.

Based on the stakeholder analysis, you develop the strategy for managing the stakeholders.

Stakeholder Management Strategy

The stakeholder management strategy is the approach developed to deal with the stakeholders in the best interest of the project. The strategy should include the following elements:

- Key stakeholders
- For each stakeholder, level of influence on the project and level of impact on the stakeholder from the project
- How to manage individual stakeholders
- How to manage groups of stakeholders

For example, you can maintain the strategy in a matrix like the one shown in Table 4.1.

Table 4.1 An Example Template for the Stakeholder Management Strategy Matrix

Stakeholder	Interest in the Project	Assessment of Impact of the Project on the Stakeholder	Level of Influence of the Stakeholder on the Project	Positive Stakeholder or Negative Stakeholder?	Strategy for Maximizing Support or Minimizing Negative Impact

SUCCESS SHOT

The stakeholder management strategy should include both the positive and the negative stakeholders. You should develop and implement the stakeholder management strategy with one goal in mind: to optimize the project success by maximizing the support from the positive stakeholders and minimizing (or mitigating) the damaging impact on the project from the negative stakeholders.

During the analysis you can draw a variable against another variable and see where the stakeholders fit in that plot. If the variables are chosen carefully, the plot will suggest how much attention should be given to various stakeholders in the plot. As an example, Figure 4.2 presents such a plot in which the X-axis represents the level of interest from very low to very high, and the Y-axis represents the capability of influencing the project from very low to very high. Stakeholders 1, 2, and 3 have a low interest in the project and low capability of influencing the project, and therefore do not deserve much of your time and effort. However, they must be monitored because the interest and the capability may change over time. On the other extreme,

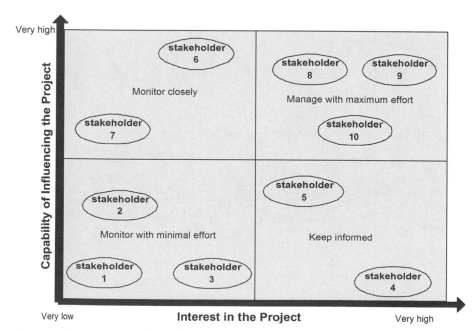

Figure 4.2 *An example of determining the strategy by plotting stakeholders against different variables.*

Stakeholders 8, 9, and 10 have a high interest in the project and have a very high capability to influence the project. Now, these stakeholders should obviously be managed with maximum effort.

It is imperative that you maintain the information from the stakeholder identification process in one or more documents. The standard name for this document or a set of documents is the *stakeholder register*.

Standardize This

You can accomplish everything discussed in this chapter without mentioning the word *process*. However, in standard project management, you do almost everything using a set of processes. The concept of a process and its three elements—input, output, and tools and techniques—were discussed in Chapter 2. The processes used by the PMI standard to initiate a project are illustrated in Figures 4.3 and 4.4. The develop project charter process is used to develop the project charter, and the identify stakeholders process is used to identify and analyze stakeholders and to

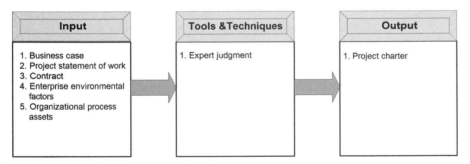

Figure 4.3 *The develop project charter process: input, tools and techniques, and output.*

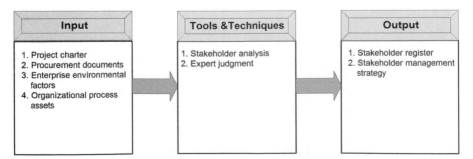

Figure 4.4 *The identify stakeholders process: input, tools and techniques, and output.*

develop the stakeholder register and the stakeholder management strategy. All the items in Figures 4.3 and 4.4 were discussed earlier in this chapter. Note that a contract is required when the performing organization and the customer of the project are two different legal entities.

You can look at Figures 4.3 and 4.4 and align what you have learned in this chapter along these two processes.

STUDY CHECKPOINT 4.3

Make a list of documents produced during the initiation stage of a project.

Answer:

Project charter, stakeholder register, statement of work, and business case.

Quick Success Mantras

- A project can originate inside the performing organization or outside of it, in order to meet business needs by meeting business or legal requirements, taking on an opportunity, offering a solution to a problem, or aiming to satisfy a social need.

- Initiating a project includes defining the project, authorizing the project, and identifying and analyzing the project stakeholders.

- Defining the project means specifying certain aspects of the project at a high level, such as project objectives and product, project scope, project budget, and success criteria.

- The project definition is stored in a document called the project charter.

- The project charter also names the project manager and determines the authority level of the project manager.

- All major stakeholders must approve the project charter as a token of their agreement on the project definition.

- Issuing an approved project charter moves the project from the initiation stage into the planning stage discussed in the next chapter.

- Overall, the initiation stage accomplishes the following:
  - Project objectives and deliverables are determined.
  - An initial scope of the project is defined.
  - Initial financial resources are estimated and committed.
  - The project is selected and approved.
  - The project manager is assigned with an appropriate authority level
  - Stakeholders are identified and analyzed.

PART II

Planning the Project

Congratulations, you have already defined your project as described in Part I. You can't wait to begin executing. But hold on! I have a couple of questions for you. First, when you are executing your project, how will you know that you are on the right track? Second, during the execution, how will you know that the project is performing in such a way that you will end up with success? To address these two and other related questions, you will need to do some planning before you begin the execution. Also, to lead the project to success, you want to monitor and control it throughout its lifetime. Planning gives you the tools and the framework to do exactly that; for example, a performance baseline against which you will be measuring the progress of the project—an important part of monitoring and controlling—is developed during planning. This baseline is constituted by the scope baseline, schedule baseline, and cost baseline, which are developed during scope, schedule, and cost planning. You will also need to plan for the resources needed to complete the project. Any management task has the potential to increase or decrease a potential risk. Therefore, all project management is inherently connected to risk management. You need to plan for managing risks.

Initiation determines *what* will be done, whereas planning embraces that *what*, refines it, and determines *how* it will be done.

Chapter 5

Scoping the Project

- Planning the Project: Big Picture
- Managing the Project Scope: Big Picture
- Collecting Requirements for the Project
- Defining the Project Scope
- Organizing the Project Work into the Work Breakdown Structure
- Standardize This
- Quick Success Mantras

Initiation determines what the project will do, whereas planning is needed to determine how it will be done. The first thing you do during planning is finalize the project definition determined during project initiation. In other words, you determine the project scope by writing down exactly what needs to be done—that is, what is included and what is not. To determine precisely what is included in the project, you need to collect the project and product requirements. With requirements at your disposal, you can draw boundaries around the project—that is, determine the project scope. Practically speaking, project scope is the work that needs to be done to deliver the planned outcome—product, service, or result—of the project. However, the work will be done by specific individuals and groups. So, the scope needs to be broken down into manageable pieces that can be assigned to these individuals and groups. This breakdown is called the *work breakdown structure (WBS)*, and the details about this structure are called the *WBS dictionary*. The WBS, WBS dictionary, and scope statement constitute what is called the *scope baseline*.

So, the central question in this chapter concerns how to develop the scope baseline? In search of the answer, you will explore three avenues with me: collecting requirements, defining the scope, and creating the WBS.

In this chapter you'll learn:

- How to develop the project management plan
- How to collect requirements
- How to define the projects scope
- How to create the work breakdown structure (WBS)
- About the relationship between collecting requirements, defining the scope, creating the WBS, developing the project management plan, and ensuring the project's success
- How to identify the standard processes to develop the project management plan, collect requirements, define the scope, and create the WBS

Planning the Project: Big Picture

Once the project has been initiated, it's time to do some planning. This planning includes determining the project scope, during which you'll refine the project objectives and determine some how to's: how the scope will be executed, how the execution will be monitored and controlled, and how the project will be brought to a proper closure. Project planning is embodied in the project management plan that is developed through progressive elaboration, a concept explained in Chapter 3. The project management plan is a document that defines, prepares, coordinates, and integrates all subsidiary plans, such as the scope and risk management plans, into one plan. The goal here is to develop a source of information that will work as a guideline for how the project will be executed, monitored and controlled, and closed.

> Project planning involves determining exactly what will be done and how it will be done.

To start with, it is important to plan the project because not all projects need all the planning processes, nor do they all need them to the same degree. Therefore, the content of the project management plan will depend upon a specific project. As the project goes through different stages, the project management plan may be updated and revised through the change control process. Following is an incomplete list of issues that a project management plan addresses:

- Which project management processes will be used for the project, what the level of implementation for each of the processes will be, and what the inputs and tools and techniques for the processes are

- The project baseline against which the performance of the project will be measured and against which the project will be monitored and controlled

- How the changes will be monitored and controlled

- What the needs and techniques for communication among the stakeholders are

- How the project lifecycle looks, including the project phases if the project is a multiphase one

---

PROJECT BASELINE

The *project baseline* is defined as the approved plan for the scope, schedule, and cost of the project. The project performance is measured against this baseline, and therefore this baseline is also called the *performance baseline*. The project baseline is also referred to in terms of its components: cost baseline, schedule baseline, and scope baseline. How do you know how the project is performing? You compare the performance to the baseline. Approved changes in scope, schedule, or cost will obviously change the baseline.

Figure 5.1 presents the big picture of project planning. Depending upon the complexity of the project, the project management plan can be either a summary or a collection of subsidiary plans and components, which might include the following:

- Standard plans from different aspects of project planning, such as the cost management plan, the communication management plan, the scope management plan, and the risk management plan.

- Other components, such as the milestones list, the resource calendar, and baselines for scope, schedule, cost, and quality. A *baseline* is a reference plan against which all the performance deviations are measured. This reference plan can be the original or the updated plan.

Figure 5.1

A high-level view of interactions and data flow between different components of project planning.

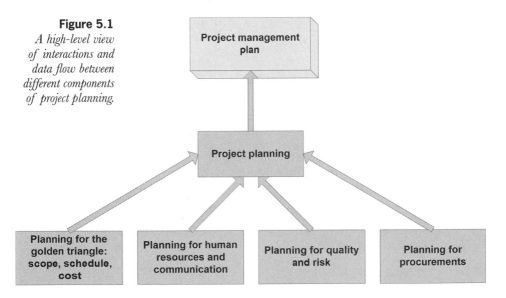

In a nutshell, project planning involves determining exactly what will be done and how it will be done. The output of all the planning processes goes into developing the project management plan. Executing a project means implementing the project management plan for that project. Therefore, the project management plan contains the project scope that defines what needs to be done to meet the project objectives. The scope needs to be managed.

> **SUCCESS SHOT**
>
> Project success is a six-wheel vehicle that you drive to the finish line, and the six wheels are: *what, how, why, when, who, and where. What* is determined during initiation and planning, and *how* is worked out during planning. In the process of determining *how*, you also end up determining *why, who, when,* and *where.* Here is an example: What will be done, how will it be done, why should it be done and why should it be done in a certain way, when will it be done, where will it be done, and who will do it? Always ask questions like these throughout the lifecycle of the project, not only during planning.

Managing the Project Scope: Big Picture

Practically speaking, the scope of a project is defined as the work that must be performed to deliver the required outcome—product, service, or result—of a project. It is about both what is included in the project and what is not. In other words, scoping a project means drawing boundaries around what is included. The importance of managing the project scope cannot be overemphasized, as it has a profound impact on the overall success of the project.

> **TIP**
>
> The scope of a project consists of the work that must be performed to deliver the required project outcome.

The major goal of scope management is to ensure that the required work—and only the required work—is included and performed in the project. As shown in Figure 5.2, this goal is accomplished by the following functions of project management:

- **Collect the requirements.** Define the project and product requirements and develop a plan to manage those requirements. This will help clarify what needs to be done.
- **Define the scope.** Develop a detailed description of the project and the product that will determine what needs to be done.

Figure 5.2
A high-level view of interactions and data flow between different components of scope management.

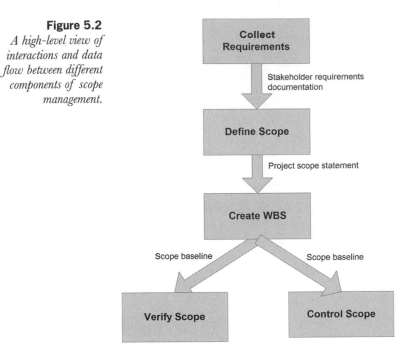

- **Create the work breakdown structure (WBS).** Break down the scope into concrete, manageable components. In other words, break down the project deliverables into manageable tasks that can be assigned to team members.
- **Verify the scope.** Formalize the acceptance of the completed project deliverables—that is, determine how to verify that the project scope has been executed as planned.
- **Control the scope.** Determine how to monitor the status of the project and the product scope and monitor and control changes to the scope.

Verifying and controlling the scope will be discussed further on in this book, whereas other components of scope management are discussed in this chapter, starting with collecting requirements.

Collecting Requirements for the Project

Recall that the project success is defined as the delivery of the planned outcome with full scope, on time, and within the schedule. To realize this success, it's very important that there is an agreement on what exactly is being delivered and with what requirements. A requirement is a condition, characteristic, or capability that a specific outcome of the project must have. For example, an online banking website is an outcome of the project, and the expectation that it must record the number of users that visit the site each day is a requirement. Stakeholder expectations and needs often materialize into requirements.

You need to do some requirement planning, which includes:

- Defining and documenting the project requirements
- Defining and documenting the product requirements
- Developing a plan to manage the requirements—the requirements management plan

You do all this to determine and fulfill stakeholder expectations and needs.

SUCCESS SHOT

How effective you are in collecting requirements will determine how effective you will be in getting agreement on these requirements from the stakeholders and in managing the stakeholder expectations and needs. Also, these requirements go right into the foundations of the WBS, along with the deliverables. Therefore, collecting requirements effectively is critical for the success of the project.

During project initiation, you created the project charter and the stakeholder register, both of which were discussed in Chapter 4. These two documents are the starting point to collecting requirements. Recall that the project charter contains the high-level product description and requirements. You get the information about the stakeholders from the stakeholder register, and you start collecting the needed information about the requirements by using various techniques, such as interviews, questionnaires and surveys, and focus groups and workshops. You can also collect requirements by making a prototype (working model) of the expected product and by simply observing the stakeholders—listening to their comments and reactions in various settings.

Requirement planning includes defining and documenting project and product requirements and developing a requirements management plan.

During this process of collecting the requirements, you will produce two documents: the stakeholder requirements document and the requirements management plan.

Stakeholder Requirements Document

This document consists of a list of requirements and any necessary detail for each item in the list. The details of the requirements and the format of the document depend on the project and the rules within the performing organization. Following are some essential elements of the requirement document:

The requirements must be well defined and not vague. As a test, always ask this question: How will I be able to measure or test it? Also, make sure that a requirement is consistent within itself and with other requirements.

- **Sources of requirements.** This describes the overall project outcome to which the requirements apply and the purpose of the project, such as the opportunity being seized or the business problem being solved.

- **Types of requirements.** For effective management, you can organize the requirements into different categories using some criteria. For example, all requirements can be broadly organized into two categories: functional requirements, referring to the functionality of the project outcome; and nonfunctional requirements, such as compliance, compatibility, and support. Furthermore, these broad categories can be subdivided into more specific types, such as the following:

  - Quality requirements, such as not more than three bugs per software module

  - Support and training requirements, such as the product being released with a manual

  - Requirements that are based on assumptions and requirements that lead to constraints—for example, Phase I of the project must be completed before a specific date

- **Impacts of the requirements.** This element describes the impact of requirements on the project and on entities external to the project, such as different groups in the organization.

The requirements that you collected will need to be managed.

Requirements Management Plan

This plan documents how the requirements will be managed throughout the project's life, which includes how they will be documented and analyzed. The requirements management plan includes the following elements:

- **Prioritization.** The process and criteria to prioritize the requirements.

- **Configuration management.** How the changes to the requirements will be processed: initiated, analyzed, tracked, and reported.

- **Reporting.** How, by whom, and to whom the activities related to the requirements will be reported.

- **Traceability.** What the traceability structure of the requirements will be. For example, which attributes of a requirement will be captured on the traceability matrix?

Requirements are usually tracked using a tool called a requirements traceability matrix.

The requirements management plan includes information about prioritization, configuration management, reporting, and traceability.

Requirements Traceability Matrix

As the name suggests, the requirements traceability matrix is a table that traces each requirement back to its origin, such as a product or business objective, and tracks its progress throughout the project's life. Linking a requirement to the business objective underlines its value. Tracking the requirement throughout the lifecycle of the project ensures that it will be delivered before the project is completed. So, this table becomes a very useful tool to remind the team how important these requirements are, when they are going to be implemented, and how they are progressing in implementing them. The requirements traceability matrix includes the following links:

- Requirements linked to the origin of the project, such as the opportunity or business need

- Requirements linked to the project objectives and deliverables

- Requirements linked to the project scope and the product scope

- Requirements linked to the product design, development, and testing

- High-level requirements linked to their details

- The attributes linked to a requirement

The key information about a requirement can be stored in the form of its attributes. Here are some examples of attributes of a requirement: a unique identifier, a description, an owner, a source, a priority, a status, and a completion date.

With the definition of the project determined during project initiation and the requirements collected during planning, you are all set to begin defining the project scope.

Defining the Project Scope

Defining the project scope boils down to developing the detailed description of the project and its product. It is embodied in a document called the project scope statement.

So, defining the project scope includes determining the scope and documenting it.

Determining the Scope

The project scope is developed from the initial scope, deliverables, assumptions and constraints, and requirements documented in the project charter developed during the project initiation. Now you have more information to analyze these elements in more detail. You can also use the requirement documents developed during the planning stage described in the previous section. To determine project scope, you can use various techniques, such as identification of alternatives and stakeholder analysis.

Identification of Alternatives

You can use brainstorming and lateral thinking to identify alternatives to perform project work.

This is a technique used to apply nonstandard approaches to perform project work—in this case, to define the project scope. A host of general management techniques can be used in this category; the most common ones are brainstorming and lateral thinking. Brainstorming is a creative technique generally used in a group environment to gather ideas as candidates for a solution to a problem or an issue. The evaluation and analysis of these ideas happens later. Lateral thinking is synonymous with thinking outside the box. The idea is to think beyond the realm of your experience to search for new solutions and methods, not just better uses of the current ones.

Stakeholder Analysis

This includes identifying the needs, wants, and expectations of the various stakeholders, prioritizing them according to some criteria (such as the stakeholders' influence), and analyzing them for their origin and impact. The goal here is to quantify the interests of the stakeholders into concrete requirements. For example, what does customer satisfaction mean? Unless you quantify it into a feature or a deliverable, it is a vague and uncertain concept, and with uncertainty comes risk.

You can use these techniques to iron out the project scope, which is stored in the project scope statement.

Documenting the Scope: Project Scope Statement

The project scope is stored in the document called the project scope statement. In other words, the project scope statement is the document that describes the scope of the project, which is the work that needs to be done to deliver the planned project outcome: product, service, or result. In order to describe what needs to be done to deliver the outcome, it has to describe what the deliverables are. So, the project scope statement basically states what needs to be accomplished by the project: the deliverables along with their requirements and the work required to create those deliverables.

Some specific elements of the project scope statement are discussed in the following list.

Project objectives. A project might include a variety of objectives, such as business, schedule, technical, and quality objectives. A project objective might have attributes assigned to it, such as cost. The objectives might also include how to measure the success of the project. Success criteria must be measurable. For example, customer satisfaction and substantial increase in revenue are not measurable criteria, whereas a five-percent increase in revenue is measurable.

> The project scope statement includes project objectives, deliverables, requirements, assumptions and constraints, and boundaries, as well as a product description.

Project deliverables. A deliverable is a unique and verifiable product, a capability to provide a service, or a result that must be produced to complete a project, a process, or a phase of the project. The deliverables can include project management reports and documents.

Project requirements. The requirements include the conditions that the project items must satisfy, the capabilities (or characteristics) that the project items must possess, or both. These requirements fall into the following categories:

- **Requirements on deliverables.** These are the requirements imposed on deliverables that might stem from a contract, a standard, or a specification or from an analysis of stakeholders' needs, wants, and expectations. The scope statement lists the specification documents to which the project must conform.

- **Approval requirements.** The scope statement also identifies the approval requirements that will be applied to specific items, such as objectives, documents, deliverables, and work.

- **Configuration management requirements.** Configuration management refers to controlling the characteristics of a product, service, or result of a project. It includes documenting the features of a product or a service, controlling and documenting changes to the features, and providing support for auditing the products for conformance to requirements. The project scope statement specifies the level of configuration management requirements, including change controls to be implemented during the project execution.

SUCCESS SHOT

You must make a distinction between objectives, deliverables, and requirements. For example, in a project to launch a website, the website is a deliverable. That the website must print a warning message at the login time is a requirement, and that the website should increase the company revenue by three percent is an objective.

Project assumptions and constraints. Assumptions and constraints are initially included in the project charter. However, at this stage, you have more information about the project, and therefore you can revisit the initial assumptions and constraints, and you might be able to identify more assumptions and constraints. You should document the specific assumptions related to the project scope and also analyze their impact in case they turn out to be false. Due to the uncertainty built into them, the assumptions are potential sources of risk.

The constraints related to the project scope must also be documented in the scope statement. Because the constraints limit the team's options, the constraints' impact on the project must be evaluated. The constraints can come from various sources, such as a predetermined deadline (also called a *hard deadline*) for the completion of the project or a schedule milestone, limits on the funds available for the project, and contractual provisions. However, the following are common constraints to consider across all projects:

- Quality
- Resources
- Scope
- Time (or schedule)

Project boundaries. This involves drawing boundaries around the project by specifying what is included and what is not, especially focusing on the gray areas where the stakeholders can make their own assumptions, different from each other's.

Product description. The scope statement must describe the product scope and the product acceptance criteria:

- **Product scope description.** Product scope is defined as features and functions that characterize a product, service, or result to be delivered by the project. Do not confuse the *product* scope with the *project* scope, which is the scope of the whole project and is defined as all the work required to create the project deliverables. Product scope and project scope, although related, are different concepts.

- **Product acceptance criteria.** This defines the process and criteria for accepting the completed products that the project will deliver.

- **Initial risk identification.** Although a detailed risk analysis will be performed later, the risks that can be identified at this stage should be recorded in the scope statement.

The project scope statement serves the following purposes:

- It serves as a component to the baseline that will be used to evaluate whether the request for a change or additional work falls within or beyond the scope of the project.

- It's used as a scope baseline to verify whether the scope of the project has been completed.

- By providing a common understanding of the project scope, the scope statement helps bring the stakeholders onto the same page in their expectations.

- Because the scope statement describes the deliverables and the work required to create those deliverables, it is used to create a WBS, which helps in scheduling the project.

- It serves as a guide for the project team to do more detailed planning, if necessary, and to perform work during project execution.

- It serves as a reference to making scope-related project decisions throughout the lifecycle of the project.

To summarize, the project scope statement specifies the scope of the project in terms of the products, services, or results with specified features to be delivered by the project. From the perspective

It is important to understand the difference between the project scope and the product scope. As an example, consider a project to launch an e-commerce website. The description of the functional website with predetermined features is the product scope. The project scope is the work that needs to be done to produce this product scope, which includes writing software, testing software, putting all the software pieces together on a web server, and making the website live.

The scope statement should include not only the work that is included but also the work that is excluded. The exclusions are used to draw boundaries around what is included, and they also help to set the right stakeholder expectations.

of actually performing the work, the scope statement is still a high-level document. To be able to schedule the project, identify and assign resources, and manage the project successfully, these deliverables need to be broken down into manageable pieces. This is accomplished by creating an entity called the work breakdown structure (WBS).

STUDY CHECKPOINT 5.1

Question: You noticed in the previous chapter that the project charter may have schedule milestones and budget. This schedule and budget may also be part of the project scope statement. Why might such a schedule milestone and budget become a constraint?

Answer: The actual schedule and budget will be determined based on the scope statement and the work breakdown structure. If a schedule milestone and budget in the charter and in the project scope statement are final and cannot be changed, then that is a constraint the project team has to work with.

Organizing the Project Work into the Work Breakdown Structure

What is the secret behind accomplishing seemingly impossible tasks or solving complex problems in any area? The answer is to break down the required work or problem into smaller, manageable pieces. The process of dividing project deliverables (and hence the project work to produce them) into smaller, more manageable pieces is called creating the work breakdown structure. Put another way, to be able to actually execute the project, the project scope is broken down into manageable tasks by creating what is called the work breakdown structure (WBS). So, the WBS is a deliverable-oriented hierarchy of the work that must be performed to accomplish the objectives of and create the deliverables for the project.

As you already know, the project scope statement contains the list of deliverables and objectives, which are the basis for creating the WBS. Stakeholder requirements are also a good input into this process. You should always consider organizational process assets while going through this and several other project management processes. Even though each project is unique, there are similarities among sets of projects in an organization. These similarities can be used to prepare templates —an example of process assets—that will be used as a starting point for the WBS, to avoid duplication of work. With or without templates, you will need to go through breaking down or decomposing the deliverables, a very important step in creating the WBS.

SUCCESS SHOT

Remember two crucial points about the WBS:

1. The WBS holds the total scope of the project and hence the work required to deliver the outcome of the project.
2. In the context of the WBS, *work* refers to the components of the project outcome and not to the actual efforts made to produce that outcome. For example, planning and a piece of software are outcomes of efforts and not the efforts themselves, and they are called *work* or *work packages*.

Decomposition

Decomposition is a technique for subdividing the project deliverables into smaller, manageable tasks called work packages. The WBS is a hierarchical structure with work packages at the lowest level of each branch. Based on their complexity, different deliverables can have different levels of decomposition, as shown in the examples presented in Figure 5.3.

Decomposition allows you to subdivide the project deliverables into manageable tasks.

STUDY CHECKPOINT 5.2

Question: In Figure 5.3:

a. Identify the components at the second level that will be accomplished by using project management processes.
b. Identify the components at the second level that will be accomplished by using product-oriented processes.

Answer:

a. Project management
b. User experience, server back end, server front end

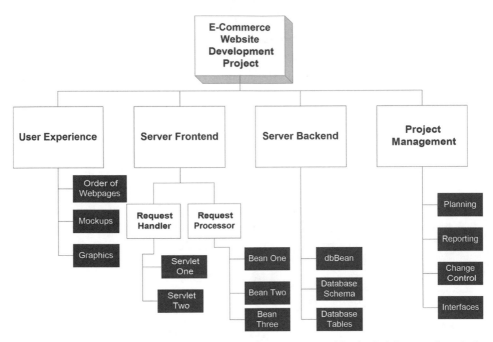

Figure 5.3 *An example of WBS. The work packages are represented by the dark boxes at the end of each branch.* Servlet *and* Bean *refer to the software programs that will need to be written.*

You decompose the project deliverables by executing the following steps:

1. Identify the deliverables and hence the work involved by analyzing the project scope statement.

2. Structure and organize the first level (just below the root of the hierarchical tree) of the WBS hierarchy. Based on the project at hand, you can use one of the following approaches:

   • Use the deliverables as components in the first level.

   • Use the phases of the project as components in the first level.

   • Use the subprojects as components in the first level. A subproject is a part of the project that is independent enough of the rest of the project that it can be performed by another project team. This approach is useful when you want to outsource parts of the project.

   • Depending on what you are dealing with, you can use different approaches within each branch of the WBS—for example, a subproject and deliverables in the first level.

3. Decompose the upper level into more detailed components for the lower level.

4. Keep decomposing to lower levels until necessary and sufficient decomposition has been achieved.

5. For a complex project, you usually assign identification codes to the WBS components to better organize them.

As the work is decomposed to lower levels of detail, work components become more concrete and manageable. However, you should avoid excessive decomposition because it will lead to a large number of work packages, and it will not be possible to manage all of them effectively. In other words, excessive decomposition leads to inefficient use of management and other resources. Necessary and sufficient decomposition is the key.

> Avoid excessive decomposition, which can lead to ineffective management of a large number of work packages.

SUCCESS SHOT

During decomposition, the components should be defined in terms of how the project work will actually be executed and controlled. For example, it's not a good idea to make a work package that involves two teams or groups. Further, you must verify the correctness of the decomposition at each level by requiring that the lower-level components are necessary and sufficient to the completion of the corresponding higher-level deliverables.

In the process of creating the WBS, you get the WBS document and some other outputs.

What You Get from Creating the WBS

During your effort to create the WBS, you should create the items discussed in the following list.

Work breakdown structure. You, the project manager, create this document with the help of the project team. Following are some important characteristics of the WBS:

• Each component in the WBS hierarchy, including work packages, is assigned a unique identifier called a *code of account* identifier. These identifiers can then be used in estimating costs, scheduling, and assigning resources.

• The WBS embraces the full scope of the project. If a task is not included in the WBS, it will not be done as part of the project.

- Because the project manager creates the WBS with the help of the project team, it is also the beginning of the team-building process on the part of the project manager.

- The WBS decomposes the project work into manageable pieces (work packages) that can be assigned to individuals. This helps define the responsibilities for the team members and is the starting point for building the schedule.

- Throughout the project, the WBS works as a reference for communication regarding what is included in the project and what is not.

Do not confuse the WBS with other information breakdown structures, such as the organizational breakdown structure (OBS), which provides a hierarchy of the performing organization and can be used to identify organizational units for assigning the WBS work packages. Remember, the end goal of the WBS is to specify the project scope in terms of work packages; this is what distinguishes the WBS from other information breakdown structures.

WBS dictionary. This could be a part of the WBS document or a supporting document for the main WBS document to provide details about the components of the WBS. The details about a component might include a code of account identifier, a statement of work, a list of milestones schedule, resources required, cost estimates, the organization responsible for the component, or any other useful information.

Updates. During the effort of creating the WBS, the project team might realize that something out of the existing scope must be included in order to accomplish something in the scope. This will give rise to a change request, which might also come from other stakeholders during or after the first creation of the WBS. After the change request has been approved, not only the WBS will be changed—the scope statement must also be updated accordingly. The impact of the approved change request on the project scope management plan must be evaluated, and the plan must be updated accordingly.

Scope baseline. The scope statement, the WBS document, and the WBS dictionary combined constitute the scope baseline against which all the change requests will be evaluated. The scope baseline becomes an important component of the project management plan.

In creating the WBS, you create the work breakdown structure, the WBS dictionary, updates, and the scope baseline.

You might wonder who creates the WBS. Well, it is your responsibility, and you perform it with the help of the team. Which team? The work packages do not exist before the WBS is complete; therefore, no assignments have been made yet. Yes, you are right—depending upon the project, the final project team might not even exist yet. However, with the help of the functional managers, you put together a group of experts and the likely team members. This is the group you will use to create the WBS.

Standardize This

The process of developing the project management plan falls in the knowledge area of integration management because it coordinates the various planning processes and activities. In standard project management, the process to develop the project management plan is called develop project management plan, and it is illustrated in Figure 5.4.

Collecting requirements, defining scope, and creating the work breakdown structure, all discussed in this chapter, are performed through three processes illustrated in Figure 5.5.

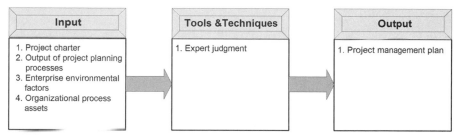

Figure 5.4 *The develop project management plan process: input, tools and techniques, and output.*

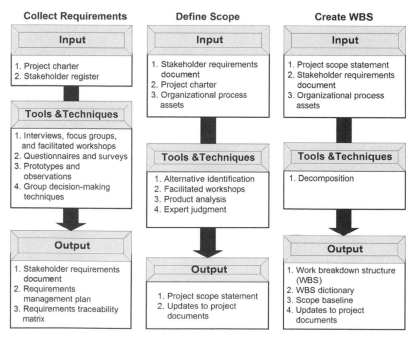

Figure 5.5 *The standard processes: collect requirements, define scope, and create the WBS.*

Quick Success Mantras

- Project planning involves determining exactly what will be done and how it will be done. Executing a project means implementing the project management plan for that project.

- Project planning produces the project management plan, which guides you on how to execute, monitor and control, and close the project.

- Project performance is measured against the project baseline, which is the approved plan for the project scope, schedule, and cost.

- How effective you are in collecting requirements will determine how effective you will be in getting agreement on these requirements from the stakeholders and in managing the stakeholders' expectations and needs.

- The project scope is the work that needs to be done to deliver the planned outcome—product, service, or result—of the project.

- The project scope statement states what needs to be accomplished by the project: the deliverables and the work required to create those deliverables.

- The work breakdown structure (WBS) is a deliverable-oriented hierarchy of the work that must be performed to accomplish the objectives of and create the deliverables for the project.

- The WBS holds the total scope of the project and hence the work required to deliver the outcome of the project. If it's not in the WBS, it will not be done.

- The scope baseline is determined by the scope statement, the WBS document, and the WBS dictionary. Any change request will be evaluated against this baseline to see whether it affects the project scope.

Chapter 6

Scheduling the Project

- Managing Time: Big Picture
- Defining Schedule Activities
- Sequencing Schedule Activities
- Estimating Activity Resource Requirements
- Estimating Activity Time Requirements
- Estimation Techniques
- Scheduling Activities
- Standardize This
- Quick Success Mantras

One of the key elements that determines the project success is completing the project on time—that is, according to the planned schedule. The schedule is developed from the scope baseline discussed in the previous chapter and is basically the set of activities required to complete the project within the timeline assigned to them. As you learned in the previous chapter, the project deliverables are broken down into manageable pieces called *work packages*. The work to accomplish these work packages is performed in the form of activities. A project schedule contains not only the activities to be performed, but also the order (sequence) in which the activities will be performed. Once the activities are determined from the work packages and other components of the scope baseline, they are sequenced according to the dependencies among them. Subsequently, you estimate the type of resources required for each activity and the amount of that type of resource available for the activity. This resource requirement and availability estimate will help determine the duration for the activity. Once you know the sequence of activities and the duration for each activity, you can schedule them and hence iron out the project schedule.

So, the core question in this chapter is, how is the project schedule developed? In search of the answer, you will explore three avenues with me: determining and sequencing activities required to perform the project work, estimating the resource and time requirements for each activity, and organizing the activities into the project schedule.

In this chapter, you will learn:

- How the project activities are determined
- How and why the project activities are sequenced
- How the estimates of activity resources and activity duration are made
- How to identify the various estimation techniques
- How the project schedule is developed
- How determining project activities, estimating activity resources and durations, sequencing activities, and developing a schedule are related to each other
- How to identify the standard processes used in the planning part of time management

Managing Time: Big Picture

Time management is so crucial to project management that project managers are often looked upon as the individuals who are there to keep track of the schedule. *Deadlines, windows of opportunities*, and *first to market* are some terms that underline the importance of time management. For example, if the project is completed after the window of opportunity has passed, it's a total failure. Project time management includes the processes that are used to plan and accomplish the timely completion of the project. The most important output from the planning part of time management is the project schedule, which will need to be executed and controlled. Here are the main elements of project time management shown in Figure 6.1:

• *Scope planning* generates the list of activities, called *schedule activities*, that need to be performed to produce project deliverables.

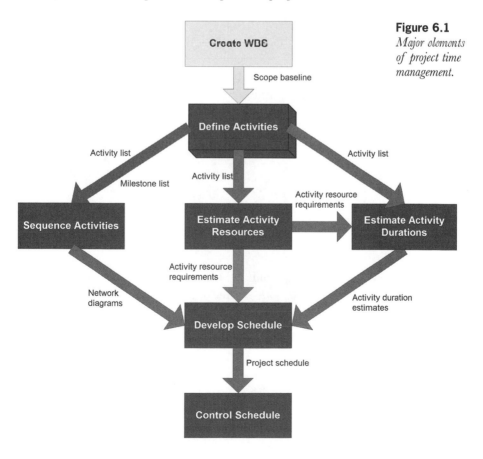

Figure 6.1
Major elements of project time management.

This activity list is the main input to the *activity sequencing*, *activity resource estimating*, and *activity duration estimating* parts of time management.

- The activity sequencing is performed to identify dependencies among the schedule activities. These dependencies are displayed in the schedule network diagrams, the main output of the activity sequencing. These network diagrams, along with activity resource requirements from the activity resource estimating and activity duration estimates from the activity duration estimating, are input items to the schedule development process.

- The schedule development generates, well, the project schedule. The approved project schedule, also called the *schedule baseline*, is executed and controlled throughout the course of the project.

SUCCESS SHOT

The underlying philosophy of effective project management for schedule development is to first develop the schedule based on the work required to complete the project tasks and the resources available, and then see how you can make it conform to other constraints, calendar requirements, and strategic goals of the organization. The point here is that you, the project manager, build the schedule through cold, hard mathematical analysis and you don't blindly accept whatever schedule goals come down the pipeline from elsewhere, such as from the customer or the project sponsor. Deadlines built into the schedule but not into the schedule math are a built-in project failure.

The main elements of project time management are scope planning, activity sequencing, activity duration estimating, schedule development, and schedule control.

We'll explore controlling the schedule in an upcoming chapter, whereas all other components of time management are discussed in this chapter.

In a nutshell, the path to schedule development includes defining activities, arranging the activities in the correct order, and estimating the resources required to complete the activities. In other words, the work necessary for completing the project is expressed in terms of activities, and the resources are required to complete the activities. So, the first step toward schedule planning after creating the WBS is defining activities that will constitute the schedule.

Defining Schedule Activities

Defining activities means identifying the specific schedule activities that must be performed to produce the project deliverables. The starting point for defining the activities is the items at the lowest level of the WBS: the work packages. Each work package can be broken down into one or more activities, or one or more work packages can be grouped together into an activity. It depends how detailed your work breakdown structure is and what the group structure and dynamics are in the performing organization.

Preparing for Defining Activities

As already mentioned, identifying project activities starts with the work packages in the WBS, which in turn are derived from the project scope statement. These are two obvious items that you need to define activities. These two items along with others are discussed in the following list.

WBS and WBS dictionary. The work packages in the WBS are decomposed into project activities. To assign appropriate resources to these work packages, you need to know their details, which are provided in the WBS dictionary.

Project scope statement. The WBS is built from the project scope statement. While dealing with the WBS, you might need to go back to the project scope statement. The following elements of the project scope statement are especially important to consider while identifying activities:

- Assumptions related to the activities or schedule planning, such as work hours per week
- Constraints that will limit the schedule options, such as predetermined deadlines on project milestones
- Project deliverables, to ensure everything is covered in WBS work packages

Recall that the WBS, WBS dictionary, and project scope statement constitute what is called the *project scope baseline*.

Enterprise environmental factors. The enterprise environmental factors relevant to identifying schedule activities include project management information systems and project scheduling software tools.

To define activities, you need the WBS, the WBS dictionary, the project scope statement, enterprise environmental factors, and organizational process assets.

Organizational process assets. Following are examples of organizational process assets that can be useful in the process of identifying activities:

- Organizational policies related to activity planning
- Organizational procedures and guidelines used in defining activities
- Knowledge base of lessons learned from previous projects regarding activity lists

So, the major items you need before you can begin defining activities are the scope baseline and necessary procedures and guidelines.

How Do You Really Define the Activities?

The major task in defining activities is to decompose the work packages in the WBS into activities. This decomposition, along with other relevant tools and techniques, is discussed here.

You create the WBS and decompose the work packages to project activities with the help of the project team. Even though the schedule is not yet developed and resources are not fully assigned, the project team in some initial form will be there. In decomposing a work package into activities, involve the individuals who either are familiar with the work packages or will be responsible for them.

Decomposition. Recall from the previous chapter that you use the decomposition technique in creating the WBS by subdividing the project deliverables into smaller, manageable tasks called *work packages*. Decomposition is also used in the activity definition process for subdividing the work packages into smaller, more manageable components called *schedule activities*.

Expert judgment. When decomposing the work packages into schedule activities, you can use the help of the team members and other experts who are experienced in developing WBS and project schedules.

Organizing WBS components for rolling wave planning. If there are areas of the project scope for which sufficient information is not available yet, there will definitely be corresponding components in the WBS that are not decomposed to the level of work packages. You can only develop a high-level schedule for these WBS components. You accommodate this kind of high-level scheduling by using the technique called *rolling wave planning*, which is used to plan the project work at various levels of detail depending upon the availability of information. Work to be performed in the near future is planned to the low level of the WBS, whereas the work to be performed far into the future can be planned at a relatively high level of the WBS.

Templates. As a timesaver and a guide, a standard activity list or an activity list from a previous project similar to the project at hand can be used as a template. The template can also contain information about the activities in it, such as required hours of effort.

Using these techniques, you convert the work packages in the WBS into schedule activities, which, along with some other items, make up the output of your efforts.

Results of Defining Activities

The key output item of defining activities is a comprehensive list of all the schedule activities that need to be performed to produce the project deliverables. This and other output items are discussed in the following list.

Activity list. This is a list of all the activities that are necessary and sufficient to produce the project deliverables. In other words, these activities are derived from the WBS and hence are within the scope of the project. Also, the scope of each schedule activity should be described to sufficient detail in concrete terms, so that the team member responsible for it will understand what work needs to be performed. Examples of schedule activities include a book chapter with a summary of content, a computer program that will accomplish a well-defined task, and an application to be installed on a computer.

Activity attributes. These attributes are in addition to the scope description of the activity in the activity list. They help manage the execution of the activity properly. The list of attributes of an activity can include the following:

- Activity identifier and code
- Activity description
- Assumptions and constraints related to this activity, such as imposed date
- Predecessor and successor activities
- Resource requirements
- Team member responsible for performing the work and information about the work

These attributes can be used to arrange the activities in the correct order (sequencing) and to schedule them.

Once developed, the milestone list becomes part of the project management plan.

Milestone list. A schedule milestone is a significant event in the project schedule, such as the completion of a major deliverable. A milestone can be mandatory, such as one required by a contract, or optional, such as one determined by the team to run the project more smoothly. The milestone list includes all the milestones and specifies whether a milestone is mandatory or optional. Milestones are used in building the schedule.

To summarize, the major outputs of defining activities are a schedule activity list, a list of attributes for each activity, and a list of milestones. But before you can schedule them, the identified activities need to be arranged in the correct order, which is called *sequencing*.

Sequencing Schedule Activities

Activity sequencing is the process of arranging the schedule activities in the appropriate order, which takes into account the dependencies among the activities. For example, if activity B depends upon the product of activity A, then activity A must be performed before activity B. So activity sequencing is a two-step process—identifying the dependencies among the schedule activities and ordering the activities accordingly.

Determining Dependencies

A dependency relationship between two activities includes a predecessor and a successor.

Dependency determination is the prerequisite to determining the order in which the activities will be performed. Therefore, most of the tools and techniques used for sequencing are focused on determining and displaying the dependencies. In other words, to properly sequence the schedule activities, you need to determine the dependencies among them. As illustrated in Figure 6.2, a dependency relationship between two activities is defined by two terms: predecessor and successor. When two activities are in a dependency relationship with each other, one of them is a predecessor of the other, and the other one is the successor. In Figure

Figure 6.2

Predecessor / successor relationship between two activities.

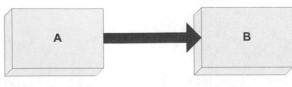

Activity A is predecessor
of activity B

Activity B is successor
of activity A

6.2, activity A is a predecessor of activity B, and activity B is successor of activity A. That means A must start before B.

By definition, the successor activity must start after the predecessor activity has already started. But exactly *when* can the successor activity start after the predecessor activity has been started? Well, both the predecessor and the successor have a start and a finish, and there are at maximum four possible combinations between the start and finish points of the predecessor and the successor activities. Accordingly, there are four kinds of dependencies, also called *precedence relationships*, listed here:

- **Finish to start.** The initiation of the successor activity depends upon the completion of the predecessor activity—that is, the successor activity cannot be started until the predecessor activity has already been completed.

- **Finish to finish.** The completion of the successor activity depends upon the completion of the predecessor activity—that is, the successor activity cannot be completed until the predecessor activity has already been completed.

- **Start to start.** The initiation of the successor activity depends upon the initiation of the predecessor activity—that is, the successor activity cannot be initiated until the predecessor activity has already been initiated.

- **Start to finish.** The completion of the successor activity depends upon the initiation of the predecessor activity—that is, the successor activity cannot be completed until the predecessor activity has already been initiated.

The four kinds of dependencies are finish to start, finish to finish, start to start, and start to finish.

These types of dependencies describe the logical relationships between activities. Where do these relationships come from? To answer this question, the dependencies can be grouped into three categories:

- **Mandatory dependencies.** These are the dependencies inherent to the schedule activities. For example, a software program must be developed before it can be tested.

- **Discretionary dependencies.** These are the dependencies at the discretion of the project management team. For example, it was possible to perform activities A and B simultaneously or to perform A after B was finished, but the team decided, for whatever reason, to perform B after A was finished. Some of the guidelines for establishing discretionary

There are three categories of dependencies: mandatory, discretionary, and external.

dependencies can come from the knowledge of best practices within the given application area and from the previous experience of performing a similar project.

- **External dependencies.** An external dependency involves a relationship between a project activity and a non-project activity—that is, an activity outside the project. For example, in a movie production project, think of a project activity that involves shooting scenes with lots of tourists skiing. This scene is planned to be shot at a ski resort during the ski season. This is an example of an external dependency.

After nailing down the dependencies among the schedule activities, you are ready to bring order to those activities.

Putting the Activities into an Order

The dependency between two schedule activities is an example of the logical relationships defined in the previous section. Logical relationships can be displayed in schematic diagrams, called *project schedule network diagrams*, or just *network diagrams* for brevity. There are two commonly used methods to construct these diagrams: the precedence diagramming method (PDM) and the arrow diagramming method (ADM).

Precedence diagramming method (PDM). The precedence diagramming method (PDM) is the method to construct a project schedule network diagram in which a box (for example, a rectangle) is used to represent an activity and an arrow is used to represent dependency between two activities. The boxes representing activities are called *nodes*. Figure 6.3 presents an example

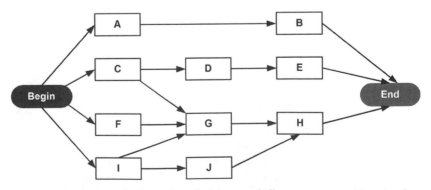

Figure 6.3 *An example of a project schedule network diagram constructed by using the precedence diagramming method (PDM).*

of a network diagram constructed by using PDM, in which activity A is a predecessor of activity B, activity C is a predecessor of activities D and G, and so on.

In this diagram, only C and I have more than one successor. In general, PDM supports all four kinds of precedence relationships discussed earlier, but the most commonly used dependency relationship in PDM is finish to start.

Although PDM is the most commonly used method, if you are only going to use the finish-to-start dependencies, the arrow diagramming method is another option to consider.

Arrow diagramming method (ADM). The arrow diagramming method (ADM) is the method to construct a project schedule network diagram in which a node (represented by a circle) acts as a junction between the predecessor activity and the successor activity, and the activity itself is represented by an arrow. The arrow representing an activity also points to the successor activity through a junction. However, there is a problem inherent to this definition. The problem arises from the fact that an activity might have multiple successors, multiple predecessors, or both. In such cases, you might need more arrows to show the dependencies than the number of activities. But an arrow does not just show the relationship; in ADM, it also represents an activity. So, you cannot have more than one arrow for one activity. How would you then represent, for example, that an activity has more than one successor? This problem is solved by introducing the concept of a dummy activity, represented by a broken arrow that is just used to show the relationship and does not represent any real activity.

Logical relationships between schedule activities can be displayed in schematic diagrams using various methods, such as the precedence diagramming method (PDM) and the arrow diagramming method (ADM).

Figure 6.4 displays a set of dependencies identical to that shown in Figure 6.3. The only difference between the two diagrams is that Figure 6.4 uses ADM instead of PDM, which was used in Figure 6.3. Note the use of dummy activities in Figure 6.4 to show the dependencies between C and G and between I and G.

Note that ADM is only used to represent finish-to-start types of dependencies.

While working on schedule network diagrams, you can use standardized templates, if available, to save time. You can also use network diagrams from previous projects and modify them for the project at hand.

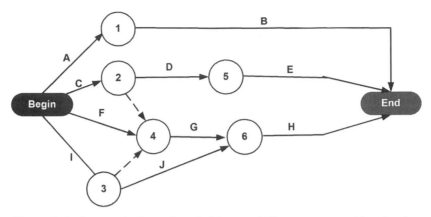

Figure 6.4 *An example of a project schedule network diagram constructed by using the arrow diagramming method (ADM).*

> **APPLYING LEADS AND LAGS**
>
> The finish-to-start dependency means that the successor activity starts where the predecessor activity finishes. Applying a lead means you allow the successor activity to start before the predecessor activity finishes, and applying a lag means you start the successor activity a few days after the predecessor activity finishes. Sometimes you might need to make such adjustments in the schedule.

Finish to start is the most commonly used precedence relationship in the precedence diagramming method, although this method can also be used to represent the other three precedence relationships: finish to finish, start to start, and start to finish. The arrow diagramming method can only be used to show the finish-to-start relationship.

You can make the activity list, and you can sequence the activities. These are important steps that must be executed. However, to perform the activities, you need resources.

Estimating Activity Resource Requirements

The resource requirements for an activity are estimated by using the activity resource estimating process. The main purpose of estimating activity resource requirements is two-pronged:

- Estimate the types of resources needed for a given activity.
- Estimate the quantities of each type of resource needed for the activity.

What You Need to Make the Resource Estimates

To estimate the resource requirements for your project, you need not only the list of activities but also the attributes of each activity. These and other necessary information items are discussed in the following list.

- **Activity list and activity attributes.** The activity list that you have already developed identifies the schedule activities that will need the resources. The activity attributes provide the details for the activities, which will be helpful in estimating the quantity of the resources.

- **Enterprise environmental factors.** Information about the infrastructure of the performing organization, such as existing facilities, will be used in identifying the resources and their availability.

- **Organizational process assets.** The organizational process assets useful for activity resource estimating include organizational policies for staffing and purchase of supplies, historical information on what types of resources were used for similar activities in a previous project, and the like.

- **Availability of resources.** Resource estimating will require information on the available quantity of resources of different types, such as human, equipment, and material. Resource calendars can be helpful here. The resource calendar contains the following useful information about the resources:

  - Days and times of day when a resource is available
  - The passive time for the resource—for example, holidays for human resources
  - The quantity of each type of available resource
  - The capability of each resource

> To estimate resource requirements for your project, you need the activity list and activity attributes, enterprise environmental factors, organizational process assets, and the availability of resources.

Once you understand the activities, you can use some tools and techniques to determine the resources required to perform those activities. The tools and techniques that can be used in estimating the resource requirements include alternative analysis and bottom-up estimating and are discussed further on in this chapter.

What You Get from Resource Estimates

From your efforts at making resource estimates, you obtain the items discussed in the following list.

It's important to realize that the duration of an activity depends on the quantity of resources available. For example, two people can generally finish an activity sooner than one. The duration may also depend on the expertise and experience level of the activity performer. Therefore, it's important to estimate the resource requirements before estimating the time duration.

Activity resource requirements. The main purpose of the activity resource estimating process is to determine the resource requirements for each schedule activity, and therefore this is the major output item from this process. You identify the types of resources required to perform each activity and estimate the required quantity of each identified resource. If a work package in the WBS has multiple activities, the resource estimates for those activities can be aggregated to estimate the resource requirements for the work package, if needed.

Resource breakdown structure. The resource breakdown structure (RBS) is a hierarchical structure of resource types required to complete the schedule activities of a project. The RBS can be used to identify and analyze the project human resource assignments.

Updated activity attributes. The identified types of required resources for an activity and the estimated quantity for each identified resource become activity attributes and must be added to the attribute list for the activity.

Requested changes. The activity resource estimating process might generate change requests in the activity list—for example, to add or delete an activity. These change requests must be processed through the integrated change control process.

Once the activities have been identified and the resources required to perform each activity have been estimated, you have enough information to begin estimating the time needed to complete each activity, which is called the *activity duration*.

Estimating Activity Time Requirements

Activity duration is generally considered as the time in calendar units between the start and finish of a schedule activity. For example, an activity that will take three weeks might start on November 3 and finish on November 24. However, the estimates are made in work periods, where a work period is a measurement of time when the work is continually in progress; it is measured in hours, days, or months, depending upon the size of the activity. This estimate can be converted to calendar units of time by factoring in the resource's passive time, such as holidays and non-work hours during the workday. For example, suppose you have estimated that it will take one programmer 32 hours to write a software program. That is four workdays with eight work hours in a day. You also know that the work will start on a Friday and there will be no work on Saturday and Sunday. Therefore, the activity duration estimate is 32 hours measured in work periods and 6 days measured in calendar units. Always distinguish between the two to avoid confusion.

So, activity duration estimates are quantitative assessments of the required time units to finish activities, such as 5 days or 10 weeks. You can also assign an uncertainty to the estimate, such as 20 ± 2 days to say that the activity will take at least 18 days and at most 22 days. The duration of an activity can be considered as an attribute of the activity. Therefore, you update the activity attributes, originally developed in the activity definition process, to include the activity durations.

To estimate the activity duration, you will obviously need the activity list and the information about each activity, the attributes. Other items that you will need are discussed in the following list.

Activity resource requirements. The work periods required to complete an activity depend on the quantity of a given type of resource assigned to the activity. However, while assigning additional resources to an activity, always consider the following:

- Sometimes assigning additional resources might reduce the overall efficiency and productivity. For example, think of two engineers with different skill levels assigned to work on the interrelated components of an activity—one could slow down the other.

- Most activities have a threshold beyond which assigning additional resources does not help. For example, installing an operating system on a machine will take the same amount of time regardless of how many system administrators have been assigned to this activity.

Resource calendar. The resource calendar usually contains the type, quantity, availability, and capability of each resource, including the skills of a human resource, which must be considered during activity duration estimating. For example, an experienced programmer can finish the same program in less time than a beginner can. Capability and quantity of available resources, both human and material, can affect the activity duration estimate. For example, if an activity will take four workdays for an engineer to finish, and the engineer can work only four hours a day on this activity, it will take eight workdays to finish.

While making estimates, always ask whether the activity was performed in the past and what it took to complete it. Using historical information is vital to the accuracy of the estimates because this would factor in the actual performance.

Project scope statement. Some assumptions and constraints in the project scope statement can affect activity duration estimates and therefore must be considered. For example, there might be an assumption that part of the work related to an activity has already been performed in a previous project and can be used in this project. If the assumption is true, the activity duration will be less than otherwise. An example of a constraint might be that a specific work package must be finished before a predetermined deadline. This will put a maximum limit on the duration for the activities corresponding to this work package.

Enterprise environmental factors. Examples of enterprise environmental factors are some databases that contain reference data relevant to the activity duration—for instance, how long it takes for a specific government agency to respond to a request.

Organizational assets. Organizational assets that will be useful in estimating activity duration include information from previous projects and a calendar of working days and non-working days.

So, now you have all the information you need to make duration estimates, which determine the schedule. For example, the duration estimates of activities on the critical path will determine the finish date of a project for a given start date. However, duration estimation is an involved task. For instance, there might be many uncertainties involved in the estimate. As an example, two programmers, due to the differences in their experience, will take different amounts of time to write the same program. The good news is that there are a number of tools and techniques that you can use in activity duration estimating to perform this task effectively and reliably.

Note that, in general, a combination of techniques is used to estimate the duration of an activity. For example, you can use the analogous technique and expert judgment to estimate the productivity rate of resources and then use that productivity rate in parametric analysis to calculate the activity duration. These techniques are discussed in the following section.

Estimation Techniques

There are standard estimation techniques you can use to estimate various quantities, such as activity resource requirements, activity duration, and cost.

Alternative analysis. As the name suggests, alternative analysis looks at the alternatives to the obvious solutions or availabilities. It may also deal with selecting from various available options. For example, during resource estimating, you will need to consider alternatives available for resources required for some schedule activities. For example, you might need to decide whether you want to buy or develop a tool needed to perform an activity, what types of machines (for example, Windows or Linux) to use, which computers to use to do the development, or what level of skills is needed.

Analogous estimating. This technique relies on analogies. For example, you can use analogous estimating techniques to estimate the duration of an activity based on the duration of a similar activity in a previous project. The accuracy of the estimate depends upon how similar the activities are and whether the team member who will perform the activity has the same level of expertise and experience as the team member from the previous project. This technique is useful when there is not enough detail information about the project or a project activity available—for example, in the early stages of a project.

Bottom-up estimating. Bottom-up estimating techniques are based on estimating the given quantity, such as cost or duration, for components and then adding them up to make the estimate for the whole. For example, you might discover that it is rather complex to estimate resources for a given schedule activity. If the problem is inherent to the activity, it might be helpful in certain cases to decompose the activity into smaller components for the purpose of resource estimating, then estimate the resource for each component, and then aggregate the resources to get an estimate for the whole activity. In aggregation, you must consider the possible relationships (overlaps and such) among different components of the activity so you don't double-count the resources.

Parametric estimating. These are quantitative techniques that depend on making mathematical calculations from the known standard values. For example, parametric estimating can be used to calculate the activity duration when the productivity rate of the resource performing the activity is available. You use a formula such as the following one to calculate the duration:

Activity duration = Units of work in the activity / Productivity rate of the resources

For example, if you know that a team assigned to the activity of burying 40 miles of cable can bury two miles of cable in one day, the duration calculation can be performed as follows:

Activity duration = 40 miles / (2 miles/day) = 20 days

Three-point estimating. This method addresses the issue of uncertainty in estimating quantities such as activity cost or activity duration. For example, the uncertainty in the duration estimate can be calculated by making a three-point estimate in which each point corresponds to one of the following estimate types:

- **Most-likely scenario.** The activity duration is calculated in the most practical terms by factoring in resources likely to be assigned, realistic expectations of the resources, dependencies, and interruptions.
- **Optimistic scenario.** This is the best-case version of the situation described in the most-likely scenario.
- **Pessimistic scenario.** This is the worst-case version of the situation described in the most likely scenario.

The spread of these three estimates determines the uncertainty. The resultant duration is calculated by taking the average of the three estimates. For example, if the duration for an activity is estimated to be 20 days for the most likely scenario, 18 days for the optimistic scenario, and 22 days for the pessimistic scenario, then the average duration is 20 days and the uncertainty is ± 2 days, which can be expressed as:

Duration = 20 ± 2 days

It's equivalent to saying that the activity duration is 20 days, give or take two days.

> **STUDY CHECKPOINT 6.1**
>
> **Problem:** You are estimating the cost for an activity. The cost is $2,500 in the most likely scenario, $1,500 in the optimistic scenario, and $3,000 in the pessimistic scenario. What is the final cost estimate?
>
> **Solution:**
>
> The cost estimate from the three-point estimating
>
> = $(2,500+3,000+1,500)/3
>
> = $2,333

Reserve analysis. Reserve analysis is used to incorporate a time cushion into your schedule; this cushion is called a *contingency reserve*, a *time reserve*, or a *time buffer*. The whole idea is to accommodate the possibility of schedule risks. One method of calculating the contingency reserve is to take a percentage of the original activity duration estimate as the contingency reserve. Later, when more information about the project becomes available, the contingency reserve can be reduced or eliminated.

Standard estimation techniques include alternative analysis, analogous estimating, bottom-up estimating, parametric estimating, three-point estimating, reserve analysis, and expert judgment.

Expert judgment. Expert judgment can be used to estimate the whole duration of an activity even when not enough information is available. It can also be used to estimate some parameters to be used in other methods—for example, what percentage of the original activity duration estimate should be used as a contingency reserve—and in comparing an activity to a similar activity in a previous project during analogous estimating. Expert judgment can also be used to make the resource estimates.

> **SUCCESS SHOT**
>
> Understand that estimation is a serious business. For example, underestimating the activity durations may lead to an unrealistic schedule. On the other extreme, overestimating the activity duration may overrun the budget. Furthermore, you should involve the team member who will actually do the work in estimating the duration, which will improve the accuracy of the estimates and the commitment of the team member.

By now, you have learned how to identify schedule activities, arrange them in proper sequence, determine resource requirements for them, and estimate their durations. All these tasks and accomplishments are a means to an end called *project schedule development*.

Scheduling Activities

The project work is composed of individual activities, which need to be scheduled. Until you have a realistic project schedule, you do not have a project. A project schedule has schedule activities sandwiched between the project start date and the project finish date.

What You Need to Schedule Activities

The following items already discussed in this chapter directly support the schedule development process:

- Activity list and activity attributes
- Project schedule network diagrams showing the dependencies among activities
- Activity resource requirements and resource calendars
- Activity duration estimates
- Project scope statement

The assumptions and constraints in the project scope statement can affect the project schedule and therefore must be considered in developing the schedule. The following two types of time-related constraints should get special attention.

Hard deadlines on start and finish dates and time constraints on deliverables should both get special attention because they can affect the project schedule.

- **Hard deadlines on start and finish dates.** Some activities or work packages might have constraints on their start or finish dates. For example, there might be a situation in which an activity cannot be started before a certain date, must be finished before a certain date, or both. Where do these date constraints come from? They can come from various sources, such as a date in the contract, a date determined by the market window, delivery of material from an external vendor, and the like.

- **Time constraints on deliverables.** These constraints can come from the customer, the sponsor, or any other stakeholder in terms of deadlines for certain major deliverables or milestones. Other projects inside or outside your organization might be depending on these constraints. So, once scheduled, these deadlines are constraints and can only be changed through the approval process.

So, the output of various time management processes is used as input to the schedule development process, which uses a variety of tools and techniques to iron out the project schedule.

Tools and Techniques for Schedule Development

Once you have the network diagrams for the activities, as well as the activity duration estimates, you are well-equipped to start scheduling the project. The remaining primary concerns include:

- The actual start date
- Uncertainty about the availability of resources
- Identification of and preparation for activities on the critical path
- Risks involved, or "what if" scenarios
- The hard start/finish dates for activities or for the project that came down the pipeline from very important stakeholders

Various tools and techniques discussed in the following sections can be used to address these concerns while you are hammering out the project schedule.

Schedule Network Analysis

A schedule network analysis is a technique used to generate a project schedule by identifying the early and late start and finish dates for the project. The analysis accomplishes this task by employing a schedule model and various analytical techniques, such as critical path method, critical chain method, "what if" analysis, and resource leveling. These techniques are discussed in the following list.

Schedule model. You know by now that the resource requirements and activity durations are the estimates based on some assumptions, such as that a typical programmer will take five days to write a certain program. However, you use this data to build the project schedule. Changing the assumptions will change the data and hence the schedule. So, a set of assumptions on which this data is based is called a *schedule model*. While trying to make some accommodations during scheduling, it's always a good idea to revisit the schedule model or to take a close look at the schedule model.

Critical path method. This is the schedule network analysis technique used to identify the schedule flexibility and the critical path of the project schedule network diagram. The critical path is the longest path (sequence of activities) in a project schedule network diagram. Because it is the longest path, it determines the duration of the project and hence the finish date of the project given the start date. An example will explain this. Consider the network diagram presented in Figure 6.5. The boxes in the figure represent activities, such as activity A followed by activity B, and the number on top of a box represents the duration of the activity in time units, such as days.

The table in Study Checkpoint shows the calculations for the duration of each path of the network diagram by adding the durations of the individual activities on the path. You can see from Table 6.1 that the path Start-A-B-Finish is the critical path because it is the longest path in the diagram, at 22 days. This means if the project start date is January 2, the project finish date will be January 24 (2+22), assuming that the duration is shown in calendar time units.

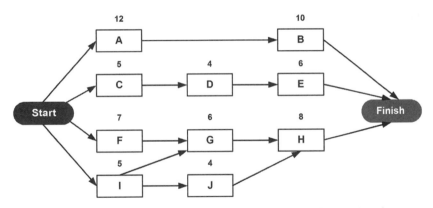

Figure 6.5 *An example of a project schedule network diagram. The duration of an activity is represented by the number shown above the box that represents the activity.*

Table 6.1 Path Durations Calculated from the Network Diagram Shown in Figure 6.5

Path	Durations of Activities	Path Duration
Start-A-B-Finish	12+10	22
Start-C-D-E-Finish	5+4+6	15
Start-F-G-H-Finish	7+6+8	21
Start-I-G-H-Finish	5+6+8	19
Start-I-J-H-Finish	5+4+8	17

The second important feature of the critical path method is to identify the flexibility in the project schedule by calculating the early and late start and finish dates of each activity on each path. The schedule flexibility of an activity is measured by the positive difference between the late start date and the early start date for the activity and is called the *float time* or *total float*.

The table in Study Checkpoint 6.2 shows calculations for the early and late start and finish dates and the float time for each activity in the network diagram being analyzed. The early start and finish dates of activities on a path are calculated by using the *forward-pass method*, which means you start your calculations from the start point (leftmost) and make your way forward. As an example, consider the path Start-C-D-E-Finish in the network diagram shown in Figure 6.5. Because C is the first activity on the path, its early start is day 0. Because D depends on the completion of C, and C takes five days to finish, the early start date for D is the early start date of C plus the duration of C—that is, 0+5 = 5. Similarly, the early start dates for E is 5+4=9. The late start and finish dates are calculated using the *backward-pass method*, which means you start your calculations from the finish point. The project finish date determined by the critical path is day 22, given that the project start date is day 0. Because activity E has a duration of six days, it must be started no later than day 16 (22–6=16). Therefore, day 16 is the late start date of activity E. Activity D has a duration of four days, so given that E must start on day 16, D must not start later than day 12 (16–4=12). Therefore, the late start date for D is day 12. Similarly, the late start date for activity C is 12–5=7. The float times are calculated as follows:

Float time for C = late start – early start = 7–0=7

Float time for D = late start – early start = 12–5=7

Float time for E = late start – early start = 16–9=7

CAUTION

Note that each of the activities on the critical path (Start-A-B-Finish) has a float time of zero. This obviously is a source of schedule risk. Each activity on a critical path has zero float time and therefore poses a schedule risk. Therefore, you must monitor the activities on all critical paths very closely during the execution of the project. Yes, a project schedule may have more than one critical path.

STUDY CHECKPOINT 6.2

Problem: Calculate the early start, early finish, late start, late finish, and float time for each activity in Figure 6.5.

Solution:

Activity	Early Start	Early Finish	Late Start	Late Finish	Float Time
A	0	12	0	12	0
B	12	22	12	22	0
C	0	5	7	12	7
D	5	9	12	16	7
E	9	15	16	22	7
F	0	7	1	8	1
G	7 (not 5)	13	8	14	1
H	13	21	14	22	1
I	0	5	3 (not 5)	8	3
J	5	9	10	14	5

Critical chain method. This is an alternative schedule network analysis technique that takes into account the uncertainties of the activity durations due to the uncertainty of the availability of resources. It uses the schedule network diagrams to identify the critical paths and the schedule flexibility, just like the critical path method. The only difference is that in this technique, you work from more than one network diagram. For example, the durations in the first network are based on the planned scenario regarding the availability of resources. You can draw another network diagram based on the pessimistic scenario regarding the availability of resources. The durations of some activities in the second diagram will be longer than in the first diagram, and the second diagram might even have a different or an additional critical path. The extra durations in the second diagram are called *duration buffers*. So, the focus of the critical chain method is on managing the duration buffers and the uncertainties in the availability of resources applied to the planned schedule activities.

Resource leveling. Resource leveling is not an independent schedule network analysis method. It is applied to the schedule that has already been analyzed using other methods, such as the critical path method or the critical chain method. The resource leveling technique is applied to address the resource needs of activities that must be performed to meet specific delivery dates. Resource leveling involves taking a part of the resources from one activity and assigning it to another. This will change the activity durations and can also result in a change of critical paths.

"What if" scenario analysis. The purpose of the "what if" scenario analysis is to calculate the effects of a specific scenario on the schedule—for example, how the schedule will be affected if a vendor does not make the delivery of a major component on the promised date. Because a "what if" scenario by definition represents uncertainty, this analysis often leads to risk planning, which might include changing the schedule or changing the network diagram to get a few activities out of harm's way if possible.

As you have seen, the critical path method is used to develop a schedule for given resources, whereas the critical chain method factors in the uncertainty of the availability of resources. The resource leveling technique is used to move the resources around to meet the resource needs of the activities that must be accomplished on a specific date. In other words, in an ideal world in which the required (or planned) resources are guaranteed, you do not need the critical chain method and resource leveling; just the critical path method will do.

During the use of various scheduling tools and techniques, always remember that the two most common and vital mistakes are misaligning the calendar with the project work and over-allocating resources. Obviously, either of these mistakes will result in an erroneous schedule.

Let's assume you have used the critical path method to determine the schedule for a project. You have also applied other techniques, such as the critical chain method and resource leveling. The final realistic schedule that you have come up with has an unacceptable project duration (the length of the critical path). What do you do? This is where the schedule compression technique comes to your rescue.

Schedule Compression

It is true that you, the project manager, build the schedule through cold, hard mathematical analysis and you don't just accept whatever schedule goals come down the pipeline from elsewhere, such as from the customer or the project sponsor. However, once you have the schedule built through analysis, you can attempt to accommodate some critical stakeholder expectations or hard deadlines, such as a predetermined project finish date. I have already discussed one such method, called *resource leveling*, to accommodate hard deadlines for activities. In this section,

I will discuss two more methods for schedule compression: crashing and fast tracking.

Crashing. This is a project schedule compression technique used to decrease the project duration with minimal additional cost. A number of alternatives are analyzed, including the assignment of additional resources.

Fast tracking. This is a project schedule compression technique used to decrease the project duration by performing project phases or some schedule activities within a phase in parallel that would normally be performed in sequence. For example, testing of a product can start when some of its components are finished, rather than waiting for the whole product to be completed.

> **CAUTION**
> Crashing usually involves assigning more resources and hence increasing the cost. However, guard yourself against the misconception that additional resources will linearly improve the performance. For example, if one programmer can develop a program in eight days, it does not necessarily mean that two programmers will develop the same program in four days, because there will be overheads, such as the initial less-productive stage of the newly assigned resource, the time taken to reallocate the work, the interaction among the resources, and so on.

After you have the data for the schedule development created by the processes discussed in this chapter, it is a common practice to use project management software to build the actual schedule. Make sure you master the project scheduling software; errors in the schedule may lead to undesired consequences, such as errors in the schedule and resulting confusion and delays.

In a nutshell, the main techniques to develop a project schedule include network diagram analysis (critical path method and critical chain method), schedule compression (fast tracking and crashing), and resource leveling. You use these techniques to generate the output of the schedule development process.

Output of the Schedule Development Process

The planned project schedule is an obvious output of the schedule development process. This and other output items are discussed in this list.

Project schedule. The project schedule includes a planned start date and a planned finish date for each schedule activity. The schedule will be considered preliminary until the resources have been assigned to perform the activities according to the schedule. Although a schedule for a simple project might be presented in a tabular form, typically a project schedule is presented in one of the following graphical formats:

- **Project schedule network diagram.** These diagrams present the schedule activities on a timescale with a start and a finish date for each activity and hence show the dependencies of activities on each other.

- **Bar chart.** In these charts the activities are represented by bars, with each bar showing the start date, the finish date, and the duration of the activity.

- **Milestone chart.** These are typically the bar charts representing only the milestones, not all the schedule activities.

Schedule data. This is the supporting data for the project schedule and consists of the following:

- Schedule activities, schedule milestones, activity attributes, and documentation of all identified assumptions and constraints
- Resource requirements by time periods
- Alternative schedules—for example, schedules based on best-case and worst-case scenarios
- Schedule contingency reserves

This data is used to create the version of the schedule that is approved by the project management team and becomes the schedule baseline.

Schedule baseline. This is a specific version of the project schedule that is approved by the project management team as a baseline against which the progress of the project will be measured. This version of the schedule is developed from the schedule network analysis of the schedule model data.

Changes and updates. The process of schedule development can generate requests for changes, which must be processed through the integrated change control process. Furthermore, some updates may be added to the following items:

The output of the schedule development process includes the project schedule, schedule data, schedule baseline, and changes and updates.

- **Resource requirements.** The schedule development process might change the initial estimate for the types and quantities of the required resources.

- **Activity attributes.** Resource requirements or any other activity attributes that have changed must be updated.

- **Project calendar.** Any update to the project calendar must be documented.

- **Project management plan.** This plan should include any updates to reflect any changes that were realized during the schedule development regarding how the project schedule will be managed. Only the approved changes should be included.

> **SCHEDULE BASELINE**
> Project schedule development is an iterative process. For example, it might be necessary to review and revise the duration and resource estimates for some activities to create a project schedule that will be approved. The approved project schedule will act as a baseline against which project progress will be tracked.

The approved project schedule is used as a baseline to track the project progress. To some extent, schedule development (or modification) continues throughout the project execution due to the approved changes and the risk occurrences.

Standardize This

In the project management standard, the elements of time management discussed in this chapter are performed by using the processes illustrated in Figures 6.6 and 6.7. We have already explored the items in these figures.

STUDY CHECKPOINT **6.3**

Problem: List the processes in Figures 6.6 and 6.7 in the order you will perform them.

Solution:

1. Define activities.
2. Estimate resource requirements.
3. Estimate time durations.
4. Develop schedule.

Sequence activities must be performed before you develop the schedule and after you define the activities.

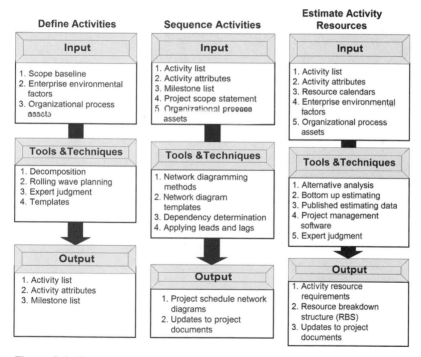

Figure 6.6 *Input, tools and techniques, and output for three processes: define activities, sequence activities, and estimate activity resources.*

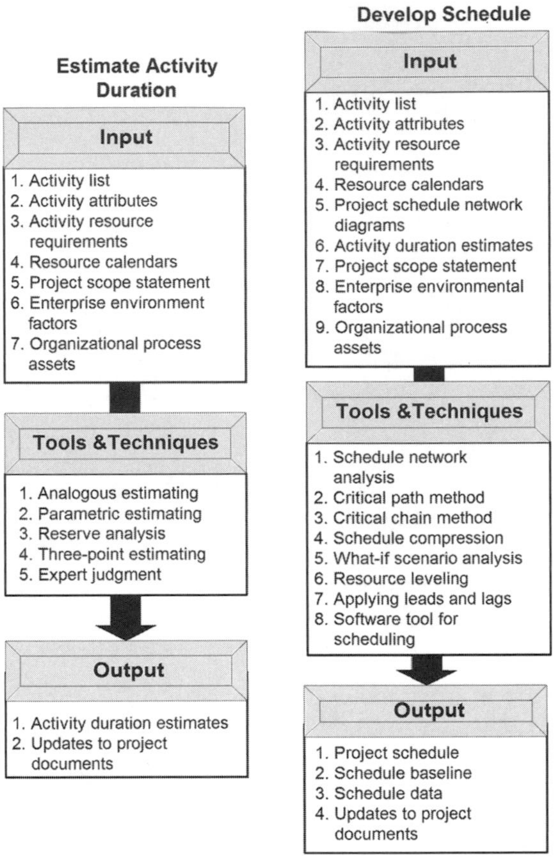

Figure 6.7

Input, tools and techniques, and output for two processes: estimate activity duration and develop schedule.

Estimate Activity Duration

Input
1. Activity list
2. Activity attributes
3. Activity resource requirements
4. Resource calendars
5. Project scope statement
6. Enterprise environment factors
7. Organizational process assets

Tools &Techniques
1. Analogous estimating
2. Parametric estimating
3. Reserve analysis
4. Three-point estimating
5. Expert judgment

Output
1. Activity duration estimates
2. Updates to project documents

Develop Schedule

Input
1. Activity list
2. Activity attributes
3. Activity resource requirements
4. Resource calendars
5. Project schedule network diagrams
6. Activity duration estimates
7. Project scope statement
8. Enterprise environmental factors
9. Organizational process assets

Tools &Techniques
1. Schedule network analysis
2. Critical path method
3. Critical chain method
4. Schedule compression
5. What-if scenario analysis
6. Resource leveling
7. Applying leads and lags
8. Software tool for scheduling

Output
1. Project schedule
2. Schedule baseline
3. Schedule data
4. Updates to project documents

Quick Success Mantras

- The major output of the planning part of time management is the project schedule.
- A project schedule contains not only the activities to be performed, but also the order (sequence) in which the activities will be performed.
- The sequencing of activities is determined by the dependencies among the activities, which can be displayed in figures called network diagrams.
- Make sure you have figured out all the dependencies. An undiscovered logical dependency can delay your project.
- The activities are determined from the work packages in the WBS.

- The time duration for an activity depends on the resources available for the activity.

- A realistic project schedule can be created bottom-up by identifying the activities and estimating the resources for the activities and the duration that each activity will take for the given resources available for it.

- To develop a realistic schedule, it's necessary to make realistic estimates of resources and time duration. This can be accomplished with the help of the experts and the team members who will perform (or have performed in the past) the activities on which the estimates are being made.

- The approved project schedule acts as the schedule baseline against which project progress is tracked.

- The critical paths on the schedule network diagrams should be closely monitored because a delay in any activity on the critical path will delay the whole project.

- Fast tracking compresses the schedule by performing activities simultaneously that would otherwise be performed in sequence, whereas crashing compresses the schedule by assigning more resources.

- Use schedule compression techniques to accommodate the predetermined hard deadlines.

- Become proficient in the scheduling software; the project work depends on the schedule, and any technical mistake on your part can cause confusion or mess up the project all together.

Chapter 7

Planning for Project Resources

- Planning for Resources: Big Picture
- Developing the Human Resource Plan
- Estimating Costs and Determining Budget
- Procuring the Project Resources
- Standardize This
- Quick Success Mantras

Once you have developed the project schedule, as discussed in the previous chapter, you need resources to execute the schedule. For example, you need the team members—the human resources—to perform the project activities, such as a computer programmer to design and develop a program. You also need financial resources to support these human resources and to make purchases and acquisitions required for the project. These financial resources are managed in the form of cost management, which includes cost planning. Some of the expected outcome items of the project will be developed by the project team; others will be purchased or acquired in a process called *procurement*, which may also include items that are needed to complete the project and are not necessarily the end product of the project.

So, the core question in this chapter is, how do you plan for the project resources? This issue breaks down into three avenues that we will explore: human resource planning, cost planning, and procurement planning.

In this chapter, you will:

- Understand the big picture of resource planning
- Describe human resource planning
- Identify the difference between cost estimates and the budget
- Understand procurement planning
- Identify the standard processes for resource planning: human resource planning, estimating costs, determining budget, and procurement planning

Planning for Resources: Big Picture

As you learned in the previous chapter, resource requirements are estimated by using the estimate activity resources process, and the schedule is developed by using the develop schedule process. As illustrated in Figure 7.1, the activity resource requirements estimated this way are used to develop a human resource plan for the project. The human resource plan and the project schedule, in turn, are used to make cost estimates for activities, which are aggregated to determine the project budget.

The approved budget with a timeline assigned to it is called the *cost baseline* against which the project performance is measured.

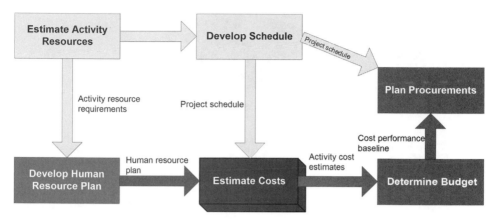

Figure 7.1 *Relationships among major elements of resource planning.*

This baseline is also used to plan for procurements—that is, purchases and acquisitions that are needed to complete the project but cannot be produced by the project team.

While developing the project schedule, the availability of resources required to perform the schedule activities is an obvious assumption. An important category of resources is human resources—for example, a computer programmer who will write a computer program.

Developing the Human Resource Plan

To avoid confusion, you must understand the logical relationships among the project, activity resource requirements, roles, and responsibilities, as illustrated in Figure 7.2. Roles are determined from the resource requirements, and responsibilities are assigned to the roles to perform the project activities. In a nutshell, project work is generally performed in the form of roles and responsibilities. Project roles, responsibilities of the roles, and reporting relationships among the roles need to be determined in order to perform a project. The use of the concept of a role is so that you can talk about it during planning, even before hiring a person who will play this role. So, a role is a defined function to be performed by a team member, such as a programmer or tester. The other issue that needs to be addressed before the project can be performed is how and when the project team members (who will perform the project work) will be acquired. The human resource planning process addresses these issues.

Figure 7.2
Relationship among project, project activity requirements, roles, and responsibilities.

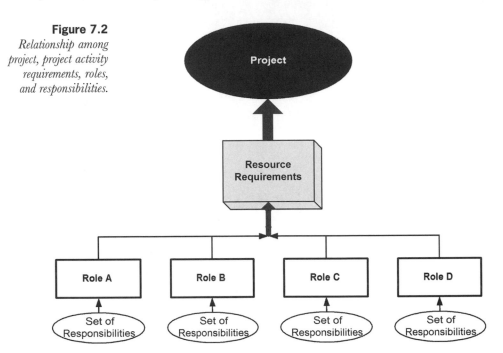

Project work is performed in the form of roles and responsibilities.

Therefore, two main goals of the human resource planning process are the following:

- Identify and document project roles, responsibilities for each role, and reporting relationships among the roles.
- Develop the staff management plan.

All this planning will go into a document called the *human resource plan*.

Preparing for Resource Planning

Before you can assign the resources to a project, you need to know the resource requirements of the project—the resource requirements are the main item you need to plan resources. The other two items are the familiar ones: enterprise environmental factors and organizational process assets.

Enterprise Environmental Factors

The enterprise environmental factors that can influence the human resource planning include human resources that already exist in the organization and are available for the project, organizational culture, organizational structure, human resource and personnel administration policies of the organization, and marketplace conditions. For example, how do the different departments and the people within the performing organization interact with each other? This will have a profound effect on defining the roles and responsibilities. Overall, while planning human resources, you must consider the following enterprise environmental factors:

- **Interpersonal.** The interpersonal environmental factor should be explored while considering the candidates within the performing organization for the project team members. You should seek answers to interpersonal questions, such as the following:

  - What are the job descriptions of the candidates? This will tell you what kind of project activities they might be able to perform.

  - What are the skills and experiences of the candidates beyond their current job description?

  - What types of formal and informal reporting relationships exist among the candidates? This will help determine who can fit in where.

  - What cultural or language differences will possibly affect the working relationships among the candidates? This should be used to optimize the project work results by honoring cultural diversity.

- **Logistical.** The logistical factor deals with the issue of how the project team is spread out geographically. For example, a relevant question to ask is, are the team members spread out in different buildings, time zones, or countries? Virtual communication, discussed in the next chapter, will be an important consideration here.

- **Organizational.** The organizational factor relevant to human resource planning can be identified by the answers to the following questions:

  - Which departments of the performing organization will participate in the project?

  - What are the current relationships between these departments? In other words, how do these departments interact?

> While planning human resources, you must consider interpersonal, logistical, organizational, political, and technical enterprise environmental factors.

- **Political.** Playing politics could be a dirty term for a social reformer, but you need to deal with it tactically by recognizing it as a project reality. To explore the effect of the political factor on human resource planning, you should ask questions such as the following:
  - What are the individual goals and agendas of the project stakeholders?
  - Which individuals or groups are influential in areas important to the project?
  - What are the formal or informal alliances that exist between individuals or departments relevant to the project?
- **Technical.** Almost all the projects these days include the use of some kind of technology. To explore the effects of technical factors on human resource planning, you should explore answers to questions such as:
  - What are the technical specialties, such as software, programming languages, and technical equipment, needed to perform the project?
  - Which of these specialties need to be coordinated?
  - Are there any technical challenges this project might face?

Organizational Process Assets

The organizational process assets that can be useful in human resource planning include checklists, templates, organizational standards and procedures, standardized role descriptions, and historical information from the previous projects. Some examples of checklists are common project roles in your organization, typical competencies, training programs to consider, team ground rules, and safety considerations. Examples of templates and organizational standards include project organizational charts and standard conflict management approach, respectively. Conflict management will be discussed in an upcoming chapter.

Activity Resource Requirements

In the previous chapter, we explored the process of determining the resource requirements for the schedule activities. These requirements include human resource requirements, which are needed to develop the human resource plan.

The human resource requirements, a subset of activity resource requirements, are the raw material to determine the roles that will perform the activities. Various tools and techniques are available to convert requirements into roles.

Performing Resource Planning

At the heart of resource planning lays the art of converting activities and activity resource requirements into roles and responsibilities. For example, consider an activity in a project—writing a software program. The program will be written by a programmer, which is a human resource. However, before you even know the name of the programmer, you can work with this programmer as a role whose main responsibility is to write the program, and you can assign a real individual to fill this role later. This approach allows for planning before hiring. The tools and techniques used to determine the roles for a project are discussed in the following list.

Organizational charts and position descriptions. These charts identify and document the roles of the project team members, the responsibilities assigned to the roles, and the reporting relationships among the roles. Most of the chart formats fall into three categories—hierarchical, matrix, and text-oriented. The text-oriented charts are the simplest form of charts; basically, the information is spelled out in simple text in a file. The other two forms of charts are discussed in the following bullet points.

- **Hierarchical.** Hierarchical charts are the traditional way to represent the reporting relationships in an organization, in a top-down format. Such a chart is also called an organizational breakdown structure (OBS), and it is arranged according to the organization's existing departments, units, or teams. The OBS will help you to identify team members for the project.

- **Matrix.** A matrix is used to specify the relationships between schedule activities, roles to perform those activities, and team members assigned to the roles. Such a matrix is generally called a responsibility assignment matrix (RAM). Different matrices can show these relationships at different levels. For instance, you can use the RAM to document resource requirements for each activity, as shown in Table 7.1. For example, for activity B in Table 7.1, the RAM shows that it will take six developers, six workstations on which the developers will work, and one server to perform the activity. You can also use a RAM to document the specific responsibilities assigned to particular team members for the schedule activities, as shown in Table 7.2.

Organizational charts are usually hierarchical, matrix, or text-oriented.

Depending upon the project needs, you can use both RAM and text-oriented charts to document roles and responsibilities of those roles. Also, remember that the RAM can be used for various purposes. For example, the RAM in Table 7.1 documents the resource requirements for the schedule activities, while the RAM in Table 7.2 depicts the roles of team members for schedule activities.

The RAM in Table 7.2 is also called the RACI chart because it assigns four roles to team members for various activities: responsible (R), accountable (A), consult (C), and inform (I). For example, Susan has the responsibility of designing the product, Cathleen will be held accountable for the design, Kiruba will play the role of a consultant for designing the product, while Pappu and Maya will play the role of keeping everybody informed of the status and progress.

Table 7.1 A Responsibility Assignment Matrix (RAM) Depicting the Resources Required to Perform Schedule Activities

Activity	Designer	Developer	Tester	Marketer	Workstation	Server
A	1					
B		6			6	1
C			3		3	2
D				2		
E	1	1	1		1	

Table 7.2 A Responsibility Assignment Matrix (RAM) Depicting the Roles Assigned to the Team Members for Various Activities

Activity	Susan	Cathleen	Pappu	Maya	Kiruba
Design	R	A	I	I	C
Develop	I	I	R	I	C
Test	C	R	A	I	C
Deploy	I	I	A	I	R

Letters are used as symbols to represent roles: R for responsible, A for accountable, C for consult, and I for inform.

SUCCESS SHOT: OWN IT BEFORE YOU BREAK IT
Each activity or task should have an owner who is responsible for its successful completion. There may be more roles assigned to complex tasks and activities, but there must be only one principal owner. Joint ownership usually gives rise to confusion, finger pointing, conflict, more overhead, and dilution of commitment.

Networking. Burn it in your head: Networking is one of the golden secrets you have for succeeding as a project manager, especially in an organization in which functional managers hold all the powers (hiring, firing, bonuses), and the project managers are running around with nothing in their hands other than the project schedules and status reports. To network effectively, you should understand the influence of political and interpersonal factors in your organization that might impact various staffing management options. Some of the essential networking happens at the beginning of each project, and you must make full use of it. However, networking is a regular practice, and you should be using all the human resource network activities, such as proactive correspondence, informal conversations, luncheon meetings, and trade conferences.

Organizational theories. Various organizational theories provide information and insight on how people behave in a team or an organization, what motivates team members, and the like. If you have knowledge of these theories, it will help you plan human resources quickly and use them more effectively.

To summarize, organizational charts, networking, and organizational theories are the main tools and techniques used to determine roles and develop the human resource plan.

What the Human Resource Plan Contains

The results of your efforts of planning human resources are documented in what is called the *human resource plan*. The following sections discuss the main elements of this document.

Roles and Responsibilities

This section contains roles and the responsibilities assigned to each role. The schedule project activities will be completed by individuals working in certain roles and performing responsibilities that come with the roles. So, roles and responsibilities are an important output of human resource planning. While determining roles and responsibilities, you must be clear about the following concepts:

Roles must be clarified by specifying the responsibilities and the authorities assigned to each role. A good match between the levels of responsibility and authority for each team member generally produces the best results. This gives the team members a sense of ownership. If you own it, you will less likely break it.

- **Role.** In real life, most activities are performed by people playing certain roles, such as a parent, a teacher, or a student. Similarly, in project management, a role is essentially a set of responsibilities, such as the responsibilities of a developer, a tester, or a manager. A role is assigned to a team member who will perform the responsibilities included in the role to complete one or more project activities.

- **Responsibility.** A responsibility is a piece of work (task) that must be performed as part of completing a project activity. Responsibilities can be grouped together as a role.

- **Competency.** Competency is the ability of a team member to play a certain role—that is, to perform the responsibilities assigned to the role. While assigning a role to a team member, you should know whether the team member possesses the skills required to perform the responsibilities of the role. You might need to respond to a mismatch with training, hiring, schedule changes, or scope changes.

- **Authority.** Authority is a right assigned to a role that enables the person playing the role to apply project resources, make certain decisions, or sign approvals. Poorly defined or undefined authorities can cause confusion and conflicts.

Project Organizational Charts

A project organizational chart displays the project team members and the reporting relationships among them. The level of formality and detail of these charts depends upon the size and needs of the project at hand.

Staff Management Plan

After you have determined the roles to perform the activities, you need to identify individuals to fill those roles. The staff management plan describes when and how human resource requirements for a project will be met. When preparing the staff management plan for your project, you must consider the following items:

- **Staff acquisition.** This will document how the staff for the project will be acquired. To be specific, while planning staff acquisition, you might need to struggle with some of the following questions:
  - What are the levels of expertise needed for the project, and what are the assigned costs?
  - Will the human resources come from within the organization, outside the organization, or both?
  - Will the team members be required to work in a central location, or can they work from distant locations?
  - Will you need the assistance of the human resources department of your organization to acquire the staff?

- **Timetable and release criteria.** You need to have a timetable for the human resource requirements, describing when and for how long a staff member is needed. The project schedule will help you determine that. You should also determine the release criteria and the time to release each team member from the project. Planning of release criteria is very important for a smooth transition of team members from one project to another and for the optimal use of the resources.

- **Training needs.** If some team members lack the adequate level of skills needed for the project, a training plan can be developed as part of the project.

- **Compliance and safety.** The staff management plan can also include strategies for complying with relevant government regulations, union contracts, and human resource policies. Your organization might have some policies and procedures that protect the team members from safety hazards. These policies and procedures must be included in the staff management plan.

- **Recognition and rewards.** Recognition and rewards are good tools to promote and reinforce desired behavior. However, to use this tool effectively, you must have clear criteria for rewards based on activities and performance of team members. The potential candidate for a reward must have an appropriate level of control over the activity for which the reward will be offered. For example, if a team member is to be rewarded for completing the project within the budget, the team member must have an adequate level of control over the decision-making that affected the spending.

> When preparing the staff management plan, you must consider staff acquisition, timetable and release criteria, training needs, compliance and safety, and recognition and rewards.

In a nutshell, human resource planning accomplishes two things: It determines roles to perform the schedule activities, and it develops a staff management plan to fill those roles with team members.

Human resources are going to cost you, and this leads us to cost management, which starts with making cost estimates, as discussed next.

Estimating Costs and Determining Budget

It's important to distinguish between cost and budget.

First of all, we need to distinguish between cost and budget. *Cost* is the value of the inputs that have been (or will be) used to perform a task or to produce an item: product, service, or result. This value is usually measured in units of money. For example, you paid two programmers $500 each for developing a software program, and you paid $100 to a tester to test the program. So, the cost for the task of developing and testing the software program is $1,100. You can add the costs of components of a system, and the sum will represent the cost of the system, but it's still a cost, and not a budget. Budget is an aggregated cost with a timeline. You aggregate the costs of all the resources needed to perform the project and put a timeline on it: the availability of funds over time. That is called a *budget.*

As illustrated in Figure 7.3, cost management consists of estimating project costs, determining budget from the cost estimates, and controlling the cost while the project is being executed. In this chapter, we explore estimating costs and determining budget. Cost control is discussed in a forthcoming chapter.

Cost management starts with making cost estimates.

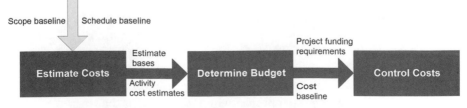

Figure 7.3 *Big picture of cost management.*

Estimating Project Costs

Estimating project cost means estimating the costs required to complete the project scope by executing schedule activities. Therefore, you need the scope baseline and the schedule baseline for estimating costs. Recall that the scope baseline is constituted by the scope statement, the WBS, and the WBS dictionary; and the schedule baseline is the approved project schedule. Other items that you may need to determine the costs include the following:

- **Human resource plan.** The information in the human resource plan useful for estimating costs includes the list of roles and responsibilities, personnel rates, and recognitions and rewards.

- **Risk register.** Both kinds of risks—threats and opportunities—have impact on the cost in the form of risk mitigation costs and revenues or savings from the opportunities.

- **Enterprise environmental factors.** Enterprise environmental factors relevant to estimating costs include market conditions and published commercial information. This will provide information related to the availability of products and services and their cost and rates.

- **Organizational process assets.** This includes the organization's policies regarding cost estimates, cost estimating templates, and information from the previous projects.

> To estimate project costs, you may need the human resource plan, the risk register, and some enterprise environmental factors and organizational process assets.

Some tools and techniques that can be used in cost estimating and budgeting are discussed in the following list.

Analogous estimation. Analogous cost estimation is a technique that uses cost information, such as rate, cost of a component, or cost of an activity from similar tasks and activities in the previous projects. This technique is useful when very limited component information is available, especially in the beginning of a project. It's generally less costly than other techniques, but it also is less accurate. Its accuracy and reliability improves if the person making the estimate is an expert and the components or activities being compared are actually similar.

Parametric estimation. This is a technique that uses some parameters and statistical relationships among them to make the estimate. For example, if the unit cost is known, the cost of the whole package containing a number of units can be calculated.

This technique can generate quite accurate results depending on the accuracy of the quantity of resources and other data that goes into the estimation.

Bottom-up estimation. This technique involves estimating the cost of the parts of a component and then aggregating the cost of those parts to calculate the cost of the whole component. This technique can generate accurate results when you can generally make a better estimate of a part than the whole, which is usually the case.

STUDY CHECKPOINT 7.1

Problem: An activity cost estimate goes like this: It will take 20 hours of a programmer's time to write this program. The average rate to hire a programmer is $50 per hour. Therefore, the cost of writing this program, assuming that everything else needed to write the program, such as a computer, is in place, is 20×$50=$1,000.

What kind of estimation technique is at work here?

Solution: Parametric estimation.

Contingency reserves may artificially overestimate the costs. So if they are included in the cost estimates, they should be put into a separate category. These contingency reserves are usually not part of the budget included in the cost baseline used to evaluate the project performance.

Contingency reserve analysis. There are the following two problems associated with the estimates:

- Estimates are approximations, and approximations imply uncertainty, which means risk.

- Some stakeholders will always push the envelope on the project scope, and each organization has some tolerance for overrunning the objectives. This will mean more cost.

You will need some funds to deal with both of these situations. What comes to your rescue here is called *contingency reserve*. The contingency reserve, in general, is an amount of resource (funds or time) allocated in addition to the calculated estimates to reduce the risk arising from various sources—for example, from the overruns of project objectives to a level acceptable to the performing organization. In other words, the contingency reserves are the funds reserved to deal with events that are anticipated but not certain. Contingency reserves can be used at the discretion of the project manager. The overall cost estimate should include the contingency reserves.

Vendor bid analysis. The bids from the qualified vendors on parts of the project or even the whole project can help in estimating the project cost.

Cost of quality. Cost of quality, discussed in the next chapter, should also be considered when making cost estimates.

> **SUCCESS SHOT**
> Note that the accuracy of cost estimates depends on many other estimates, such as the activity duration estimates and resource requirement estimates, which go into developing the schedule baseline used for making cost estimates. It is important to keep this in mind just in case you need to re-estimate the cost for some element of the project.

Some tools and techniques you can use for cost estimating and budgeting include analogous estimation, parametric estimation, bottom-up estimation, contingency reserve analysis, vendor bid analysis, and cost of quality.

The outcome of estimating costs will include cost estimate for each project activity and the basis for that estimate, which can be used to determine the project budget.

Determining Project Budget

Determining project budget is the process of aggregating the cost estimates for all project activities and assigning a timeline to them. Cost aggregation is the technique used to calculate the cost of a whole by summing up the costs of the parts of which the whole is made. You can use the bottom-up estimation technique to aggregate the costs of all the components and activities to calculate the total cost of the project. The timeline assigned to this cost will be important to reconcile the expenditure with the funding limits. The reconciliation may require rescheduling some activities.

The standard practice is not to include the contingency reserves in the budget. So, make sure you include the contingency reserve when determining funding requirements.

Do not leave out the cost of the internal employees of the organization that will work on the project. They are not free for two reasons: The organization pays for them, and they do not have an infinite number of hours to put into the project. Their cost to the project will be determined just like any other project role, based on the hours of work they will put into the project.

The approved budget that includes the aggregated cost with timeline is called the *cost baseline*. The cost performance of the project is monitored, measured, and controlled against this baseline. This is why it's also called a *cost performance baseline*. Funding requirements for the project are derived from the cost baseline and the contingency reserve analysis.

151

Your organization may just not have the resources to complete all parts of the project. For those parts of the project, you will need to use what is called *procurement*.

Procuring the Project Resources

Procurement management includes planning, conducting, administering, and closing procurements.

Procurement refers to obtaining—purchase or renting—products, services, or results from outside the project team to complete the project. Procurement management is an execution of a set of processes used to obtain (procure) the products, services, or results from outside the project team to complete the project. There are two main roles involved in procurement management:

- **Buyer.** The party purchasing (procuring) the product or service.

- **Seller.** The party delivering the product or service to the buyer.

As illustrated in Figure 7.4, procurement management includes the following components:

- **Planning procurements.** This involves making and documenting purchasing decisions, identifying potential sellers, and determining the approach toward these issues.

- **Conducting procurements.** This involves soliciting seller responses, selecting sellers, and awarding contracts.

Figure 7.4
Big picture of procurement management.

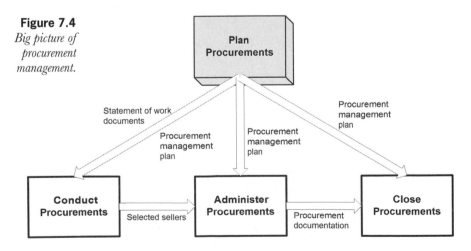

- **Administering procurements.** This involves monitoring the contract execution, making approved changes and corrections, and managing relationships among the parties involved in the procurement.
- **Closing procurements.** This involves completing each project procurement and giving it a proper closure, as planned.

In this chapter, we will explore the plan procurements part of procurement management. Other components will be discussed in the forthcoming chapters.

Planning for Procurement

Planning procurements includes making and documenting purchasing decisions, identifying potential sellers, and developing a procurement approach. Although the procurement planning should be done early in the project, like any other planning, it might be necessary at any stage of the project as the need arises due to approved changes or other circumstances.

During procurement planning, you will be looking at lots of information, such as the scope baseline, stakeholder requirements, partner agreements, risk registers, activity resource requirements, and cost baseline. You will also need to know how to take make-or-buy decisions and what the different contract types are.

Make-or-Buy Decisions

Obviously, procurement refers to buying something as compared to making it in-house. The decision to buy or make can be based on one or more of the reasons listed in Table 7.3.

Buy can mean to purchase or rent. The decision to purchase or rent should be based on the effective cost in the long term. For example, if it is a piece of hardware that will be used only in this project, you do not anticipate its use in any future project, and renting is significantly cheaper than buying, you should probably rent it. You might decide to buy it if this hardware is of common use in the kind of work your organization does and therefore will be used in other projects as well.

Before you can buy, you need to get information from the sellers. In other words, you need to request seller responses. Make-or-buy analysis is a technique used in the plan purchases and acquisitions process. Also in this process, you need to use a technique to determine the type of contract you will use for the procurement.

An output of the procurement planning process is the statement of work (SOW), which is a document summarizing the work to be performed. The SOW can be written by the buyer or the seller to specify what products will be delivered or what services will be performed. It is also called the *contract statement of work*.

Table 7.3 Reasons to Make or Buy

Factor	Reasons to Make In-house	Reasons to Buy
Cost	Less cost	Less cost
Skills availability	Use in-house skills	In-house skills don't exist or are not available
Skills acquisition	Learn new skills that will be used even after this project	These skills are not important to the organization
Risks	Deal with the risk in-house	Transfer the risk
Work	Core project work	Not core project work
Human resource availability	Staff available	Vendor available

Determining Contract Types

A contract is a mutually binding agreement between a buyer and a seller that obligates the seller to provide the specified product, service, or result and obligates the buyer to make the payment for it. Contracts generally fall into the three categories discussed in this list.

Fixed-price (lump-sum) contracts. A fixed-price contract, also called a *lump-sum contract* or a *firm fixed-price contract*, is an agreement that specifies the fixed total price for the product, service, or result to be procured. An example of a fixed-price contract is a purchase order for the specified item to be delivered by a specified date for a specified price. This category of contracts is generally used for products and services that are well defined and have good historical information. A fixed-price contract for a poorly defined product or a service with very little historical record is a source of high risk for both the seller and the buyer.

Cost-reimbursable contracts. A contract in this category includes two kinds of costs:

- **Actual cost.** This is the payment (reimbursement) to the seller for the actual cost of the item, which includes the direct cost and the indirect cost (overhead). An actual cost, such as the salary of the project staff working on the item, is incurred directly from the work on the item, whereas an indirect cost, such as the cost of utilities and equipment for the office of the staff member, is the cost of doing business. Indirect cost is generally calculated as a percentage of the actual cost. The actual cost is also called the project cost. The project here refers to the project of the seller to produce the items for the buyer.

- **Fee.** This typically represents the seller's profit.

As discussed in the following list, there are three types of cost-reimbursable contracts:

- **Cost plus fee (CPF) or cost plus percentage of cost (CPPC).** The payment to the seller includes the actual cost and the fee, which is a percentage of the actual cost. Note that the fee is not fixed; it varies with the actual cost.

- **Cost plus fixed fee (CPFF).** The payment to the seller includes the actual cost and a fixed fee, which can be calculated as a percentage of the estimated project cost. Note that the fee is fixed and does not vary with the actual project cost.

- **Cost plus incentive fee (CPIF).** The payment to the seller includes the actual cost and a predetermined incentive bonus based on achieving certain objectives.

> Both fixed-price contracts and cost-reimbursable contracts can optionally include incentives—for example, a bonus from the buyer to the seller if the seller meets certain target schedule dates or exceeds some other predetermined expectations.

Because cost overrun can occur in any type of cost-reimbursable contract, and the cost overrun will be paid by the buyer, this category of contract poses risk to the buyer.

Time and material (T&M) contracts. This category of contracts is a hybrid that contains some aspects from both the fixed-price category and the cost-reimbursable category. The contracts in this category resemble the contracts in the cost-reimbursable category because the total cost and the exact quantity of the items are not fixed at the time of the agreement. The contracts resemble fixed-price contracts because the unit rates can be fixed in the contract. These types of contracts are useful when you do not know the quantity of the procured items. For example, you do not know how much time a contract programmer will take to develop a software program, so you determine the hourly rate in the contract, but not the total cost for writing the program. In this category of contracts, the risk is high for the buyer because the buyer agreed to pay for all the time the seller takes to produce the deliverables.

> Contracts are usually fixed-price (lump-sum), cost-reimbursable, or time and material contracts.

Table 7.4 lists different types of contracts and the corresponding risk bearers.

The major output of the procurement planning is the procurement management plan.

Table 7.4 Risk Bearers in Different Categories of Contracts

Contract Type	Risk Bearer	Explanation
Fixed-price	Buyer and seller	The cost overrun is borne by the seller, whereas the price fixed higher than the actual cost hurts the buyer.
Time and material	Buyer	The increased cost due to the increased quantity of resources, such as work hours by a contractor, is borne by the buyer.
Cost plus fixed fee	Buyer	Cost overrun is paid by the buyer.
Cost plus percentage of cost	Buyer	Cost overrun is paid by the buyer. Because the fee increases with the increase in cost, this type poses maximum risk to the buyer.
Cost plus incentive fee	Buyer	Cost overrun is paid by the buyer.

Procurement Management Plan

This document describes how the procurement will be managed throughout the project. The plan includes the following:

- How the make-or-buy decisions will be made and handled
- Contracts:
  - What types of contracts will be used for this project
  - The form and format for the statement of work related to a procurement or a contract
  - Metrics to be used to evaluate potential sellers and to manage contracts
  - Requirements for performance bonds or insurance contracts that might be put in place to mitigate some project risks
- Management and coordination:
  - How to manage multiple sellers
  - How to coordinate procurement with other aspects of the project, such as the project schedule, scope, budget, and status progress reporting
  - Evaluation criteria for selecting sellers and measuring their performance

- A list of assumptions and constraints that could affect the procurement
- Any needed standardized procurement document

In a nutshell, the major tasks of procurement planning are making buy-or-make decisions, preparing the procurement management plan, preparing the statement of work, determining the suitable type of contract, and preparing or acquiring the procurement documents. Once you have these elements in place, you are ready to implement the procurement plan, which will be discussed further on in the book.

Standardize This

Figures 7.5 and 7.6 present standard processes for planning human resources, cost, budget, and procurements. All the items in these diagrams were discussed in the chapter.

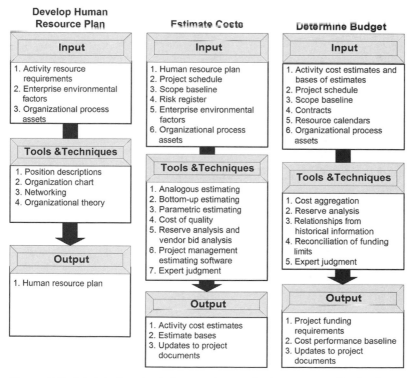

Figure 7.5 *Input, tools and techniques, and output for three processes: Develop human resource plan, estimate costs, and determine budget.*

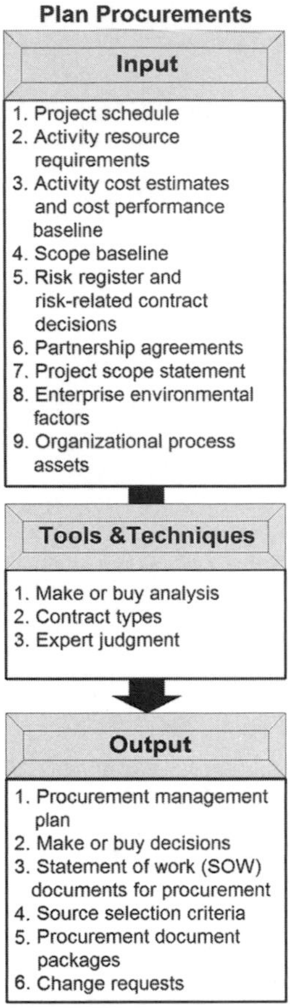

Figure 7.6

Input, tools and techniques, and output for the plan procurements process.

Plan Procurements

Input

1. Project schedule
2. Activity resource requirements
3. Activity cost estimates and cost performance baseline
4. Scope baseline
5. Risk register and risk-related contract decisions
6. Partnership agreements
7. Project scope statement
8. Enterprise environmental factors
9. Organizational process assets

Tools &Techniques

1. Make or buy analysis
2. Contract types
3. Expert judgment

Output

1. Procurement management plan
2. Make or buy decisions
3. Statement of work (SOW) documents for procurement
4. Source selection criteria
5. Procurement document packages
6. Change requests

Quick Success Mantras

- Human resource planning accomplishes two things: It determines roles to perform the schedule activities, and it develops a staff management plan to fill those roles with team members.

- The accuracy of cost estimates depends on the accuracy of other estimates, such as activity duration estimates and the activity resource requirements estimates.

- Project budget is the time-phased project cost obtained by aggregating the individual activity costs.

- The major tasks of procurement planning are making buy-or-make decisions, preparing the procurement management plan, preparing the statement of work, determining the suitable type of contract, and preparing or acquiring the procurement documents

- Of all the contract types discussed in this chapter, only the firm fixed-price contract can present risk to the seller.

- The contract type that presents the most risk to the buyer is the cost plus percentage of cost because the fee (which is a percentage cost) also increases if the cost overrun occurs.

Chapter 8

Planning for Project Communication

- Managing Project Communication: Big Picture
- Communication Types and Models
- Basic Types of Communication
- Virtual Communication Models
- Communication Networks and Systems
- Planning Project Communication
- The Many Faces of Communication
- Standardize This
- Quick Success Mantras

Communication is a common thread that runs through most project activities and processes. Without effective communication, a project is destined to fail. Communication can be as complex as it is important, and therefore it needs to be managed properly. You need to prepare a communication management plan as part of planning for the project. Communication is performed according to the communication management plan during the execution of the project by distributing the required information and by managing stakeholder expectations. Communication is also performed while monitoring and controlling the project by reporting performance in a timely manner to the right stakeholders. Like any other important aspect of the project, communication itself needs to be monitored and controlled. In the project management standard, the communication management knowledge area offers processes to accomplish all these tasks. First, you need to plan for communication.

So the core question in this chapter is how to plan for project communication. In search of an answer, we will explore three underlying fundamental topics: basic communication concepts and types, methods and models of virtual communication, and project communication planning in the context of the big picture of communication management.

In this chapter you will look at:

- The big picture of project communication management
- Basic concepts, types, and modes of communication
- The difference between communication networks and technology networks, such as computer networks and telephone networks
- Basic models of virtual communication
- Communication planning in the context of the big picture of communication management
- The standard process for communication planning

Managing Project Communication: Big Picture

There is a common thread that runs through almost all activities and processes in project management, and that is communication. The project and its activities will fail without effective communication. Communication is an exchange of information among persons and groups by using an effectively common system of signs, symbols, and behavior. I used the term "effectively common" to take into account the fact that even if two communicating entities are using two different systems, the "translators" between the communicating entities produce the results as if the two entities were using a common system. For example, I might be using a Windows computer and you might be using a Macintosh, but we can exchange emails without having to deal with the differences between the two machines.

The importance of communication in project management cannot be overemphasized. Even a well-scheduled and well-funded project can fail in the hands of a hardworking team of experts due to the lack of proper communication. As a project manager, you may be dealing with a wide functional variety of individuals ranging from executives, to marketing personnel, to sales folks, to technologists. You should be able to wear different communication hats depending upon whom you are communicating with. For example, you will not be talking in terms of technical jargon to executives or marketing folks, and you will not speak marketing lingo to software developers. You will be speaking to different stakeholders in their language, while filling the language gap between different functional groups and eliminating misunderstandings due to miscommunication. The key point is that you put on the appropriate communication hat depending on which individual you are communicating with. Be able to switch communication hats quickly and avoid the technical jargon and acronyms that are not understood by the person or the group you are communicating with. The goal is the clarity of the language to convey the message accurately.

In a project, you will be communicating with project stakeholders. The different components of project communication management are illustrated in Figure 8.1.

> Communication is a common thread that runs through almost all activities and processes in project management.

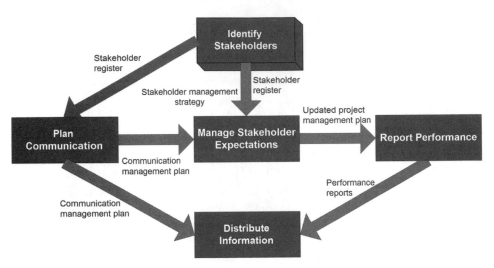

Figure 8.1 *Big picture of project communication management.*

In this chapter we discuss communication in general and how to plan for it. Other components of communication management will be discussed in forthcoming chapters.

Communication Types and Models

In science, a model is a mathematical, physical, or logical representation of a system of entities, phenomena, or processes in order to explain the observed reality and possibly use it. In modeling, often the ideas from different disciplines are unified to explain a complex phenomenon or to invent something new and useful—or both.

A communication model is a set of assumptions about communication entities and the relationships among those entities that describes how the information is exchanged between the sender and the receiver. To be on the same page throughout this discussion, let's first define the following terms:

- **Entity.** Any individual or device, which is usually a part of the system.

- **Communication entity.** An individual or device that has a well-defined role in a communication system.

- **Communicating entity.** A communication entity that is playing the role of a sender or a receiver. A mediator in a communication can also be looked upon as a communicating entity because it receives a message and then sends it to some-one else, so it has a double role as a receiver and a sender.

- **Communication system.** A collection of communication entities that acts as an integrated whole to facilitate communication.

- **Communication network.** An interconnected set of communicating entities arranged in such a way that an entity can send a message to one or more other entities and can receive messages from them. In other words, it's a collection of nodes and communication lines, where a node is an original sender or an ultimate recipient. Here are the fundamental elements of a communication network:

  - **Message.** A unit of information that is exchanged between the sender and the receiver.

  - **Sender.** An entity—an individual or a device—that sends the message. The original sender is called a node.

  - **Receiver.** An entity—an individual or a device—that receives the message. The ultimate receiver is called a node.

  - **Medium.** The part of the communication system between the sender and the receiver through which the message travels from the sender to the receiver.

Here, we are only concerned with the topology of the communication system—that is, the patterns of connections between senders and receivers—without going into the technical details of how that topology is implemented. For example, one-to-one communication is a part of a pattern that is called *unicast*, and one-to-many communication is part of a pattern called *multicast*. In this discussion of topology of communication, we are not concerned whether this unicast or multicast is performed through email, letters, or phone.

The original sender and the ultimate receiver of the message are the two most important communicating entities. They play important roles in defining the types of communication.

Basic Types of Communication

In its most basic form, communication is the exchange of information between two entities. Even communication among several entities is better handled by looking at it as a set of exchanges between two entities. For example, A communicating with B, C, and D is a set of exchanges between A and B, A and C, and A and D. In other words, exchange between two entities is the basic building block of communication. So we can always break down a communication as an exchange between a sender and a receiver.

From the perspective of how the sender and the receiver are involved with each other through the communication system, communication can be classified into the following two categories:

There are two categories of communication: interactive and one-way.

1. **Interactive communication.** In this type of communication, the receiver receives the message and sends a response to it. This way the communicating entities keep switching the roles of senders and receivers. There are two kinds of interactive communication:

The two types of interactive communication are asynchronous and synchronous.

- **Asynchronous communication.** A communication in which the two communicating entities do not have to be present on both ends of the communication line at the same time. Email is an example of asynchronous communication because when the sender of the email clicks the Send button, the intended recipient of the email message does not have to be logged on to the email server. The recipient can log on later, retrieve the message, and read it.

- **Synchronous communication.** A communication in which the two communicating entities have to be present on both ends of the communication line at the same time. It's a live, real-time communication; if you are not present when the sender is sending the message, you miss the message. Speaking with someone face to face or conversing with someone on the phone is an example of synchronous communication.

2. **One-way communication.** There are two kinds of one-way communications:

The two types of one-way communication are pull and push.

- **Pull communication.** In this kind of communication, the receiver pulls the information from a pool of information. Downloading from websites is an example of this communication.

- **Push communication.** In this kind of communication, the sender broadcasts the information to a set of entities without waiting for the request for information and without the need to confirm that the information reached its destination. Marketing emails and letters are examples of push communication.

The pull and push methods can also be used in conjunction with each other. For example, the sender can also push the information to a pool, and the receivers can pull it from there at their own convenience.

Communication types discussed here are also called communication *methods*. Depending on the purpose, the project manager can decide which of these communication methods to use. Quite often a hybrid approach is used in the real world—that is, a mix of more than one method.

Communication in its most primitive form can be defined as an exchange of a message between two living individuals face to face—all communication is local. This was the form of communication most commonly used in ancient times. Then appeared the role of a mediator—a messenger who would receive the message from the original sender and deliver it to the ultimate receiver. This way, the messenger acted as a receiver on one hand and a sender on the other. This was the beginning of virtual communication.

Virtual Communication Models

Virtual communication is a form of communication that does not require the communicating individuals to be present at the same location; they can be at places remote to each other. Conference calls, emails, blogs, and online bulletin boards are all examples of virtual communication. As mentioned earlier, a messenger was the first entity that extended local communication to its virtual horizons. Virtual communication is the evolution of communication rather than the alternative to local communication. In this information age, virtual communication is rapidly developing as a main form of communication.

> Virtual communication methods, such as conference calls, emails, blogs, and online bulletin boards, do not require the communicating individuals to be present at the same location.

The very definition of virtual communication extends the definition of communicating entities, which in the virtual world don't need to be just living individuals. They could be robots, devices, or software programs. In the virtual world (or the Internet age) that we live in, a communication entity is a component of the communication system that plays a well-defined role in the communication. For example the sender and receiver of a message are both communication entities and so is the communication line whose role is to transport the message. Following are some categories of communication entities:

Communication node. A communication node is a communicating entity that is the original sender or the ultimate receiver. It's a subset of communicating entities, which also include the mediators.

Communication line. A communication line is a communication entity that helps transport the message from the sender to the receiver. Communication lines are used to make connections between two communication entities. Topologically speaking, a communication line has two ends: a sender's end and a receiver's end.

COMMUNICATION LINE AND VIRTUALITY

In a face-to-face conversation, the communication line is the vibrating air or the pressure wave, called the *sound wave*, between the sender and the receiver. In a remote communication, the communication lines become more complex. For example, a letter has to go through several post offices and trucks before it completes its journey, and an email has to go through the whole Internet infrastructure: the phone lines, cables, routers, email servers, and so on. However, the original sender and the ultimate receiver do not have to worry about the complexity of the system between them. They can simply imagine it as a line, an imaginary line, a virtual line—hence the name *virtual communication*.

Communication channel. A communication channel is a buffer or part of the storage media to which a message is put and from which the message is retrieved during communication. A cable or satellite system is an example of a communication channel.

Communication hub. A communication hub is a central communication entity through which each communication message in the communication system has to pass.

Communication bus. A communication bus is a communication channel accessible to and shared by each communication node. An online bulletin board, a discussion form, or a blog site is an example.

A communication network is a collection of nodes that can communicate with one another by using one or more communication modes. There are three communication modes:

- **Unicast.** This is the communication mode in which one node communicates with only one other node at a time. This means the message sent by an original sender is received only by one specific ultimate receiver.

- **Broadcast.** In this mode, the message sent by the sender node is received by all the nodes in the network.

- **Multicast.** In this mode, the message sent by the receiver is received by a predetermined subset of the nodes in the communication network.

> The three communication modes are unicast, broadcast, and multicast.

You can think of nodes as individuals or devices without worrying about the technology that makes these modes of communication possible. In this spirit of topology, the communication can be grouped into a few categories based on the patterns of the connections between communicating entities. Because virtual communication is not face to face, it needs some connections—that is, communication lines—between the nodes and the channels to which the message can be put at some point and from which the message can be retrieved at another point. So, a virtual communication model is a topological model that basically determines the patterns used to connect the nodes and some other communicating entities in the communication network to each other. Most of the concepts and the models discussed here are based on the knowledge base and experience in the computer networking. However, the term *network* in this chapter does not necessarily mean the computer network; instead, it refers to the network of communication between entities, including individuals.

STUDY CHECKPOINT 8.1

Problem: You communicate with your project team through conference calls, one-on-one phone calls, and emails. In this communication identify the following:

A. Communication network
B. Communication system
C. The difference between the communication system and the communication network

---

> **Solution:**
> A. You and your team members are the nodes of the communication network. The communication lines between these nodes are set up through phone or email. The collection of these nodes and communication lines is the communication network.
> B. Your communication network and the technology that supports it (phones, email servers, and so on) combined make the communication network.
> C. In a communication network, we only look at nodes and the connection between the nodes at a virtual level. In the communication system, all the communication entities are included—nodes and the technological devices that connect the nodes and make the communication possible.

Because these communication models describe the communication that goes on in the real world, you can improve your communication by understanding these models. There are four main models discussed here.

Bus Communication Model

As shown in Figure 8.2, nodes in a network based on a bus communication model share a single main channel (hence the name *bus*), and each node is attached to this channel through its own individual connection. This means that the channel is part of the communication line between any two nodes on the network. This model can support any mode of communication: unicast, multicast, or broadcast.

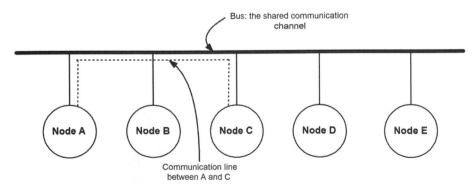

Figure 8.2 *Illustration of the bus communication model. All communication nodes are attached to a single shared communication channel.*

One disadvantage of a communication network based on this model is that a single fault in the shared channel can bring down the whole network. An online bulletin board is an example of a shared channel. If the website supporting the bulletin board goes down, the communication network supported by the bulletin board also goes down.

Another way of connecting nodes in a network is to connect a node directly to another node rather than through a single shared channel. This is done in the ring model.

Ring Communication Model

As shown in Figure 8.3, each node in a network based on a ring model is connected directly to its two neighbor nodes: a predecessor and a successor. A communication network that uses the ring communication model can be called a *ring communication network*.

As a typical example of how a node in a ring network communicates with another node, assume node A in Figure 8.3 sends a message to node D. The message will travel in the ring from A to B, B to C, and C to D. Node D will receive the message and send a copy of it to node E, and the message will eventually reach the sender A by traveling through E, F, G, and H. In other words, the

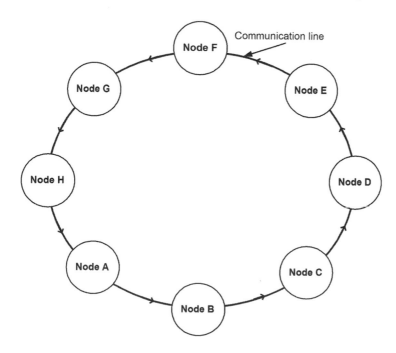

Figure 8.3
Illustration of the ring communication model. Each node in the ring communication network is connected to its two immediate neighbors.

message from the sender A keeps going until it completes the circle and reaches back to A. This is also called *short circuit communication*. The point here is to realize that each node and each connection in the ring is a single point of failure. In this method, there is a greater chance for the message to be changed. Rumors usually are spread by using this model. If the accuracy of the message is important, this is not a good method of communication. Following are some variations of this model:

- Following the previous example, when a message reaches from A to D through B and C, D responds back to A through C and B. This is also a ring in which B and C appear twice.

- D does not send the same message to A that it received through E, F, G, and H, but sends the acknowledgment of it or a response to it.

Another example that closely fits this model is one method of communication in a functional organization when the project manager wants to communicate with an employee in a functional department: The project manager talks to the functional manager, the functional manager talks to the employee, and the employee talks to the project manager.

Ring networks used to be in full swing in olden times, because in some communities rumor mills were an important source of entertainment. In this information age, the virtual communication model that is more in use (in addition to the bus model) is the star communication model.

Star Communication Model

As shown in Figure 8.4, all nodes in a communication network based on the star model are connected to a central entity called a *communication hub* or just a *hub*. The communication network that uses the star communication model can be called the *star communication network*. A message from the sender node goes to the recipient through the hub.

The advantage of this model is that it's easy to figure out who is talking to whom (the hub knows it), and the troubleshooting is relatively easy if something goes wrong with the communication. It is fault tolerant in the sense that if a node goes down or a connection of a node to the hub goes down, the rest of the network keeps functioning. However, the hub is the single point of failure. As an example, think of a project team in which the team

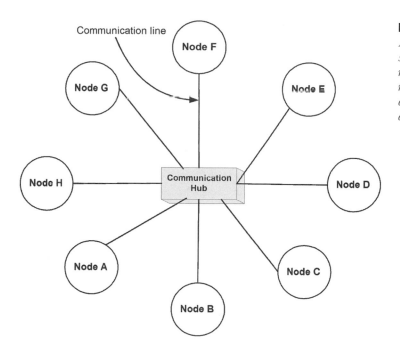

Figure 8.4
Illustration of the star communication model, in which each node is connected to a central entity called a hub.

members are the nodes and the project manager acts as a hub. All the project-related communication is performed through the project manager. If the team member A wants something from team member C, and C is not responding, the project manager will immediately become aware of it and solve the problem. However, if the project manager herself cannot be found, then the whole communication network goes down.

The star communication model supports all three modes of communication: unicast, multicast, and broadcast. For example, A can communicate with C through the hub. A can also send a message to the hub, and the hub will send it to B, C, and D. This is an example of a multicast. If A sends the message to the hub, and the hub sends it to all the nodes connected to the hub, it is an example of a broadcast.

It's important to remember that the communication entities in a virtual network can be individuals, devices, or both; usually it's a mix of the two. In our previous example of a project team, the project manager acts as a hub, the project team members are nodes, and the phones or emails can be considered as setting up the communication lines. In a different scenario, the email server can act as a hub and the email senders and recipients as the nodes.

Mesh Communication Model

The mesh communication model is the communication network with the maximum possible communication lines.

In the mesh communication model, each node is connected to every other node in the communication network, and the communication network based on this model is called the *mesh communication network*. In this network everybody is speaking to everybody else. This is the communication network with the maximum possible communication lines. As an example, Figure 8.5 presents the mesh communication network of four nodes. Each of these four nodes is connected with three other nodes, and if we multiply 4 by 3, we are double-counting each communication line. Therefore, the total number of communication lines in this network is $4\times3/2=6$. In general the number of communication lines in a mesh network of n nodes is $n(n-1)/2$: a lot more communication lines than the nodes. This represents the complexity and importance of communication management because in the absence of proper management and planning, all communication lines tend to get active to cause confusion and disarray, or the right communication lines may stay passive while the wrong ones become active.

Figure 8.5

Illustration of the communication network of four nodes based on the mesh communication model.

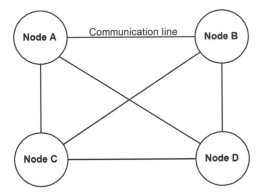

STUDY CHECKPOINT 8.2

Problem: The communication in your 10-member project team is currently a total mess. Everybody is communicating with everybody else on important matters. What is the total number of communication lines in this communication network?

Solution:

Total number of nodes = 10

Total number of communication lines = $n(n-1)/2$

= $10\times9/2$

= 45

To implement these models, there are two important points to remember:

- Models are models. Which model you should use and in which way depends on the situation and the environment you are dealing with.

- In the real world, often a hybrid approach of communication that may include elements from more than one model is used.

Communication Networks and Systems

To avoid confusion, it's important to understand the distinction between three concepts: communication network, technology network, and communication system. These three concepts were defined earlier and are presented together in the following list:

- **Communication system.** A communication system is a collection of communication entities that act as an integrated whole to facilitate communication.

- **Communication network.** A communication network is an interconnected set of communicating entities arranged in such a way that an entity can send a message to one or more other entities and can receive messages from them. In other words, it's a collection of nodes and communication lines— the virtual communication lines.

- **Technology networks.** These are the networks formed by connecting technology devices, such as computer networks and telephone networks, called telecommunication networks. These networks support the communication networks.

The relationship among communication network, technology networks, and communication system is illustrated in Figure 8.6. In this illustration, a communication network is constituted by two nodes (A and B) and a communication line between them. It's a virtual communication line that is supported by the technology networks, such as computer networks and telephone networks. The actual communication path, of course, goes through these technology networks, but the communicating entities, the nodes, don't need to deal with that technical detail. They can assume that they are directly connected to each other through the virtual communication. The communication network composed of these nodes and links is the network that is managed by the project manager. Technology networks are managed by technology administrators, such as network system administrators.

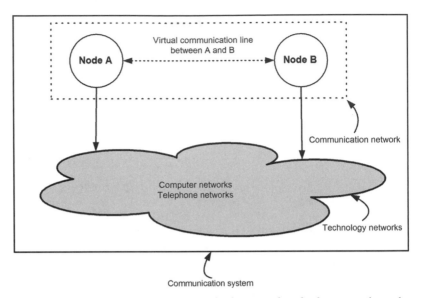

Figure 8.6 *Relationship between communication network, technology networks, and communication system.*

Planning Project Communication

In a project environment, communication means communicating with the project stakeholders. Planning communication is the process of determining the information needs of the project stakeholders and accordingly the communication approach.

Communication planning is the process of determining the following:

- The communication and information needs of the program stakeholders
- The four Ws: what information is needed, when it is needed, who needs it, and who will deliver it
- How the information will be delivered—for example, by email, phone call, or presentation

In Chapter 4, you learned how to identify stakeholders. During the process of identifying stakeholders, you create the stakeholder register and develop the stakeholder management strategy. Both of these items are used in planning the project communication.

Recall that communication is transferring information from one point to another. It expends resources. To optimize the use of resources and the benefits of communication, you need to analyze the communication requirements and determine the communication technology to be used.

Communication Requirements Analysis

Communication requirements, needed for the communication planning process, need to be analyzed. This analysis will generate the communication needs of the project stakeholders. For example, a communication requirement may specify the type of information and the format in which this information should be delivered. The analysis of this requirement will estimate the value of this communication requirement—for example, the fulfillment of this requirement will significantly contribute to the success of the project, or the lack of it will result in the failure of the project or one of its components. So, one of the purposes of communication requirements analysis is to optimize the use of resources in communication

Communication requirements need to be analyzed to generate the communication needs of the project stakeholders.

Complexity of communication can be appreciated by realizing that there are $n(n-1)/2$ possible communication channels among n stakeholders, as discussed earlier in this chapter. For example, if there are 30 stakeholders, the possible number of communication channels is $30\times29/2=435$.

Communication Technology Determination

Depending on the communication needs and nature of the information, a communication technology may vary from a conversation in a hallway to a sophisticated information system. The following factors can contribute to determining the communication technology to be used for your program:

- **Availability.** If you are considering a number of options, obviously the technology that's already in place is more likely to be chosen.

- **Project environment.** The project environment can also affect the choice of communication technology. For example, the communication technology requirements for a program team that meets face to face will be different from that of a virtual team.

The factors that can contribute to determining the communication technology to be used include availability, project environment, project length, the urgency of the information need, and the preparation level.

- **Project length.** The length of the project affects the communication technology requirements in the following ways:

  - Is it worth it to spend on a technology for the given length of the project?

  - Will the technology under consideration change during the course of the project? If yes, that will mean extra cost for the new technology and for training the team members to use it.

- **Urgency of the information need.** How frequently the information needs to be updated will also play a role in determining the communication technology. For example, the information that does not need to change frequently can be delivered in written reports, whereas the information that can change very frequently can be delivered through web pages.

- **Preparation level.** Another factor that can be considered in making the communication technology decision is the users' (project team and other stakeholders) level of preparation for using a given technology. Are the users already fluent in this technology or will they need to be trained?

You use these tools and techniques to generate the output of the communication planning process: the communication management plan.

Communication Management Plan

This is the document that describes the communication expectations, needs, and plans for the project. It specifies what information will be communicated, when and how it will be communicated, and who will communicate it and to whom. It includes the following:

- Communication requirements of the project stakeholders

- Information to be communicated: content, format, and level of detail

- Who will communicate the information, who will receive it, and why

- The person responsible for authorizing the release of confidential information

- Methods of communication that will be used, such as email, presentation, and press release

- The frequency of communication, such as daily or weekly

- The method and procedure for escalating the issues that cannot be resolved at a lower staff level, such as project level
- A glossary of common communication terminology
- Methods and procedures for updating and refining the communication management plan if needed as the program progresses

The communication management plan may also include the technology requirements plan. Executing a project in this information age, more likely than not, you will need multiple technologies for communication, such as email, web calendars, and video conferencing. Therefore, it is important that you plan for the communication technology requirements. This planning has two components: the tools that are needed and the usage of those tools. To determine which tools are needed, ask questions such as the following:

- How frequently do you need to update the information?
- Will the team hold face-to-face or virtual meetings?

For the information that does not change often, the written reports will be sufficient, whereas the information that needs to be updated frequently and on a moment's notice needs web communication tools. To plan the effective usage of the tools, ask the following questions:

- Are the tools (communication systems) already in place and ready to be used?
- Will the available communication tools change before the program ends?
- Are the team members familiar with the tools, or do they need training to use them?

The Many Faces of Communication

While planning for communication, you should consider the multiple facets of communication in the following list:

- **Multiple kinds of receivers.** You should consider all kinds of project stakeholders that will need different kinds of information. For example, stakeholders in the project team and outside the project team, stakeholders who are down the hierarchy point from where you are and those who are higher than you on the hierarchy tree, and stakeholders who are your peers.

Communication with your peers is called horizontal communication, and communication up and down the hierarchy is called vertical communication.

While planning for communication, you should consider that there are multiple kinds of receivers and multiple forms of communication.

- **Multiple forms of communication.** In order to choose suitable forms of communication, consider all forms for different situations and audiences, such as formal and informal, written and oral, and official and unofficial.

- **Volume.** Pay attention to the volume of communication, verbal and nonverbal (body language, and so on), tone of communication, and between-the-lines communication.

SUCCESS SHOT: OBSERVATION AND LISTENING

While planning for communication (or doing anything, for that matter), pay attention to details, ask questions, and probe the situation to come to a better understanding. A well-understood problem is already half solved. Be an active and effective listener.

Standardize This

The standard process for project communication planning, called *plan communications*, is shown in Figure 8.7. The figure illustrates the standard way of looking at the elements of communication planning discussed in this chapter.

Quick Success Mantras

- Communication is the common thread that runs through almost all activities and processes in project management.
- A good communicator is also a good listener.
- A project supported by all the needed resources can fail without effective communication management.
- Project communication management includes identifying stakeholders, planning for communication, distributing information, managing stakeholder expectations, and reporting performance.
- Three modes of communication are one to one, called unicast; one to many, called multicast; and one to all, called broadcast.

- A communication system is a collection of communication entities that acts as an integrated whole to facilitate communication.

- A communication network is a high-level view of the communication system and is a collection of communicating entities called nodes and the communication lines between them, called links.

- Technology networks, such as computer networks and telephone networks, are parts of the communication system and support the communication networks.

- The results of communication management planning are documented in the communication management plan.

- The communication management plan document describes the communication expectations, needs, and plans for the project. It specifies what information will be communicated, when and how it will be communicated, and who will communicate it and to whom.

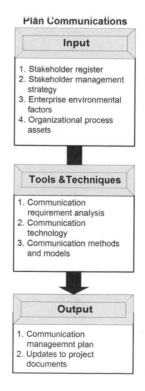

Figure 8.7

The plan communications process: input, tools and techniques, and output.

Chapter 9

Planning for Quality and Risk Management

- Understanding Quality Management
- Planning Quality
- Understanding Risk Management
- Planning Risk Management
- Identifying Risks
- Planning the Risk Response
- Standard This
- Quick Success Mantras

The basic requirement for a project to be successful is to complete it with full scope, on schedule, and within the planned budget. This is also the basic quality requirement for a project. However, to break down this basic quality requirement into details, you need to plan for quality management. Planning in any area requires of you to be proactive, and proactive project management is at its peak when you are planning how to identify and deal with the potential project risks. So, the core question in this chapter concerns how to plan for quality and risk management. In search of an answer, we will explore three avenues: planning quality, identifying and analyzing risks, and planning risk responses.

In this chapter you'll:

- Understand the big picture of quality management and risk management
- Understand how to plan for quality management
- Understand how to develop a risk management plan and how to identify risks
- Distinguish between qualitative risk analysis and quantitative risk analysis
- Learn how to prepare risk responses
- Identify the tools and techniques for quality and risk planning
- Identify the standard processes for quality and risk planning

Understanding Quality Management

Quality refers to the degree to which the project objectives and a set of characteristics of project deliverables fulfill the project requirements. When you plan to produce a deliverable, the deliverable has some requirements that it is expected to meet when it's complete. After the deliverable has actually been produced, it has some characteristics—for example, features. The question is to what degree the characteristics fulfill the requirements. Also, recall that a project is started to meet some objectives that align with the strategic objectives of the organization. The question is: to what degree do these objectives met by the finished project satisfy the required objectives planned for the project? So, the quality is the sum of project and product characteristics that help fulfill the requirements and objectives. A broader goal of quality management is to ensure that a given project will satisfy the needs for which it was undertaken.

> **SUCCESS SHOT: GOLDEN RULE OF QUALITY MANAGEMENT**
> **Quality is planned instead of inspected.** In the long term,
> the cost of planning and implementing quality is less than the
> cost of inspecting and fixing the quality problems and living
> with the consequences of poor quality.

Quality management has two components: project quality management and product quality management. While product quality management techniques depend upon the specific product that the project is going to produce, project quality management applies to all projects independent of the nature of the products. The performing organization may have its own quality policy and procedures in addition to the three quality management processes shown in Figure 9.1 and explained in the following list.

The three project quality management processes are plan quality, perform quality assurance, and perform quality control.

- **Plan quality.** A process used to identify which quality requirements and standards are relevant to the project at hand and to determine how to meet them.

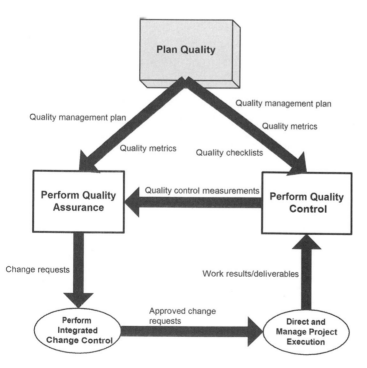

Figure 9.1

Illustration of relationships among different components of quality management and the relationships of quality management with other components of project management.

- **Perform quality assurance.** A process used for auditing the fulfillment of quality requirements to ensure that the project employs all the planned quality requirements and standards.
- **Perform quality control.** A process to monitor and control the results from the quality-related activities with a two-pronged purpose: to assess performance in implementing quality and recommend needed changes.

Quality assurance and quality control are used during the project execution and control stages and are therefore discussed in upcoming chapters. Quality planning is performed during project planning stage and is discussed next.

Planning Quality

As mentioned earlier, quality is defined as the degree to which project objectives and a set of characteristics of project deliverables fulfill the project requirements. Therefore, any characteristic that influences the satisfaction of the stakeholders is included in determining the quality. Project quality management includes performing quality planning, quality assurance, and quality control. Quality planning is the quality process that is performed during the planning stage to accomplish the following goals.

- Identify which quality requirements and standards are relevant to the project at hand
- Determine how to satisfy these requirements and standards

You need to have a few items at your disposal before you can begin quality planning.

Preparing for Quality Planning

The items needed for quality planning include:

Project performance baseline. The project performance baseline comprised of the scope baseline, schedule baseline, and cost baseline contains the list of all the deliverables and objectives to which the quality needs to be applied. For example, the following components of the project scope statement are especially relevant to quality planning:

- Project deliverables.
- Project objectives.

- Project requirements.

- A product scope description that may contain the details of technical issues and other quality-related concerns.

- Product acceptance criteria. The definition of acceptance criteria has an impact on the quality cost.

THE MOTHER OF ALL QUALITY REQUIREMENTS

One fundamental quality requirement for a project is to complete it on time, with full scope, and within planned budget—that is, to successfully implement the schedule baseline, the scope baseline, and the cost baseline. That's why you need these three baselines, collectively called the *project baseline*, to prepare for quality planning.

Enterprise environmental factors. Guidelines, regulations from a government agency, rules, and standards relevant to the project at hand are examples of enterprise environment factors that must be considered during quality planning.

Organizational process assets. The following organizational process assets can affect the project from the perspective of quality planning:

- Information from the previous projects and lessons learned

- An organizational quality policy, which is composed of overall intentions and high-level direction of an organization with respect to quality, established by the management at the executive level

- Procedures relevant to the application area of this project

If the performing organization lacks a quality policy, the project team will need to develop a quality policy for the project. Once a quality policy is in place, it is your responsibility to ensure that the project stakeholders are aware of it and are on the same page.

Stakeholder register and risk register. A stakeholder register may help in identifying the stakeholders that will have interests in quality. A risk register will help identify positive risks (opportunities) and negative risks (threats) that may have an impact on quality.

The items needed for quality planning are a project performance baseline, enterprise environmental factors, organizational process assets, and a stakeholder register and risk register.

How You Actually Plan for Quality

The tools and techniques used for quality planning include benchmarking, cost/benefit analysis, experiment design, and brainstorming.

Benchmarking. Benchmarking is comparing practices, products, or services of a project with those of some reference projects for the purpose of learning, improving, and creating the basis for measuring performance. These reference projects might be the previous projects performed inside or outside of the performing organization. Improvement and performance are of course quality-related factors. For example, you might have a similar project performed in the past that accepted no more than two defects in each feature. You might use that as a quality criterion—a benchmark—for your project.

The tools and techniques used for quality planning include benchmarking, cost/benefit analysis, experiment design, and other quality-planning tools, such as brainstorming, flowcharting, control charts, and statistical sampling.

Cost of quality and cost/benefit analysis. The cost of quality is the total cost incurred in implementing conformance to the requirements, reworking due to the defects resulting from failure to meet the requirements, and updating the product or service to meet the requirements. During quality planning, you must consider the tradeoff between the cost and the benefit of quality and strike the appropriate balance for a given project. Implementing quality has its costs, including quality management and fulfilling quality requirements. The benefits of meeting quality requirements include less rework, resulting in overall higher productivity; lower costs of maintaining the product or service; and higher customer satisfaction.

Design of experiments. This is a statistical method that can be used to identify the factors that might influence a set of specific variables for a product or a process under development or in production. By using the results from these experiments, you can optimize the products and processes.

Other quality-planning tools. Other tools that you can use in quality planning, depending upon the project, include brainstorming, flowcharting, control charts, and statistical sampling. Statistical sampling involves randomly selecting a part of the population for study. In quality control, you can select a subset of features for inspection. This can save a substantial amount of resources. However, during quality planning, you will need to decide on some sampling issues, such as sample size and frequency. Brainstorming, control charts, and flowcharting are discussed further on in this book.

You can use one or more of these techniques to plan for quality.

What You Get from Quality Planning

A major output of the quality planning process is the quality management plan. In the following list, I discuss the quality management plan and other items resulting from quality planning.

Quality management plan. The quality management plan describes how the quality policy for this project will be implemented by the project management team. It also addresses quality assurance and quality control, as explained in the previous section. This plan becomes a component of the overall project management plan.

Whether the quality management plan is informal and high level or formal and detailed depends upon the size, complexity, and needs of the project.

The quality management plan also contains the quality baseline that sets the criteria that specifies the quality objectives for the project and thereby makes the basis for measuring and reporting the quality performance. The quality management plan becomes part of the project management plan. Therefore, quality planning updates the project management plan.

Quality metrics. This is an operational criterion that defines in specific terms what something (such as a characteristic or a feature) is and how the quality control process measures it. For example, it is not specific enough to say the defects in the product will be minimized. Rather, specifying something, such as that no feature will have more than two defects, is a measurable criterion and hence a metric. The metrics that you set during quality planning will be used in quality assurance and quality control.

Quality checklist. A checklist is a structured tool used to verify that a predetermined set of required steps has been performed. The checklists can come in imperative form ("to do" lists) or in interrogative form ("have you done this" lists). Checklists are prepared (or identified if they already exist in the organization) in quality planning and used in quality control.

Process improvement plan. This plan describes how to improve some of the processes that will be used in the project. For example, one purpose of improvement is to prevent activities in the processes that are not needed for this project. This is accomplished by describing the purpose, start, and end of a given process, the input to the process, and the output of the process.

Note that quality planning might influence other planning processes. For example, implementing the identified quality standards will impact the cost and the schedule. Furthermore, the implementation of a quality characteristic might require a risk analysis of the problem that the quality characteristic addresses.

Understanding Risk Management

Risk is an uncertain event or condition that has a positive or negative effect on meeting the project objectives.

Risk management is an integral part of project management. To most of us, risk means danger—if it happens, it will result in negative, undesired consequences. However, in the profession of project management, risk is an uncertain event or condition that, if it occurs, has a positive or negative effect on meeting the project objectives related to components such as schedule (time), cost, scope, or quality. For example, one of the obvious schedule objectives for a project is to complete the project by the scheduled deadline. If a risk related to the schedule occurs, it can delay the completion of the project or it can make it possible to finish the project earlier. For example, replacing a team member with a new team member poses an uncertainty: The new team member may be more or less productive than the old team member. The two characteristics of a risk in project management are the following:

- It stems from the elements of uncertainty.
- It might have negative or positive effects on meeting the project objectives.

Project risk management includes planning risk management, identifying and analyzing the risks, preparing the response plan, implementing the risk response plan, and monitoring and controlling the implementation. Figure 9.2 illustrates these aspects of risk management, which are also explained in the following list.

- **Plan risk management.** A process to determine the how of risk management: how to conduct risk management for the project at hand.
- **Identify risks.** A process to identify and document the risks that might occur for a given project.

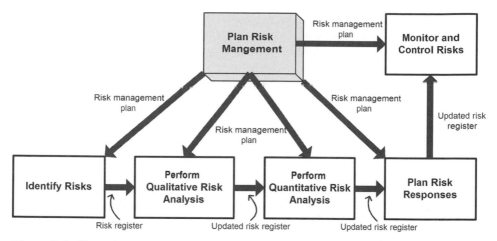

Figure 9.2 *Illustration of relationships among different components of risk management.*

- **Perform qualitative risk analysis.** A process used for estimating the overall probability for risks to occur and their impact, and prioritizing them accordingly for further analysis.

- **Perform quantitative risk analysis.** A process used to analyze numerically the effect of identified risks on meeting the project objectives.

- **Plan risk responses.** A process used to prepare a risk response plan in order to increase the positive impact and decrease the negative impact of risks on the project.

- **Monitoring and control risks.** A process used for tracking identified risks, identifying new risks, executing risk response plans, and evaluating the effectiveness of executing responses throughout the lifecycle of the project.

The data flow between the different processes shown in Figure 9.2 is true in general. However, note that depending upon the project and the experience of the risk management team, shortcuts can be taken. For example, you can go directly from risk identification to quantitative risk analysis, or even to risk response planning.

Monitoring and controlling risks is part of monitoring and controlling the project and therefore is discussed further on in this book. The other five processes are discussed next, starting with planning risk management.

Planning Risk Management

Risk management planning is used to decide how the risk management activities for the project at hand will be performed. The major goals for planning risk management are threefold: Ensure that the type, level, and visibility of risk management are proportionate to the actual risk involved in the project and the importance of the project to the organization; secure sufficient resources, including time for risk management activities; and set up an agreed-upon basis for evaluating risks. To be specific, you use the risk management planning process to determine the following:

- How to approach the risk management activities for the project
- How to plan the risk management activities
- How to execute the risk management activities

To plan for risk management, you need to consider assumptions and constraints, project objectives and requirements, product description, and initial risk identification.

To plan for risk management, you need to look at the project scope statement, which contains elements such as the following, which are relevant to risk management planning:

- **Assumptions and constraints.** Assumptions should be evaluated for their uncertainty and thereby the possible risks. Constraints represent fixed parameters, such as available funds and deadlines, that can also pose risks to the project.
- **Project objectives and requirements.** You must address the risks that might prevent the team from meeting the project objectives and requirements.
- **Product description.** There might be risks involved in performing the work for meeting the product description.
- **Initial risk identification.** The project scope statement might contain some of the risks you initially identified. Now you have more information to build on that work.

The cost management plan may have information on risks related to budget, contingency, and management reserves. The schedule management plan may have information on how the schedule contingencies will be used and reported. The communication management plan should have information on who should be informed about the different risks.

The enterprise environmental factors relevant to risk planning include the organizational attitude toward risks and the risk tolerance level of the organization. This information can be found from the policy statements of the organization and from actual experience with previous projects. The organizational process assets relevant to risk planning include organizational approaches toward risk management, definitions of concepts and terms used within the organization, standard risk templates you can use, a roles and responsibilities list, and authority levels for decision making.

You develop the risk management plan by holding planning meetings, which might include the following attendees:

- Project manager
- Selected members from the project team
- Selected stakeholders
- Any member from the performing organization who has the responsibility for risk planning and executing

The only output of risk management planning is the document called the *risk management plan*, which includes the following elements.

Methodology. This specifies the system of approaches, tools, and data sources that will be used to perform risk management on the project at hand. These tools and approaches might vary over the projects, so you have to make the best selection for the given project.

Identifying and assigning resources. This identifies and assigns the resources for risk management, such as human resources, cost, and time.

- **Roles and responsibilities.** This specifies the roles and responsibilities for each role involved in risk management. These roles are assigned to the members of the risk management team. The risk management team might include members from outside the project team.

- **Budgeting.** The cost for risk management activities needs to be estimated and included in the budget and the project cost baseline.

- **Timing and scheduling.** The plan specifies how often the risk management processes will be performed and which risk management activities will be included in the project schedule, which is planned and developed by using processes discussed in Chapter 6.

It's a good idea for the risk management team to include members from outside the project team to ensure unbiased risk evaluations.

Risk categories. This element specifies how the risks will be categorized. The risk categories typically correspond to the sources of risks. Depending upon the size and complexity of the project, you might need to develop a risk breakdown structure (RBS), which is a hierarchical structure that breaks the identified risk categories into subcategories. In developing this structure, you will end up identifying various areas and causes of potential risks.

Some project management literature and some PMP exam questions might use the terms *risk sources* and *risk categories* synonymously.

The performing organization might already have prepared a categorization of typical risks. However, you need to examine this categorization for each project and tailor it according to the needs of the project at hand. The risk categorization helps you identify the risks to the extent that you will be identifying various areas and causes of potential risks for your project.

Risk probability and impact. Defining different levels of risk probabilities and impacts is necessary to ensure the quality and credibility of the qualitative risk analysis that we will discuss later in this chapter. The basic issues are defining the scale of likelihood that the risk will happen and defining the scale of the strength of its impact if the risk occurs. These definitions, even if they already exist in the organization, must be examined and tailored to the needs of the specific project.

The output of risk management planning is the risk management plan, which includes sections on methodology, identifying and assigning resources, risk categories, and risk probability and impact.

You can define the risk probability scale from very unlikely to almost certainly; this is called the *relative scale*. As an alternative, you can define a numerical scale in which the probability is represented by numbers, in which a value close to 0.0 means very unlikely and a value close to 1.0 means almost certainly. The impact scale represents the size of the risk impact on the given project objective should the risk occur. Just like the probability scale, you can define the impact scale relatively or numerically. The relative scale can range from very low impact to very high impact, with points in the middle such as low, moderate, and high. As an alternative, you can define the impact numerically; it might be linear, such as the first point at 0.1, the second point at 0.2, and the tenth point at 1.0, or it might be nonlinear, such as the first point at 0.001, the second point at 0.01, and the third point at 0.1. Figure 9.3 shows an example of linear and nonlinear impact scales, in which the impact scale for objective 1 is nonlinear and the impact scale for objective 2 is linear. You can think of the X axis as a variable on which the risk impact depends.

Risks are prioritized according to the size of their impact on the project objectives, which can be recorded in what is called an *impact matrix* or *lookup table*. Even if your organization already has a typical impact matrix, you should examine it and tailor it to the needs of the specific project at hand. I will discuss the probability and impact matrix in more detail later in this chapter.

As an example, Table 9.1 shows the risk impact definitions for four project objectives: cost, time, scope, and quality. Note that this example only shows the negative impact. The first row of the table presents the impact scale, and each cell in the following rows from column 2 to column 6 specifies the impact on a specific objective corresponding to a point on the overall impact scale. For example, the cell corresponding to second row and fifth column reads that high impact (0.65) means a 50 to 80 percent increase in cost.

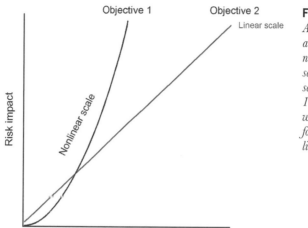

Figure 9.3

An example of a linear and a nonlinear impact scale. The impact scale for objective 1 is nonlinear, whereas the scale for objective 2 is linear.

Table 9.1 Risk Impact Definitions for Four Project Objectives: Cost, Time, Scope, and Quality

Risk Impact	Very Low (0.05)	Low (0.10)	Moderate (0.35)	High (0.65)	Very High (0.90)
Cost	Less than 1% cost increase	1–20% cost increase	20–50% cost increase	50–80% cost increase	80–100% cost increase
Time	Insignificant time increase	1–10% time increase	10–30% time increase	30–60% time increase	60–100% time increase
Scope	Scope decrease unnoticeable	Scope of only a few minor areas affected	Sponsor approval necessary for scope reduction	Scope reduction unacceptable to the sponsor	Project and the item are effectively useless
Quality	Unnoticeable quality reduction	Only a few applications will be affected	Quality requires sponsor approval	Quality reduction unacceptable	Project and item are effectively useless

Risk reporting and tracking. This element describes the format of the risk reports, such as the risk register, a document that contains the results of risk analysis and risk response planning. Furthermore, it describes how different aspects of risk activities will be recorded so that the risks can be monitored for the current project. Also, should the performing organization decide to audit the risk management process, one should be able to track these activities. Another reason for recording these activities could be to save the information for the benefit of future projects in the form of lessons learned.

During the process of planning risk management for a specific project, you revisit the tolerance levels of the stakeholders for certain risks, and these levels may be revised. In a nutshell, risk management planning is the process that generates the risk management plan document, which contains the information that will be used in risk identification, risk analysis, and risk response planning.

Identifying Risks

An unidentified risk is a danger lurking out of your sight and waiting to attack the project. The significance of risk identification cannot be overemphasized. You perform the risk identification process to accomplish the following tasks:

* Identify which risks might affect the project at hand
* Document the characteristics of the identified risks in a document called the *risk register*

Note that the risk identification process has the risk management plan as an input item, in addition to all the input items that the quality planning and risk management planning processes have.

What Goes into Identifying Risks

The risk management plan, the project management plan, and the project scope statement are the key input items to the risk identification process. As in many other processes, the enterprise environmental factors and organizational process assets relevant to the project at hand must also be considered. These and other items to be used in identifying risks are discussed in the following list.

Enterprise environmental factors. The environmental factors internal or external to the performing organization that can influence the project must be considered in the risk identification process. This might include academic and industry studies, benchmarking, and commercial databases.

Organizational process assets. This might include information from previous projects (the knowledge base), including lessons learned.

Project scope baseline. Assumptions in the project scope statement are potential sources of uncertainty, hence the risk. Constraints pose a risk by presenting predetermined factors, such as hard deadlines and fixed cost, thereby posing questions such as, "What is the probability that we can meet this constraint with the available resources?" The WBS, another component of the scope baseline, can be used to recognize risks at different levels of the WBS hierarchy.

Management plans. In the process of identifying risks, you need to look at the cost management plan, schedule management plan, risk management plan, and quality management plan. The approach that you will take in this project toward any of these plans may pose some risks of its own or may enhance some other risks. The key items from the risk management plan useful for risk identification are risk categories, roles and responsibilities, and the budget and timing available for the risk management activities.

Estimates. Estimates such as cost estimates and activity duration estimates by definition have a degree of uncertainty built into them. They should be looked at to identify the potential risks hiding behind this uncertainty.

Stakeholder register. If you look at the stakeholder register, you might find some stakeholders who can give useful input to identifying risks.

Toolbox for Risk Identification

Risk identification is crucial to risk management: If you fail to identify a risk, you will not be able to manage it. There are a multitude of tools and techniques available to aid you in identifying risks.

Assumptions analysis. Assumptions in the project scope statement represent uncertainty. You analyze these assumptions to identify the risks. Assumptions analysis is the technique used to examine the validity of the assumptions and thereby to identify the risks resulting from the inaccuracies, inconsistencies, or incompleteness of each assumption. For example, assume that there is only one person in the organization who has a rare skill needed for the project. An obvious assumption would be that the person will not quit the organization before completing the assignment. The inaccuracy of this assumption amounts to the risk.

Checklist analysis. The carefully prepared checklists in any process are great no-brainer timesavers. The projects in the same organization will more often than not have similarities. As a result, you can develop a risk identification checklist based on the information gathered from a similar set of projects previously performed. Also, if you developed the risk breakdown structure (RBS) in risk planning, the lowest level of the RBS can be used as a checklist.

Risk identification checklists are rarely exhaustive. Always explore what is left out of the checklist you are using. Also, improve the checklist when you close the project to enhance its value for future projects.

Diagramming techniques. These techniques use diagrams to identify risks by exposing and exploring the risks' causes. Here are a few examples:

- **Cause-and-effect diagram.** A cause-and-effect diagram illustrates how various factors (causes) can be linked to potential problems (effects).

- **Flowchart diagram.** A flowchart depicts how the elements of a system are related to each other and shows the logical flow of a process. By examining the flowchart of a process, the risk management team can identify the points of potential problems in the flowchart diagram.

- **Influence diagram.** An influence diagram is a graphical representation of situations that shows relationships among various variables and outcomes, such as causal influences and time-ordering of events. By examining these diagrams, the risk management team can recognize the potential problem areas and thereby identify risks.

Documentation reviews. A structured review of the relevant parts of input documents, such as the project scope statement and the project management plan, will certainly help in identifying risks. Furthermore, the knowledge base related to risk management from the previous projects can also be reviewed.

Information-gathering techniques. To identify risks, you need to gather risk-related information. Following are some of the information-gathering techniques used in risk identification:

- **Brainstorming.** The goal here is to get a comprehensive list of potential risks so that no risk goes unidentified. The project team, along with relevant experts from different disciplines, can participate in the brainstorming session. Brainstorming is better performed under the guidance of a facilitator. You can use the categories of risks or the RBS as a framework to keep the session focused on the issue.

- **Delphi technique.** The goal here is for the experts to reach a consensus without biases toward each other. I'm sure you will have no problem recalling a time when a decision was made because somebody (usually higher in the management hierarchy) said so. Contrary to this, the Delphi technique is used to ensure that it is the quality of the information and the argument that are important, not who is saying them. A facilitator circulates a questionnaire among the experts to solicit ideas about the risks of the given project. The experts respond anonymously. The responses are compiled and circulated among the participating experts for further evaluation without attaching a name to a response. It might take a few iterations before a general consensus is reached.

- **Interviewing.** This is one of the common methods used for information gathering for risk identification. You interview the appropriate stakeholders and subject matter experts to gather information that will help identify risks for the project at hand.

- **Root cause identification.** A powerful way to identify risk is to look for anything in the project that might generate a risk. In other words, if you can spot a potential cause for risks, it's simple to identify the risks resulting from that cause. Furthermore, if you know the cause of a risk, it helps to plan an effective response. You can also look for risks at the opposite side of causes—that is, impacts.

- **SWOT analysis.** While root cause identification techniques look into the causes of the risks to identify them, a SWOT analysis looks at the potential impacts of the risks to identify them. If you examine the strengths, weaknesses, opportunities, and threats (SWOT) of a given project, you will be exposing the risks involved. Remember that a strength is an opportunity, a weakness is a threat, and opportunities and threats are posed by risks. This helps broaden the spectrum of risks considered. For example, a strength of your project might be that most of its parts are well understood from previously executed similar projects. Therefore, the risks involved in those parts will be easy to identify. A weakness of your project might be that one of the parts involves new technology that is not well tested. So, this is a source of unknown risks. An opportunity might be that your organization will be the first one to take this product to the market. An example of a threat might be that the government is considering a bill that, if it becomes a law, will have profound implications for your project.

If you fail to identify a risk, you will not be able to manage it.

You will generally be using more than one of these tools and techniques to identify the risks. During risk identification, you might discover the causes of the risks, and you might even think of some potential risk responses. All this is part of the output of the risk identification process.

Here Comes the Risk Register

The risk register is a document that contains the output of the risk identification process. You will see later in this chapter that the risk register, which is initiated in the risk identification process, will also contain the information from other risk management processes. To begin, you store the following information from the risk identification process in the risk register:

- **List of identified risks.** These are the risks that you identified in the risk identification process.
- **List of the root causes of the risks.** This is a list of events or conditions that might give rise to the identified risks.
- **Updated risk categories.** Risks categories were originally identified in the risk management planning process. However, in the process of identifying risks you might discover new categories or modify the existing categories. The updated risk categories must be included in the risk register.

- **List of potential responses.** Risk response planning is a separate process that is performed after risk analysis. However, during risk identification, you might identify potential risk responses that you must document in the risk register. These responses can be further examined and planned in the risk response planning process.

The risk register becomes part of the project management plan.

The results of the risk identification process usually lead to the qualitative risk analysis.

In the risk register, you store a list of identified risks, a list of the root causes of the risks, updated risk categories, and a list of potential responses.

Analyzing Risks

Once you have identified the risks, you need to answer two main questions for each identified risk: What are the odds that the risk will occur, and if it does, what will its impact be on the project objectives? You get the answers by performing risk analysis, which comes in two forms: qualitative and quantitative.

- **Qualitative risk analysis.** This is used to prioritize risks for further analysis by estimating the probability of their occurrence and their impact on the project.
- **Quantitative risk analysis.** This is used to perform the numerical analysis to estimate the effect of each identified risk on the overall project objectives and deliverables.

Usually, you prioritize the risks by performing qualitative analysis on them before you perform quantitative analysis. However, if the project manager and the team have enough expertise, they can combine these two steps into one.

Risk analysis comes in qualitative and quantitative forms.

Qualitative Analysis

Because the qualitative analysis is an estimate, it is less precise than the quantitative analysis, which is based on numbers and hence is more precise. However, qualitative analysis is quick and cheaper. It gives you some feel about the risks, and then you can determine which risks need to be analyzed further by using the quantitative analysis.

Raw Data for Qualitative Risk Analysis

In addition to the risk register, the qualitative risk analysis can also use the risk management plan, the project scope statement, and the organizational process assets to collect the raw data—that is, the information that will be analyzed.

Organizational process assets. While analyzing risks, you will make use of the risk-related components of the knowledge base from previous projects, such as data about risks and lessons learned.

Project scope statement. When you are performing qualitative risk analysis, you want to know what kinds of risks you are dealing with. For example, are you already familiar with these risks? If your project is similar to previous projects, it might have well-understood risks. If it is a new and complex project, it might involve risks that are not well understood in your organization. So, how do you know what kind of project you are dealing with? Simple—you take a look at the project scope statement.

Risk management plan. To generate the output of the qualitative risk analysis, you will need the following elements of the risk management plan:

- Budgeting
- Definitions of probabilities and impacts
- The probability and impact matrices
- Risk categories
- Risk timing and scheduling

If any of these input items was not developed during risk management planning, it can be developed during the qualitative analysis.

Risk register. The risk register that you created in the process of identifying risks contains the list of identified risks that will be the key input to the qualitative risk analysis.

Tools and Techniques for Qualitative Risk Analysis

Prioritizing risks based on their probabilities of occurrence and their impact if they do occur is the central goal of the qualitative risk analysis. Accordingly, most of the tools and techniques used involve estimating probability and impact.

Risk probability and impact assessment. Risk *probability* refers to the likelihood that a risk will occur, and *impact* refers to the effect the risk will have on a project objective if it occurs. The probability for each risk and the impact of each risk on project objectives, such as cost, quality, scope, and time, must be assessed. Note that probability and impacts are assessed for each identified risk.

Methods used in making the probability and impact assessment include holding meetings, interviewing, considering expert judgment, and using an information base from previous projects. A risk with a high probability might have a very low impact, and a risk with a low probability might have a very high impact. To prioritize the risks, you need to look at both probability and impact.

Probability and impact matrix. Risks need to be prioritized for quantitative analysis, response planning, or both. The prioritization can be performed by using the probability and impact matrix—a lookup table that can be used to rate a risk based on where it falls both on the probability scale and on the impact scale. Table 9.2 presents an example of a probability and impact matrix by showing both the probability scale and the impact scale. Here is an example of how to read this matrix: risk R_{35} has a probability of 0.70 (that is, 7 out of 10 chances) for occurrence and an impact of 0.45 on the project objective for which this matrix is prepared. How to calculate the numerical scales for the probability and impact matrix and what they mean depends upon the project and the organization. However, remember the relative meaning: Higher value of a risk on the probability scale means greater likelihood of risk occurrence, and higher value on the impact scale means greater effect on the project objectives. The higher the value for a risk, the higher its priority is. For example, risk R_{38} has higher priority than risk R_{27}.

Each risk is rated (prioritized) according to the probability and the impact value assigned to it separately for each objective.

Table 9.2 Risk Probability and Impact Matrix for an Objective

Probability	Impact								
0.00	0.05	0.15	0.25	0.35	0.45	0.55	0.65	0.75	0.90
0.10	R_{11}	R_{12}	R_{13}	R_{14}	R_{15}	R_{16}	R_{17}	R_{18}	R_{19}
0.30	R_{21}	R_{22}	R_{23}	R_{24}	R_{25}	R_{26}	R_{27}	R_{28}	R_{29}
0.50	R_{31}	R_{32}	R_{33}	R_{34}	R_{35}	R_{36}	R_{37}	R_{38}	R_{39}
0.70	R_{41}	R_{42}	R_{43}	R_{44}	R_{45}	R_{46}	R_{47}	R_{48}	R_{49}
0.90	R_{51}	R_{52}	R_{53}	R_{54}	R_{55}	R_{56}	R_{57}	R_{58}	R_{59}

R_{ij}, where i and j are integers, represent risks in the two-dimensional (probability and impact) space.

Generally, you can divide the matrix in Table 9.2 into three areas—high-priority risks represented by higher numbers, such as R_{59}, medium-priority risks represented by moderate numbers, such as R_{23}, and low-priority risks represented by lower numbers, such as R_{12}. However, each organization has to design its own risk score and risk threshold to guide the risk response plan.

Impact can be a threat or an opportunity. Note that impact can be a threat (a negative effect) or an opportunity (a positive effect). You will have separate matrices for threats and opportunities. Threats in the high-priority area might require priority actions and aggressive responses. Also, you will want to capitalize on those opportunities in the high-priority area, which you can do with relatively little effort. Risks posing threats in the low-priority area might not need any response, but they must be kept on the watch list.

Assessment of the risk data quality. Qualitative risk analysis is performed to analyze the risk data to prioritize risks. However, before you do it, you must examine the risk data for its quality, which is crucial because the credibility of the results of qualitative risk analysis depends upon the quality of the risk data. If the quality of the risk data is found to be unacceptable, you might decide to gather better-quality data. The technique to assess the risk data quality involves examining the accuracy, reliability, and integrity of the data, and also examining how good that data is relevant to the specific risk and project for which it is being used.

Risk categorization. You defined the risk categories during risk management planning and the risk identification processes. Now you can assign the identified risks to those categories. You can also revisit the categorization scheme, such as the RBS, that you developed for your project, because now you have more information about risks for the project. Categorizing risks by their causes often helps you develop effective risk responses.

Risk urgency assessment. This is a risk prioritization technique based on time urgency. For example, a risk that is going to occur now is more urgent to address than a risk that might occur a month from now.

You need to update the risk register with the output of the qualitative risk analysis.

The Big Update for the Risk Register

The risk register was initiated during the risk identification process and is updated with the results from the qualitative risk analysis. The updates include the following:

- **Risks categorizations.** This means arranging risks in different categories. This helps you identify the causes of the risks and the areas of the project that might require special attention. Furthermore, categorizing risks can bring order to a chaotic situation and makes the management of these risks easier and more effective.

- **Prioritized list of risks.** The risk register has lists of risks prioritized according to the probability and impact matrix discussed earlier in this chapter. A separate list can be created for each project objective, such as cost, quality, scope, and time. These lists help you prioritize efforts for preparing and executing risk responses.

- **List of risks with time urgency.** This list includes urgent risks that require attention now or in the near future.

- **Watch list of low-priority risks.** This list contains the risks that are deemed unimportant by the qualitative risk analysis, but that need to be monitored continually.

- **List of risks for additional analysis and response.** This list includes risks that need further analysis, such as quantitative analysis or a response action.

- **Trends in the analysis results.** By examining the results from the qualitative risk analysis, you might recognize a trend for specific risks. That trend might suggest further analysis or a specific risk response.

Updates to the risk register from the results of the qualitative risk analysis include risk categorizations, the prioritized list of risks, the list of risks with time urgency, the watch list of low-priority risks, the list of risks for additional analysis and response, and trends in the analysis results.

The main output of qualitative risk analysis is the prioritization of risks based on a probability and impact matrix for each objective. So each objective can have its own prioritized list of risks.

Qualitative risk analysis is a relatively quick and cost-effective way to prioritize risks for risk planning. It also does the groundwork for the quantitative risk analysis if one is required for some risks.

Quantitative Analysis

Quantitative risk analysis is generally performed on the risks that have been prioritized by using qualitative risk analysis. However, depending upon the experience of the team and their familiarity with the risk, it is possible to skip the qualitative risk analysis and move directly after the risk identification to the quantitative risk analysis. The quantitative risk analysis has three major goals:

- Assess the probability of achieving specific project objectives
- Quantify the effect of the risks on the overall project objectives
- Prioritize risks by their contributions to the overall project risk

Because quantitative analysis is more detailed and more precise, it requires more information in addition to the risk register and risk management plan, and that is the cost management plan and the schedule management plan. Obviously, the quantitative risk analysis will use techniques that are of a more numerical nature.

Tools and Techniques for Quantitative Risk Analysis

Before you can analyze the data, you need to gather it. Therefore, quantitative risk analysis can be looked upon as a two-step process—gathering and representing the data, and analyzing and modeling the data. Accordingly, all the techniques fall into two categories: data gathering and representation techniques, such as interviewing, probability distributions, and expert judgment; and analysis and modeling techniques, such as sensitivity analysis, EMV analysis, decision-tree analysis, and modeling and simulation.

Interviewing. This technique is used to collect the data for assessing the probabilities of achieving specific project objectives. You are looking for results such as, "We have an 80-percent probability of finishing the project within the schedule desired by the customer." Or perhaps, "We have a 70-percent probability of finishing the project within the budget of $100,000." The goal is to determine the scale of probabilities for a given objective; for example, there is a 20-percent probability that the project will cost $50,000, a 60-percent probability that it will cost $100,000, and a 20-percent probability that it will cost $150,000.

The data is collected by interviewing relevant stakeholders and subject-matter experts. Most commonly, you will be exploring the optimistic (best case), pessimistic (worst case), and most likely scenarios for a given objective. For example, for the project cost, the optimistic estimate might be $10 million, the pessimistic estimate might be $50 million, and the most likely estimate might be $25 million.

Probability distributions. After you have collected the data on meeting the project objectives, you can present it in a probability distribution for each objective under study. Note that a distribution represents uncertainty, and uncertainty represents risk. For example, if you know for sure the project will cost $25 million, there will be no distribution because it is only one data point. Distribution comes into the picture when you have several possible values with a probability assigned to each value. There are distributions of different shapes in which the data can be presented. Figure 9.4 shows some of them, such as for the cost objective. The X axis represents the cost, and the Y axis represents the corresponding probability that the project will be completed within that cost.

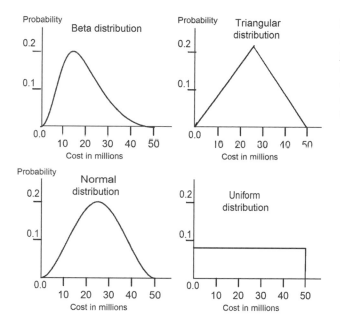

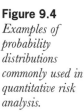

Figure 9.4
Examples of probability distributions commonly used in quantitative risk analysis.

The beta distribution and the triangular distribution are the most frequently used distributions. The other commonly used distributions that could be suitable under given circumstances are normal distribution and uniform distribution. The uniform distribution is used when all the values of an objective have the same chance of being true.

Sensitivity analysis. This is a technique used to determine which risk has the greatest impact on the project. You study the impact of one uncertain element on a project objective by keeping all other uncertain elements fixed at their baseline values. You can repeat this analysis for several objectives, one at a time. You can also repeat this study for several uncertain elements (creating risks), one element at a time. This way, you can see the impact of each element (or risk) on the overall project separate from other elements (or risks).

Expected monetary value analysis. The expected monetary value (EMV) analysis is used to calculate the expected value of an outcome when different possible scenarios exist for different values of the outcome with some probabilities assigned to them. The goal here is to calculate the expected final result of a probabilistic situation. EMV is calculated by multiplying the value of each possible outcome by the probability of its occurrence and adding the results. For example, if there is 60-percent probability that an opportunity will earn you $1,000 and a 40-percent probability that it will only earn you $500, the EMV is calculated as follows:

$$\text{EMV} = 0.60 \times \$1,000 + 0.40 \times \$500 = \$600 + \$200 = \$800$$

So the EMV in this case is $800. When you are using opportunities and threats in the same calculation, you should express EMV for an opportunity as a positive value and for a threat as a negative value. For example, if there is 60-percent chance that you will benefit from a risk by $1,000 and a 40-percent probability that you will lose $400 as a result of this risk, the EMV is calculated as follows:

$$\text{EMV} = 0.60 \times \$1,000 - 0.40 \times \$500 = \$600 - \$200 = \$400$$

Therefore, the EMV in this case is $400.

The concept of EMV can be presented in a decision-making technique, such as a decision-tree analysis.

Decision-tree analysis. This technique uses the decision-tree diagram to choose from different available options; each option is represented by a branch of the tree. This technique is used when there are multiple possible outcomes with different threats or opportunities with certain probabilities assigned to them. EMV analysis is done along each branch, which helps to make a decision about which option to choose.

Figure 9.5 presents a very simple decision-tree diagram that depicts two options: updating an existing product or building a new product from scratch. The initial cost for the update option is $50,000, whereas the initial cost for the build-from-scratch option is $70,000. However, the probability for failure is 40 percent for the update option, compared to 10 percent for the build-from-scratch option, and the impact from failure in both cases is a loss of $200,000. As Table 9.3 shows, even though the initial cost for the update option is less than the initial cost for the build-from-scratch option, the decision will be made in favor of the build-from-scratch option because when you combine the initial cost with the EMV resulting from the probability of failure, the build-from-scratch option turns out to be a better deal.

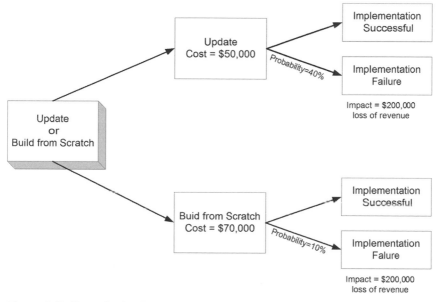

Figure 9.5 *Example of a decision-tree diagram.*

STUDY CHECKPOINT 9.1

Problem: Perform the EMV analysis of the decision tree presented in Figure 9.5 to make a decision on which option to take.

Solution:

Table 9.3 EMV Analysis for the Decision Tree in Figure 9.5

Option	Initial Cost	Risk Cost	Probability	EMV for Risk Cost	Total Cost
Update	$50,000	$200,000	40%	0.40×$200,000 =$80,000	$50,000+$80,000 =$130,000
Build from scratch	$70,000	$200,000	10%	0.10×$200,000 =$20,000	$70,000+$20,000 =$90,000

The decision will be made in favor of the build-from-scratch option because it costs less overall.

Modeling and simulation. A *model* is a set of rules to describe how something works; it takes input and makes predictions as output. The rules might include formulas and functions based on facts, assumptions, or both. A *simulation* is any analytical method used to imitate a real-life system. Simulations in risk analysis are created using the Monte Carlo technique, which is named after Monte Carlo, France—known for its casinos that present games of chance based on random behavior. Monte Carlo simulation models take random input iteratively to generate output for certain quantities as predictions. This technique is used in several disciplines, such as physics and biology, in addition to project management. In risk analysis, the input is taken randomly from a probability distribution, and the output for impact on the project objectives is predicted. The name "Monte Carlo" refers to the random behavior of the input. (In that spirit, it could easily be called Las Vegas.)

Quantitative risk analysis techniques include interviews, probability distributions, expert judgment, sensitivity analysis, EMV analysis, decision-tree analysis, modeling and simulation, and expert judgment.

Expert judgment. In the quantitative risk analysis, expert judgment can be used to validate the collected risk data and the analysis used for the project at hand.

The risk register is updated with the results of the quantitative risk analysis.

Update That Risk Register Again

The risk register that was used as an input item to the quantitative risk analysis is updated with the results of this analysis. The updates include the following:

- **Probabilistic analysis of the project.** This includes the estimates of the project schedule and cost with a confidence level attached to each estimate. Confidence level is expressed in percentage form, such as 95 percent, and it represents how certain you are about the estimate. You can compare these estimates to the stakeholders' risk tolerances to see whether the project is within the acceptable limits.

- **Probability of achieving the project objectives.** Factoring in the project risks, you can estimate the probabilities of meeting project objectives, such as cost and schedule set forth by the current project plan. For example, the likelihood of completing the project within the current budget plan of $2 million is 70 percent.

- **Prioritized list of risks.** The risks are prioritized according to the threats they pose or the opportunities they offer. The risks with greater threats (or opportunities) are higher on the list. The goal is to prioritize the response plan efforts to eliminate (or minimize) the impact of the threats and capitalize on the opportunities. The priorities are determined based on the total effect of each risk to the overall project objectives.

- **Trends in the results.** By repeating the analysis several times and by examining the results, you might recognize a trend for specific risks. That trend might suggest further analysis or a specific risk response.

The emphasis in quantitative analysis is on two tasks: Assess the probabilities of meeting each project objective and prioritize the risks based on the total effect of each risk on the overall project objectives. Subsequently, the resultant prioritized list of risks can be used to prepare the risk response plan.

> Updates to the risk register resulting from the quantitative risk analysis include probabilistic analysis of the project, the probability of achieving the project objectives, a prioritized list of risks, and trends in the results.

Planning the Risk Response

Depending on the project, the nature of the risks, and the experience of the team, risk response planning can start after risk identification, qualitative risk analysis, or quantitative risk analysis. Recall that risks can include threats (negative risks) and opportunities (positive risks). Accordingly, the central task in risk response planning is to develop actions and options to meet the following two goals:

- Minimize threats to meeting project objectives
- Maximize opportunities

Input to Risk Response Planning

The two major items you need for risk response planning are the risk register and the risk management plan.

Risk register. The risk register contains the results from risk identification, qualitative risk analysis, and quantitative risk analysis. The following elements of the risk register are especially useful for risk response planning:

- List of identified risks
- Root causes of risks
- Prioritized list of responses
- List of risks that need immediate attention
- Trends in analysis results

Risk management plan. The elements of the risk management plan that can be useful for risk response planning include the following:

• Organizations' and stakeholders' thresholds for low, moderate, and high risks to sort out those risks for which the response is needed.

• Roles and responsibilities that specify the positions and functions for each position involved in risk management. These roles are assigned to the members of the risk management team, which might include members from inside or outside the project team.

• Timing and a schedule that specify how often the risk management processes will be performed and which risk management activities will be included in the project schedule.

Because there is a wide spectrum of risks that can occur, there are a multitude of tools and techniques available to plan responses for these risks.

Tools and Techniques for Risk Response Planning

Risk, as you have already learned, can come in two categories: negative risks, which pose threats to meeting the project objectives, and positive risks, which offer opportunities. The goal is to minimize the threats and maximize the opportunities. In project management, there are three kinds of possible responses to risks—take an action, take no action, or take a conditional action. When you want to take an action, you must have different response strategies for negative and positive risks. Accordingly, there are three kinds of strategies available to handle three kinds of scenarios:

• Strategies to respond to negative risks (threats) when action is required

• Strategies to respond to positive risks (opportunities) when action is required

• Strategies that can be used to respond to both negative and positive risks when no action or a conditional action is taken

Response Strategies for Threats

There are only three commonsense ways to take action against a potential problem: Get out of harm's way, pass it to someone else, or confront it to minimize the damage. In project management, these three strategies are called avoid, transfer, and mitigate—the ATM approach.

Avoid. You avoid the risk by changing your project management plan in such a way that the risk is eliminated. Depending upon the situation, this can be accomplished in various ways, including the following:

- Obtaining information and clarifying requirements for risks based on misunderstanding or miscommunication. This answers two questions: Do we really have this risk and, if yes, how can we avoid it?

- Acquiring expertise for risks that exist due to a lack of expertise.

- Isolating the project objectives from the risk whenever possible.

- Relaxing the objective that is under threat, such as extending the project schedule.

Transfer. Risk transfer means you shift the responsibility for responding to the risk (the ownership of the risk), the negative impact of the risk, or both to another party. Note that transferring the risk transfers the responsibility for risk management and does not necessarily eliminate the risk. Risk transfer almost always involves making payment of a risk premium to the party to which the risk has been transferred. Some examples include buying an insurance policy and contracting out the tasks involving risk.

Mitigate. Mitigation in general means taking action to reduce or prevent the impact of a disaster that is expected to occur. Risk mitigation means reducing the probability of risk occurrence, reducing the impact of the risk if it does occur, or both. A good mitigation strategy is to take action early on to first reduce the probability of the risk happening, and then to plan for reducing its impact if it does occur, rather than letting it occur and then trying to reduce the impact or repair the damage. Following are some examples of mitigation:

> In project management, the ATM approach stands for *avoid, transfer,* and *mitigate*—three strategies for taking action against a potential problem.

- Adopting less complex processes

- Conducting more tests on the product or service of the project

- Choosing a more stable supplier for the project supplies

- Designing redundancy into a system so that if one part fails, the redundant part takes over and the system keeps working

Each of these three strategies has a counter-strategy to deal with the opportunities.

Response Strategies for Opportunities

Just like in the case of threats, you have three strategies to deal with opportunities. Not surprisingly, each response strategy to deal with an opportunity is a counterpart of a response strategy to deal with a threat—a one-to-one correspondence:

- Share corresponds to transfer
- Exploit corresponds to avoid
- Enhance corresponds to mitigate

You use the SEE (share, exploit, enhance) approach to deal with the opportunities presented by the positive risks.

Share. Sharing a positive risk that presents an opportunity means transferring the ownership of the risk to another party that is better equipped to capitalize on the opportunity. Some examples of sharing are:

- Forming risk-sharing partnerships
- Starting a joint venture with the purpose of capitalizing on an opportunity
- Forming teams or special-purpose companies to exploit opportunities presented by positive risks

Exploit. Exploiting an opportunity means ensuring that the opportunity is realized—that is, the positive risk that presents the opportunity does occur. This is accomplished by eliminating or minimizing the uncertainty associated with the risk occurrence. An example of exploiting is assigning more talented resources to the project to reduce the completion time and therefore to be the first to market. Another example could be providing better quality than planned to beat a competitor. Whereas exploiting refers to ensuring that the positive risk occurs, enhancing refers to increasing the impact of the risk once it occurs.

Enhance. This strategy means increasing the size of the opportunity by increasing the probability, impact, or both. You can increase the probability by maximizing the key drivers of the positive risks or by strengthening the causes of the risks. Similarly, you can increase the impact by increasing the project's susceptibility to the positive risk.

You have just learned the different strategies that you need to plan for negative and positive risks if you intend to take action. If, on the other hand, you intend to take no action or a conditional action, then the response planning strategies for both negative and positive risks are the same.

To deal with opportunities presented by positive risks, you use the SEE (share, exploit, enhance) approach.

Response Strategies for Both Threats and Opportunities

There are two response strategies that you need to plan for risks for which you need to take either a conditional action or no action.

Acceptance. Acceptance of a risk means to let it be. Generally, it is not possible to take action against all the risks. Depending upon their probabilities and impacts, some risks will simply be accepted. There are two kinds of acceptance:

- Passive acceptance requires no action.

- Active acceptance requires a conditional action, called a *contingent response.*

Contingency. Generally speaking, contingency means a future event or condition that is possible but cannot be predicted with certainty. So, your action will be contingent upon the condition; that is, it will be executed only if the condition happens. In risk management, a contingent response is a response that is executed only if certain predefined conditions (or events) happen. These events trigger the contingency response. Some examples of such triggers are missing a milestone or escalating the priority of a feature by the customer. The events that can trigger contingency response must be clearly defined and tracked.

To plan for risks for which you will take a conditional action or no action, response strategies are acceptance and contingency.

You use these strategies to generate the output of the risk response planning process.

Output of Risk Response Planning

The output of risk response planning might include risk register updates, risk-related contractual agreements, and project management plan updates.

Risk register updates. The appropriate risk responses planned and agreed upon by the risk management team are included in the risk register. The responses to high and moderate risks are entered in detail, while the low-priority risks can be put on a watch list for monitoring. After the risk register is updated, it includes the following main elements:

- A list of identified risks, descriptions of the risks, root causes of the risks, WBS elements affected by the risks, and the impacts of the risks on the project objectives.

- Roles and responsibilities in managing the risks—that is, risk owners and the responsibilities assigned to them.

- Results from qualitative and quantitative risk analyses, including a prioritized list of risks, a probabilistic analysis of the project objectives, and a list of risks with time urgency.

- Planned and agreed-upon risk response strategies and specific actions to implement each strategy.

- Symptoms and warning signs of risk occurrences, contingency plans, and triggers for contingency risks.

A residual risk is the remains of a risk on which a response has been performed, whereas a secondary risk is a risk that is expected to arise as a result of implementing a risk response; therefore, a response for a secondary risk must be planned.

- Budget and schedule requirements to implement the planned responses, including the contingency reserve, which is the amount of funds, time, or both needed in addition to the estimates in order to meet the organization's and stakeholders' risk tolerances and thresholds.

- Fallback plans in case the planned responses prove to be inadequate.

- A list of risks to remain, which include the following:

  - Passive, accepted risks

  - Residual risks that will remain after planned responses have been performed

- A list of secondary risks that will arise as a result of implementing the responses. You must plan for these risks like any other risk.

Risk-related contractual agreements. The risk-related contractual agreements might result, for example, from transferring the risks.

Updates to the project management plan. The project management plan is updated to include the risk response activities that might affect other project management areas, such as cost, schedule, quality, and procurement.

Risk response planning deals with both kinds of risks—those that pose threats to meeting project objectives and those that present opportunities. Three kinds of responses can be planned—take action, take no action, or take a conditional action.

Standardize This

This chapter has presented the essence of the standard processes used to plan for quality and risk management. All the items in these processes discussed in this chapter can be rearranged in terms of input, tools and techniques, and output, as shown in Figures 9.6 and 9.7.

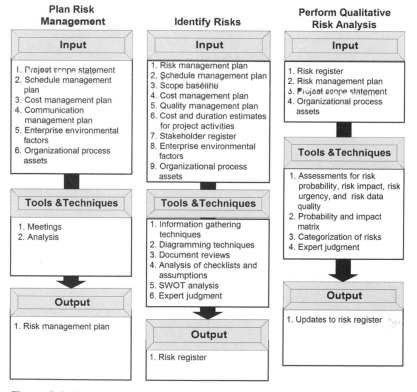

Plan Risk Management

Input

1. Project scope statement
2. Schedule management plan
3. Cost management plan
4. Communication management plan
5. Enterprise environmental factors
6. Organizational process assets

Tools &Techniques

1. Meetings
2. Analysis

Output

1. Risk management plan

Identify Risks

Input

1. Risk management plan
2. Schedule management plan
3. Scope baseline
4. Cost management plan
5. Quality management plan
6. Cost and duration estimates for project activities
7. Stakeholder register
8. Enterprise environmental factors
9. Organizational process assets

Tools &Techniques

1. Information gathering techniques
2. Diagramming techniques
3. Document reviews
4. Analysis of checklists and assumptions
5. SWOT analysis
6. Expert judgment

Output

1. Risk register

Perform Qualitative Risk Analysis

Input

1. Risk register
2. Risk management plan
3. Project scope statement
4. Organizational process assets

Tools &Techniques

1. Assessments for risk probability, risk impact, risk urgency, and risk data quality
2. Probability and impact matrix
3. Categorization of risks
4. Expert judgment

Output

1. Updates to risk register

Figure 9.6 *Input, tools and techniques, and output for three processes: Plan risk management, identify risks, and perform qualitative risk analysis.*

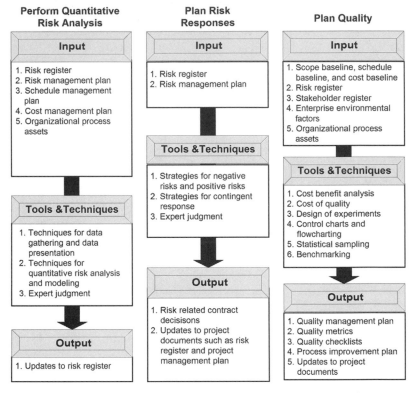

Figure 9.7 *Input, tools and techniques, and output for three processes: Perform quantitative risk analysis, plan risk responses, and plan quality.*

Quick Success Mantras

- Quality refers to the degree to which project objectives and a set of characteristics of project deliverables fulfill the project requirements.

- Quality management consists of planning quality, performing quality assurance, and monitoring and controlling quality.

- Risk management is an integral part of project management.

- Risk stems from elements of uncertainty and may have a negative or positive effect on meeting the project objectives.

- Risk identification is performed before the risk analysis, and the qualitative risk analysis, if performed, is performed before the quantitative risk analysis because it takes less effort and time and its results can be used for quantitative analysis.

- An important update added to the risk register by the qualitative risk analysis is the prioritized list of risks. Each objective may have its own prioritized list of risks.

- Two important updates added to the risk register by the quantitative risk analysis are:

  - The probabilistic analysis of the project objectives—that is, the probabilities of meeting the project objectives.

  - The prioritized list of risks based on the total effect of each risk to the overall project objectives.

- Depending upon the experience of the team and the nature of the risk, a risk can be moved directly after identification to the quantitative risk analysis, or even to risk response planning.

PART III

Executing the Project

After the project is authorized through initiation and planned, it's time to begin the execution. You will be directing and managing the project execution throughout the lifecycle of the project. In addition to producing deliverables, it will also include assuring quality, distributing information on the project progress and issues, and managing stakeholder expectations. To perform the project work, you will also need to acquire, develop, and manage the project team. Furthermore, your organization might not have the resources to finish certain parts of the project work. You will need to conduct procurement for those parts of the work.

Chapter 10

Managing Project Work

- Executing a Project: Big Picture
- Directing and Managing Project Execution
- Performing Quality Assurance
- Conducting Procurements
- Standardize This
- Quick Success Mantras

Af
fter a project has been authorized through initiation and planned, it needs to be executed. The goal of the execution stage is to complete the project work specified in the project management plan to produce the project deliverables and meet the project requirements. Throughout the lifecycle of the project, you need to proactively direct and manage its execution. Directing and managing project execution is the process of implementing the project management plan developed during project planning. The end product of this process is the project deliverables. This is a high-level umbrella process under which other execution processes are performed, such as assuring quality and conducting procurements.

So the core question in this chapter is how to execute a project as planned. In search of an answer, you will explore three avenues—directing and managing project execution, assuring quality, and conducting procurements.

In this chapter you'll learn:

- How directing and managing project execution is an umbrella process for several other processes related to project execution
- How to perform quality assurance
- How to conduct procurements
- Standard processes for directing and managing project execution, assuring quality, and conducting procurements

Executing a Project: Big Picture

Executing the project means implementing the project management plan by performing the work described in it in the way it's planned. This work is executed by using the processes in the executing process group shown in Figure 10.1. It is up to the project team to determine which of these processes are relevant for the project at hand. The processes in this group are used to accomplish a three-pronged goal:

- Coordinate people and resources used to perform the project activities
- Integrate and manage the project activities being performed
- Ensure the implementation of the project scope and approved changes

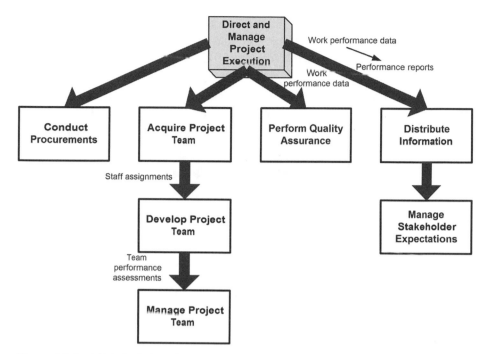

Figure 10.1 *A high-level view of interactions and data flow between different components of project execution.*

The components (or processes) shown in Figure 10.1 are defined here:

- **Direct and manage project execution.** Manage various interfaces in the project execution to complete the project work smoothly in order to produce the project outcome, such as deliverables and objectives.

- **Acquire project team.** Obtain the project team members needed to perform the project work.

- **Develop project team.** Improve the competencies of team members and interaction among team members to enhance the project performance.

- **Manage project team.** Manage the project team, which includes tracking the performance of team members, providing feedback, resolving issues, and managing changes to improve project performance.

- **Perform quality assurance.** Audit the results from the quality control measurements to ensure that the quality requirements are being met.

- **Distribute information.** Make the relevant information about the project, such as project progress, available to the stakeholders according to the communication management plan.

- **Conduct procurements.** Obtain responses from the potential sellers in terms of quotes, bids, offers, and proposals for their product or services needed for the project; select sellers; and negotiate written contracts with the selected sellers.

- **Manage stakeholder expectations.** Stay on the same page with the stakeholders by communicating and working with them on their needs and issues.

Once the project execution begins, you, the project manager, need to direct and manage it.

Directing and Managing Project Execution

While the project work defined in the project management plan is being performed, you need to continually direct and manage the project execution. In this process, you will be interacting with other departments in your organization. In general, a project team includes people from different departments. Usually the reporting relationships within the same department are very well defined and structured. However, the relationships between different departments (especially between individuals from different departments at the same level of authority) are not well defined. So, managing such project interfaces is a crucial function of a project manager during project execution. Generally speaking, project interfaces are the formal and informal boundaries and relationships among team members, departments, organizations, or functions—for example, how the development department and the QA department interact with each other while working on

---

SUCCESS SHOT: AN EFFECTIVE PROJECT MANAGER IS A LEADER

Once the project execution begins, it becomes even more crucial to use your leadership skills to coordinate everything and keep the project on the path to successful completion.
Remember, you manage processes and lead the people who accomplish the tasks to complete the project.

the same project. Directing and managing project execution involves managing various technical and organizational interfaces in the project to facilitate smooth execution of the project work.

To keep your eyes on the ball, remember that the main purposes of directing and managing project execution include:

- Producing the project deliverables by executing the project management plan. This means the deliverables satisfy the planned requirements.

- Implementing the approved changes, defect repairs, and other needed actions.

- Implementing the planned methods, processes, standards, and other quality-related requirements.

- Producing and distributing the status information.

The key words during execution are *implement*, *manage*, and *inform* (status). You manage all these tasks under the umbrella of directing and managing the project execution.

Preparing for Directing and Managing Project Execution

The process of directing and managing the project execution begins with identifying the items that need to be implemented. The information on the project work that needs to be performed to produce project deliverables is the major input to this process. The specific input items are discussed in the following list:

Project management plan. Directing and managing project execution is all about implementing the project management plan, which contains all the major subsidiary plans, such as the scope baseline, the schedule baseline, the cost baseline, and the quality baseline. It also describes how the work will be executed to meet the project objectives and produce deliverables that satisfy the planned requirements.

Approved items. The approved change requests are input to the project execution because they must be implemented.

Organizational process assets. Items in this category that can be useful or need to be considered in directing and managing project execution include standardized work guidelines, workplace security requirements, project files from previous projects, and the issue and defect management database. For example, the defect management database may contain a list of validated defect repairs with information on whether a previously performed defect repair has been accepted or rejected. This will tell you whether you need to implement the defect repair again.

Directing and managing project execution requires implementing the project management plan.

Enterprise environmental factors. Items in this category that can be useful or need to be considered in directing and managing project execution include organizational structure and culture, company infrastructure (such as facilities and equipment), personnel administration (such as hiring and firing guidelines), and the project management information system.

The project management information system, a good tool to facilitate directing and managing project execution, is a collection of tools and techniques—manual and automated—used to gather, integrate, and disseminate the output of project management processes. This system is used to facilitate processes from the initiation stage all the way to the closing stage. Microsoft Project, a product that lets you create a project schedule, is an example of such a tool.

Another tool used in directing and managing project execution is expert judgment, which—depending on the issue and the available resources—can be provided by the project manager, other individuals from other departments and groups within the organization, consultants, stakeholders, or professional associations.

What Directing and Managing Project Execution Accomplishes

When the project is being executed, at each point in time some deliverables or parts thereof have been completed, and there is a status for the project that can be reported to the stakeholders. These two important output items (deliverables and status), along with others, are discussed in the following sections.

Deliverables

A deliverable is a unique and identifiable product, service, or result identified in the project management plan that must be generated to complete the project. The core purpose of executing the project management plan is to produce deliverables.

When you are directing and managing the project execution, obviously the items are being implemented. In addition to the work that produces original deliverables, the following items are implemented during project execution:

- Approved change requests
- Approved corrective actions recommended by the QA process
- Approved preventive actions recommended by the QA process
- Approved defect repairs recommended by the QA process

Change Requests

During the execution of the project work, requests for changes may arise from sources such as issues and may affect certain aspects of the project, such as the following:

- Project scope
- Project cost
- Project schedule
- Policies or procedures

These change requests might come from inside or outside the performing organization and can be optional or mandated legally or contractually. These change requests must be approved before they can be processed and implemented. Change requests can include the following types:

- **Direct change requests.** These are the changes that are not a result of any other action, such as defect repairs. Examples are requests for changes to scope, schedule, and cost. Of course, these changes can also result from other types of change requests that come under the category of indirect change requests.

- **Indirect change requests.** These include:
  - **Defect repairs.** This is the list of the defects found during the quality assurance (QA) process that have been approved for repairs.
  - **Corrective actions.** The QA process can recommend corrective actions to improve quality, which are directions for executing the project work to bring expected project performance into conformance with the project management plan. The approved corrective actions must be scheduled for implementation.
  - **Preventive actions.** These are the directions to perform an activity that will reduce the probability of negative consequences associated with project risks. These preventive actions are recommended by the QA process during process analysis.

> Requests for changes may affect project scope, cost, or schedule, or policies or procedures.

> Change requests fall into two broader categories: direct and indirect.

After some change requests are approved, you may need to change some elements of the project management plan, such as the project baseline, the human resource management plan, the requirements management plan, or the communication management plan.

Work Performance Data

Work performance information includes schedule progress information, incurred costs compared to authorized costs, resource utilization details, how well the quality standards are met, and lessons learned and added to the knowledge base.

Monitoring the project status is one of the crucial functions of a project manager during project execution. Work performance information is basically the project status information that is regularly collected and distributed among the stakeholders during project execution. It includes the following items:

- The schedule progress information:
  - Schedule activities that have been finished and those that have started
  - An estimate to complete the schedule activities that have started and hence are in progress
  - The portion of each in-progress activity completed in a percentage—for example, activity A is 30-percent complete
  - Deliverables that have been completed and those that have not yet been completed
- Incurred costs compared to authorized costs
- Resource utilization details
- How well the quality standards are being met
- Lessons learned and added to the knowledge base

In a nutshell, the main outputs of directing and managing project execution are the project deliverables specified in the project management plan and the performance data as the work progresses. Between planning the project and producing the deliverables, many things need to happen, and you need to manage them by:

- Distributing information
- Managing stakeholder expectations
- Acquiring, developing, and managing the project team
- Performing quality assurance
- Conducting procurements

Therefore, the direct and manage project execution process is a high-level umbrella process, and to execute it you need to perform some other processes too, which are discussed in this and the next chapters. To start with, assuring quality is an integral part of managing project execution.

Performing Quality Assurance

Quality planning, discussed in Chapter 9, is used to identify which quality standards are relevant to the project at hand and to determine how to meet these standards. Implementing the quality management plan consists of two components: quality assurance and quality control. Quality assurance is the process of auditing the results from quality control measurements to ensure that the quality requirements are being met.

Performing organizations typically have a department called quality assurance (QA) that oversees the quality assurance activities and fosters continuous process improvement, which is an iterative method for improving the quality of all processes. The ultimate goal is to improve the quality of the projects and project products to optimize the benefits to the organization's strategic objectives.

One way to improve the quality of the outcome of any project is to improve the processes used to generate that outcome. Continuous process improvement enhances the efficiency and effectiveness of the processes by minimizing waste (unnecessary activities) and duplication of efforts. It includes identifying and reviewing the business processes inside the organization, such as coding of modules within software programs and the process of project approval.

Input to Performing Quality Assurance

The input to quality assurance comes largely from three sources: quality planning, directing and managing project execution, and quality control. These input items are discussed here.

Output from quality planning. The following output items from the quality planning process become the input into the quality assurance process:

- **Quality management plan.** This is the plan that needs to be implemented.

- **Quality metrics.** These are the metrics set during quality planning.

- **Process improvement plan.** The process improvement plan, developed during quality planning, must be implemented during QA.

The input to quality assurance primarily comes from quality planning, directing and managing project execution, and quality control.

Output from directing and managing project execution. When you are directing and managing the project execution, information about the work performance and the implementation of a few items will help you determine how the quality is being implemented. Therefore, during QA, you must consider the work performance data, such as cost incurred, schedule progress, and overall project performance.

Quality control measurements. Quality control involves monitoring specific project results to verify whether they meet quality standards. The quality control process sends its results back to QA as feedback.

Some tools and techniques can be used to facilitate the QA process.

Tools and Techniques for Performing Quality Assurance

Quality audits and process analysis, along with the tools and techniques used in quality planning and quality control processes, can be used in the QA process.

Quality audits reduce the cost of quality on subsequent projects and increase customer satisfaction with the product or service delivered.

Quality audits. A quality audit is a structured and independent review to determine whether project execution is meeting the planned quality requirements. It also verifies the implementation of approved change requests, corrective actions, defect repairs, and preventive actions. The audits can occur as scheduled or at random and can be conducted by a third party or by the properly trained in-house auditors of the performing organization. These audits accomplish the following:

- Because one of the objectives of a quality audit is to identify inefficient and ineffective policies, processes, and procedures being used for the project, audits reduce the cost of quality on the subsequent projects.

- Audits increase customer satisfaction and acceptance of the product or service delivered by the project.

Process analysis. This is a technique used to identify the needed improvements in a process by following the steps outlined in the process improvement plan. It examines the problems, constraints, and unnecessary (non-value-added) activities identified during the implementation of the process. Process analysis typically includes the following steps:

1. Identify a technique to analyze the problem.

2. Identify the underlying causes that led to the problem.

3. Examine the root cause of the problem.

4. Create preventive actions for this and similar problems.

Output of Performing Quality Assurance

The main output of performing quality assurance includes recommended corrective actions and change requests. These and other output items are discussed in the following subsections.

Change Requests

The goal of quality assurance is improving quality, which involves taking actions to increase the effectiveness and efficiency of the policies, procedures, and processes of the performing organization. One way to accomplish this is to implement the quality-related changes recommended and approved during the process of directing and managing the project execution, including:

- **Modifications to policies and procedures.**
- **Modifications to project scope, cost, and schedule.**
- **Recommended corrective actions.** Implementation of recommended corrective actions will increase the effectiveness and efficiency of the policies, processes, and procedures of the performing organization, and will also improve the quality of the product or service delivered by the project. Following are examples of the types of recommended actions:
    - Audits
    - Process analysis that itself might produce a list of preventive actions
    - Defect repair, such as bug fixes in a software program

Updates

As a result of the QA process, you might need to add updates to the following:

As a result of QA, you might need to update organizational process assets and the project management plan.

- **Organizational process assets.** The quality standards, policies, procedures, and processes of the performing organization are the organization assets that can be updated during the QA process.
- **Project management plan.** The quality assurance process can result in updates to the project management plan in the following ways:
- Changes to the quality management plan, which is a part of the project management plan
- Changes to the quality assurance processes

During the execution of the project, the work is performed at two possible fronts: internal to the performing organization and external to the performing organization—that is, the procurement front.

Conducting Procurements

Conducting procurement is a process of obtaining responses from potential sellers, selecting sellers based on those responses, and awarding contracts to the selected sellers. The responses can be solicited in form of bids, quotations, proposals, or offers. The responses are then evaluated according to the criteria determined during procurement planning to select sellers. The major input to conducting procurements comes from the procurement management plan.

Input to Conducting Procurements

The input items to conducting procurements include the procurement management plan, procurement documents, and procurement-related organizational process assets. These input items are discussed in the following subsections.

Procurement Management Plan

The major input to conducting procurements is the procurement management plan developed during procurement planning. The procurement management plan may have the following items of interest:

- Prequalified selected sellers
- Procurement metrics to be used to manage contracts and evaluate sellers
- Types of contracts to be used and the format for the contract statement of work
- Assumptions and constraints that could affect planned purchases and acquisitions
- Scheduled dates for the contract deliverables
- Directions to be provided to the seller on developing and maintaining a contract work breakdown structure

Procurement Documents Package

The procurement documents package is the set of procurement documents put together during procurement planning. The buyer structures these documents with two goals in mind:

- To facilitate an accurate and complete response from each prospective seller
- To facilitate easy evaluation of the responses

These documents include the following:

- A description of the desired form of the response
- A relevant contract statement of work
- Any required contractual provisions, such as a copy of a model contract, and non-disclosure provisions

Different terms are used for these documents for different purposes:

- A term such as *bid*, *tender*, or *quotation* (or *quote*) is used when the seller selection decision will be based on the price, when buying commercial or standard items.
- A term such as *proposal* is used when multiple factors are considered, such as cost, technical skills, and technical approach.
- Common names for these different kinds of documents include *invitation for bid*, *request for quotation*, *tender notice*, *request for proposal*, and *contractor initial response*.

The procurement documents should be rigorous enough to ensure consistent responses from different sellers that can be fairly compared to one another and flexible enough to allow the sellers to offer suggestions on better ways to satisfy the requirements. How are the requests sent to the potential sellers? This is done according to the policies of the buyer's organization—for example, publication of the request in the public media, such as in newspapers, in magazines, and on the Internet.

> In government contracting, some or all of the content and structure of a procurement document might already be defined by regulations.

> Bids and quotations are typically used to ask for prices, whereas proposals are used to ask for solutions. Invitations for bid, requests for quotation, and requests for proposal travel from buyer to seller, whereas bids, quotations, and proposals travel from seller to buyer.

Evaluation Criteria

Also called *source selection criteria*, evaluation criteria is developed by the buyer during procurement planning to rate the responses from the sellers. The evaluation criteria could be as simple as the price for off-the-shelf standard items, or it could be a combination of factors for a more complex proposal.

Following is a list of some examples of evaluation criteria:

- **Cost.** To evaluate the overall cost, you should consider all cost-related factors, such as:
  - Purchase price
  - Delivery cost
  - Operating cost
- **Business aspects.** This can include the following factors:
  - **Business size and type.** Does the business size or type meet a condition set forth in the contract, such as being a small business or a disadvantaged small business?
  - **Financial capacity.** Does the seller have the financial capacity to do the job, or is the seller in a position to obtain the necessary financial resources to do the job?
  - **Production capacity and interest.** Does the seller have the capacity and the interest to meet future potential requirements?
  - **References.** Can the seller provide reliable references (such as from previous customers) verifying the seller's work experience and history of compliance with contractual requirements?
- **Management approach.** If the procurement itself involves a project, does the seller have the ability to execute management processes and procedures to run a successful project?
- **Rights.** The following rights can be considered:
  - **Intellectual property rights.** Will the seller own the intellectual property rights for the work processes or services that will be used to produce the deliverables?
  - **Proprietary rights.** Will the seller have the proprietary rights for the work processes or services that will be used to produce the deliverables?
- **Technical aspects.** This includes the technical approach and capability:
  - **Technical approach.** Will the technical methodologies, techniques, solutions, or services proposed by the seller meet the procurement requirements, or will they provide more than the expected results?
  - **Technical capability.** Does the seller have or is the seller capable of acquiring the technical skills and knowledge required to produce the deliverables?

Organizational Process Assets

The organizational process assets relevant to requesting seller responses include the following:

- A preexisting list of prospective sellers
- A list of previously used or qualified sellers
- Information about the past experiences with previously used sellers
- Organizational policies that could affect evaluating the responses and selecting the sellers

Any partner agreements and make-or-buy decisions made during procurement planning should also be considered during this process of conducting procurements.

Tools and Techniques for Conducting Procurements

The first goal for the tools and techniques here is to find the sellers and provide them with the information about the request for responses. The list of potential sellers can be developed from various sources, such as the World Wide Web, library directories, relevant local associations, trade catalogs, and the performing organization's internal information base. The main techniques used in soliciting seller responses are advertising and bidder conferences. These and other techniques used in conducting procurements are discussed in the following subsections.

> Advertising and bidder conferences are the main techniques used to solicit seller responses.

Advertising

The request for seller responses can be advertised in the public media or in relevant professional journals. Whether you should use advertising depends on the organization's policy. However, some government jurisdictions require public advertising of pending government contracts.

> In some cases, after a proposal is submitted, the buyer can request the seller to supplement its proposal with an oral presentation to provide some additional information that can be used to evaluate the seller's proposal.

Bidder Conferences

Bidder conferences refer to meetings with prospective sellers prior to preparation of a response to ensure that the sellers have a clear understanding of the procurement, such as the technical and contractual requirements. These meetings can generate amendments to the documents. All potential sellers should be given the same amount of information (or help) during this interaction so that each seller has an equal opportunity to produce the best response.

These conferences are also called *contractor conferences*, *vendor conferences*, or *pre-bid conferences*.

Proposal Evaluation Techniques

Price, technical and commercial aspects, and multiple sources are all considered during the proposal evaluation process.

Different techniques can be used to evaluate responses from sellers. All these techniques use expert judgment and evaluation criteria. The common factors that can be considered in the evaluation include the following:

- **Price.** This can play a primary role in the selection of off-the-shelf standard items. However, you should consider that a lower price does not mean lower cost if the seller does not deliver on time.

- **Multiple aspects.** Proposals are usually evaluated for different aspects, such as technical and commercial. Technical aspects refer to the overall approach, whereas commercial aspects refer to the cost.

- **Multiple sources.** For products critical to the project, multiple sources (sellers) might be required. This redundancy will help mitigate such risks as failure to meet the delivery schedule or quality requirements.

The following list discusses some techniques used to make the final selection of sellers:

Sellers in procurement are sometimes also called *sources*.

- **Independent estimates.** The purpose of independent estimates is to have a check on the proposed pricing by the seller. The procuring organization prepares the independent estimate in-house or has it done by a third party. Significant differences between the proposed price and the independent estimate mean that either the market has changed or the seller has failed to offer reasonable pricing due to reasons such as failure to understand the contract statement of work. The independent estimates are also called should-cost estimates.

- **Seller rating system.** A seller's rating does not depend on a specific response that you are evaluating. Rather, the seller's rating comes from the seller's rating system, which is developed by multiple organizations based on multiple factors related to seller's past performance, such as delivery performance, contractual compliance, and quality rating.

- **Weighting system.** The purpose of putting a weighting system in place is to have an objective evaluation as opposed to a subjective evaluation influenced by personal prejudice. The weighting system uses a method to quantify the qualitative data and typically involves the following steps:

1. Assign a numerical weight to each evaluation criterion according to its importance, such as w1, w2, and w3 for three criteria, and make these weights the same for each seller.

2. Rate the seller on each criterion, such as r1, r2, and r3. These ratings depend upon the seller.

3. Multiply the weight by the rate for each criterion.

4. Add the results in the previous step to compute an overall score, such as s1 for seller 1: s1 = r1 × w1 + r2 × w2 + r3 × w3.

- **Expert judgment.** The expert judgment is made by a committee that consists of experts from each of the disciplines covered by the procurement documents and the proposed contract. The committee can include experts from functional disciplines, such as accounting, contracts, engineering, finance, legal, manufacturing, and research and development.

Screening System

A screening system consists of minimum requirements as a threshold that must be met if the seller is to stay in the list of candidate sellers. It might, for example, consist of one or more evaluation criteria. The screening system can also use the weighting system and independent estimates.

Contract Negotiations

Contract negotiations have the following goals:

- Clarify the structure and requirements of the contract.
- Reach an agreement.

The subjects covered during the negotiations might include the following:

- Applicable terms and laws
- Authorities, rights, and responsibilities
- Business management and technical approaches
- Contract financing
- Payments and price
- Proprietary rights
- Schedule
- Technical solutions

A contract is a mutually binding legal relationship subject to remedy in court. The project manager might not be the lead negotiator on the contract. However, the project manager might be required to be present during negotiations to provide any necessary clarification on the project requirements.

The conclusion of contract negotiations is a document, the contract, which can be signed by both the buyer and the seller. The final contract signed by both parties can be an offer by the seller or a counteroffer by the buyer. Sometimes for simple procurement items, the contract is non-negotiable.

Internet searches and expert judgment are other tools that can also be used while conducting procurements.

Output of Conducting Procurements

The output of conducting procurements includes the list of selected sellers and the contract awards for the selected sellers. These and other output items are discussed in the following list.

Selected sellers. This is the list of sellers you have selected as a result of response evaluations.

Procurement awards. These are the contracts awarded to selected sellers. A contract is a legal document that obligates the seller to provide the specified products, services, or results and obligates the buyer to make the payment to the seller. The contract can be a simple purchase order or a complex document, depending on the nature of the procurement. A contract can include, but is not limited to, the following sections:

- List of deliverables and statement of work
- Schedule
- Acceptance criteria
- Change-request handling
- Inflation adjustments
- Insurance
- Limitation of liability
- Penalties and incentives
- Pricing and payment
- Product support
- Roles and responsibilities
- Termination and dispute-handling mechanisms
- Warranty

Resource calendars. This contains the information on the quantity and availability of the contracted (procured) resources— for example, the dates on which a resource will be active or idle.

Changes and updates. Conducting procurements can generate changes and updates, such as the following:

- **Change requests.** The selection process can generate change requests for the project management plan and its subsidiary plans and components, such as the project schedule and the procurement management plan. These change requests must be processed through the integrated change control system before implementation.

- **Updates to the procurement management plan.** If a procurement-related change request is approved, the procurement management plan should be updated to reflect the change.

Standardize This

The three standard processes used to direct and manage project execution, assure quality, and conduct procurements are presented in Figure 10.2. All the items in this figure were discussed in this chapter.

Quick Success Mantras

- Executing the project means implementing the project management plan developed during project planning.

- Directing and managing project execution involves managing various technical and organizational interfaces in the project to facilitate smooth execution of the project work.

- You perform the processes to take the project to its success by leading the people performing the project work.

- Quality assurance is the process of auditing the results from quality control measurements to ensure that the quality requirements are being met.

- One way to improve the quality of the outcome of any project is to improve the processes used to generate that outcome. So, one quality mantra is continuous process improvement.

- Conducting procurement is a process of obtaining responses from potential sellers, selecting sellers based on those responses, and awarding contracts to the selected sellers.

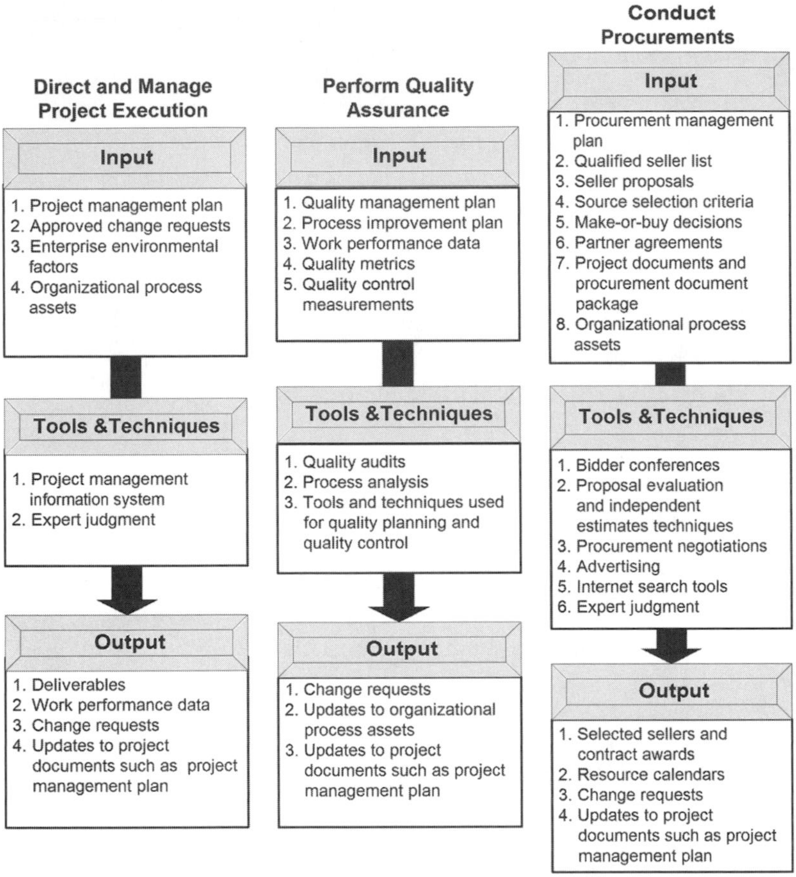

Conduct Procurements

Direct and Manage Project Execution

Input

1. Project management plan
2. Approved change requests
3. Enterprise environmental factors
4. Organizational process assets

Tools &Techniques

1. Project management information system
2. Expert judgment

Output

1. Deliverables
2. Work performance data
3. Change requests
4. Updates to project documents such as project management plan

Perform Quality Assurance

Input

1. Quality management plan
2. Process improvement plan
3. Work performance data
4. Quality metrics
5. Quality control measurements

Tools &Techniques

1. Quality audits
2. Process analysis
3. Tools and techniques used for quality planning and quality control

Output

1. Change requests
2. Updates to organizational process assets
3. Updates to project documents such as project management plan

Input

1. Procurement management plan
2. Qualified seller list
3. Seller proposals
4. Source selection criteria
5. Make-or-buy decisions
6. Partner agreements
7. Project documents and procurement document package
8. Organizational process assets

Tools &Techniques

1. Bidder conferences
2. Proposal evaluation and independent estimates techniques
3. Procurement negotiations
4. Advertising
5. Internet search tools
6. Expert judgment

Output

1. Selected sellers and contract awards
2. Resource calendars
3. Change requests
4. Updates to project documents such as project management plan

Figure 10.2 *Input, tools and techniques, and output for three processes: direct and manage project execution, perform quality assurance, and conduct procurements.*

Chapter 11

Building and Managing the Project Team

- Human Resource Management: Big Picture
- Acquiring a Project Team
- Developing the Project Team
- Tools and Techniques of Team Development
- Managing the Project Team
- Standardize This
- Quick Success Mantras

D uring project planning, you define roles and assign responsibilities to those roles. Individuals who play these roles perform the responsibilities of the roles to execute the project work. The process of obtaining the individuals to fill these roles and therefore become the members of the project team is called *acquiring the project team*. A team is a group of individuals who perform individual responsibilities to work interdependently on their independent assignments.

From a scientific viewpoint, a team is a dynamic entity, and its dynamics are determined by the interaction among its members. Therefore, for the team to be successful, it has to be effective in both dimensions: Its members must be competent in performing their individual assignments, and the interaction among them must be constructive overall. To ensure that, you need to continually develop and manage the project team. To obtain the right individuals for the project team and to develop and manage the team is an art, whereas an effective team taking the project to success is science, which will unfold itself automatically if you do the art part right.

So the core question in this chapter is how to build and manage a high-performance project team. In search of an answer, we will explore three avenues—acquiring project team members, developing the project team, and managing the project team.

In this chapter you'll:

- Understand the big picture of human resource management
- Understand what it means to acquire the team and how it is accomplished
- Know what's involved in developing the project team
- Identify the five stages of team development in the Tuckman model
- Identify key skills needed to develop a high-performance project team
- Know what's involved in managing the project team
- Identify different techniques of resolving conflicts
- Identify the standard processes for acquiring, developing, and managing the project team

Human Resource Management: Big Picture

As shown in Figure 11.1, human resource management as part of project management means developing the human resource plan and acquiring, developing, and managing the project team.

- **Acquire project team.** This is the process of filling the roles determined during human resource planning with actual staff assignments.

- **Develop project team.** This is the process of developing an optimal team by improving individual competencies, improving the interaction among individual team members, and thereby improving the team environment.

- **Manage project team.** This is the process of tracking performance of and providing feedback to the individual team members, managing changes related to the team, and resolving issues

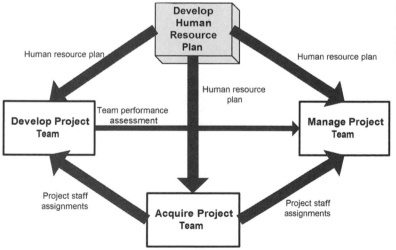

Figure 11.1
Big picture of human resource management.

SUCCESS SHOT: ROBUST SUCCESS

The science of project management will produce the project success in a robust fashion, but only if you do the art part right. A big component of doing the art part right is to obtain the right individuals for the project team and to build and manage a high-performance project team. A high-performance team has two essential components: competent team members and constructive interaction among them.

The project team has two dimensions: independence and inter-dependence. Each member has an independent assignment in the sense that the member owns that part of the work, is responsible for completing it, and must have the competency to complete it. However, all these individual assignments may have dependencies among them requiring the team members to interact effectively.

In a nutshell, you hire the individuals, but you need a team to complete the project successfully. The team needs to be developed from the individuals and then managed.

Acquiring a Project Team

The team's collective role is crucial to the success of the project.

The project work will be executed by the project team, and there-fore the collective role of the team in the success of the project is crucial. It is critical to acquire (hire or arrange from inside the performing organization) the right project team members for your project. Roles and responsibilities for the roles required to complete the project are defined during human resource plan-ning, as discussed in Chapter 7. Before the work can begin, the roles need to be assigned to real individuals who will become the members of the project team. These individuals might come from different departments, and the project management team might not have direct control over them.

Most of the work for getting ready to acquire the project team is done during project planning.

Getting Ready to Acquire the Project Team

When you are getting ready to acquire the project team, you must have or consider the human resource plan and the relevant enterprise environmental factors and organi-zational process assets.

Human resource planning, discussed in Chapter 7, generates the information you need to begin putting your team together. Getting ready to acquire the project team means making sure you have or consider the following items.

Human resource plan. You need this document because acquiring the project team is one of several processes that imple-ment the human resource plan. The human resource plan has useful items relevant to acquiring the project team, such as a list of roles and responsibilities required for the project, project orga-nizational charts, and the staffing management plan.

Enterprise environmental factors. The enterprise envi-ronmental factors are important in obtaining the project team members because the team members can come from various sources inside and outside the performing organization. For example, the team might include current employees of the performing organization and contractors hired for the project. Depending on your enterprise environment, you, the project manager (or the project management team), may or may not be able to direct or influence the hiring and staff assignments. In either case, you must try to obtain the best team you can. To determine who will be the best team member to fill in a role, you need to do your homework, which includes finding out the availability and abilities of the candidate team members. When you do have an influence on making the staff assignments, you should consider the following characteristics:

> When making staff assignments, you should consider availability, competency, experience, interests, and cost.

- **Availability.** It is important to know whether and when the candidate is available before you attempt to obtain that member.

- **Competency.** Does the candidate have the skills needed to complete the schedule activities?

- **Experience.** Has the candidate performed similar work well in the past?

- **Interests.** What is the candidate's interest level in this project and in the work that will be assigned to him or her?

- **Cost.** What is the cost attached to each candidate in terms of pay? This is even more important if the member is a contractor.

Based on this information, compose your dream team on paper and attempt to obtain that team. If the team is spread out over different departments and hence the team members are under the control of different functional managers, plan who you will ask for from each functional manager. To make a request, meet with the manager and ask for your most wanted team member first, even though it is very unlikely that you will get everyone you ask for.

Before meeting the functional managers, you need to prioritize your staffing needs. The most complex activities and the activities on the critical paths should get special attention, and you should make sure these activities have the best members because they have the highest risk potential. Having assigned staff to these activities first, you have more flexibility to agree to a different resource assigned to activities that are less complex and have a non-zero float time. Even though you want to negotiate for the best team, keep a backup plan—that is, if you don't get the best member, try to get the second best member, and so on.

> ### SUCCESS SHOT: AVOID LAYING THE FOUNDATIONS FOR FAILURE
>
> In a traditional organizational structure, you will not have direct control over the project team members, and you will need to acquire them by negotiating with the functional managers. But you still need to do the homework that you would do if you were to interview the candidates because you still want to get the best members available for the job. Failure to obtain necessary and correct team members may affect several core aspects of the project, such as cost, schedule, scope, and quality, and therefore may ultimately lead to the project failure.

In the worst-case scenario, you will not be able to negotiate for staff and you will have no influence on the staff assignments. Unless a team member is not qualified to do the job, you will have to live with the staff assignment decision and make the best of it. If you choose to challenge one of these assignments, make sure you are doing this based on hard facts, such as the lack of skills required to perform the assigned activity.

Organizational process assets. In the process of acquiring the project team, you should consider the following organizational process assets:

- Guidelines, policies, or procedures governing staff assignments that your organization may have
- Help from the human resources department in the recruitment of and orientation for the team members

To put together the best team, you need to understand the tools and techniques available for acquiring the team.

What Helps in Acquiring the Project Team

There are some concepts, such as virtual teams, and some tools and techniques that can help you acquire the right team. These items are discussed in the following list.

Acquisition. If the performing organization does not have the human resources to fill one or more roles needed to finish the project, the required team member can be obtained from outside the organization as a contractor, or the corresponding work can be given to a source outside the performing organization—a project aspect called *procurement*, which was discussed in Chapters 7 and 10.

Negotiation. You will most likely need to negotiate with functional managers for the staff assignments for your project. In these negotiations, you have a two-pronged goal—to obtain the best available person for an activity and to obtain the person for the required timeframe. As described in the previous section, you must do your homework in order to get the best results from the negotiations.

Pre-assignment. In some cases, there will be some staff members already assigned to the project. This can happen, for example, due to the following situations:

- A staff member was promised as part of a specific proposal to compete with another proposal. Acceptance of this proposal automatically affirms that staff-member assignment.

- There is only one person in the organization who has the expertise to perform a specific activity.

- A staff assignment was specified in the project charter.

Virtual teams. Welcome to the information age triggered by the Internet. The process of working for an organization from outside its physical location is called *telecommuting*. The Internet (along with other technological advances, such as teleconferencing, webinars, cellular phones, and pagers) makes it possible to telecommute from your home in the same city where the organization is or from a location on the other side of the globe with almost the same ease. Teams composed of telecommuters are called *virtual teams* because the team works together on the same project without holding face-to-face meetings. It is not difficult to find people who have worked on virtual teams and have never seen the other team members face to face. I have been working on such teams for a while, and I'm sure you either have or will in the near future. The virtual team format expands the team definition to offer the following benefits:

- People working for the same organization but living in different locations can join the same team.

- A needed expert can join a team even if the expert does not live in the same location as the rest of the team.

- The organization has the option to accommodate employees who can only work from their home offices for a certain period of time.

- Due to the availability of asynchronous communication means, such as e-mail and online bulletin boards, it is possible to form a team of members who have different work hours or shifts.

- Virtual teams eliminate or reduce the need to travel by using means of communication that are abundantly available, such as e-mail, video conferencing, and the World Wide Web. This enables organizations to perform projects that were previously impossible due to the anticipated travel expenses.

While negotiating with a functional manager, sometimes it's important to understand the functional manager's perspective in light of the politics of the organization. For example, a functional manager will weigh the benefits (for example, the visibility of your project compared to that of competing projects) in determining where to assign the best performers. In this case, it is to your advantage to explain the importance of your project and the activity for which you are asking for the best performer.

Acquisition, negotiation, pre-assignment, and virtual teams can help you acquire the right team.

SUCCESS SHOT: VIRTUAL TEAMS AND VIRTUAL COMMUNICATION

Because the virtual team members are not at the same location and do not have regular face-to-face meetings, effective communication is that much more important for the success of the project being performed by the virtual team. Therefore, communication management is crucial to the success of virtual teams. Take a good look at the virtual communication models discussed in Chapter 8.

The team you are going to acquire could be a team at one location or a virtual team, and a team member might be from your organization or from outside your organization.

What You Actually Acquire

The major output of the acquire project team process are the staff assignments to fill the roles defined during human resource planning and the list of time periods for which the staff members will be available. These and other output items of this process are discussed in the following list.

Project staff assignments. This document contains the list of individuals assigned to the project. It can also include the responsibilities assigned to each staff member, memos sent to the team members, the project organization chart, and the schedule with the names inserted.

Resource calendars. This document records the resource availability, such as the time periods for which each assigned member can work on the project. Possible schedule conflicts, commitments to other projects, and times when a team member is not available can also be recorded.

The output of the acquire project team process includes project staff assignments, resource calendars, and updates to the project management plan.

Updates to the project management plan. The project team is acquired by matching the staffing requirements specified in the staffing management plan to the candidates. Hardly ever is there a perfect match between the two. During the process of acquiring the project team, you might realize that the staffing management plan needs to be updated. It may also trigger an update in other components of the project management plan.

Some updates to the staffing management plan might come from the following sources:

- Promotions
- Retirements
- Illnesses
- Performance issues
- Changing workloads

In a nutshell, what you actually acquire are the individuals to fill the roles and perform the responsibilities assigned to those roles. After the assignments have been made to the acquired staff, you have the raw material out of which you need to develop the special team for your project.

Developing the Project Team

As mentioned earlier, your project team can consist of members from different departments and disciplines, regular employees and contractors, and experts from different disciplines, depending on the project needs. Some of these individuals might not have much appreciation for others' disciplines. You have a challenge to develop this diverse group into a cohesive and efficient team that will perform the project on time, within budget, and with quality. Keep two things in mind. First, from the project's perspective, one single goal of team development is the project success. Second, team development is a two-pronged process:

- Improve the individual competencies of team members
- Improve the interaction among team members

This will help you develop a cohesive, competent, and high-performance team to meet the project objectives effectively.

Team development starts with a list of team members and the staff assignments made during acquiring the project team. The resource availability listed in resource calendars provides information about when the team members are available for team development activities. Furthermore, the following items of the staff management plan (or human resource plan) can be useful for team development:

- Training strategies
- Plans for developing the project team
- Recognition and rewards systems

With this information at hand, you can use some tools and technique to continually develop your team.

Tools and Techniques of Team Development

To develop an effective team, you need effective communication, the ability to influence the organization, leadership, motivation, negotiation and conflict management strategies, and problem-solving skills.

As discussed in the following list, there are some standard tools and techniques that you can use to develop a winning team.

Interpersonal skills. General management skills, especially interpersonal skills, are necessary to develop an effective team. You and the project management team can minimize problems and maximize cooperation by understanding the sentiments of each team member, anticipating their actions, acknowledging their concerns, and following up on their issues. To accomplish this, the following interpersonal management skills are necessary:

- **Effective communication.** This is needed to facilitate the smooth flow of necessary information among the team members.

- **Ability to influence the organization.** This is needed to get things done.

- **Leadership.** A project manager is a leader. This is necessary for developing a vision and strategy and for motivating people to achieve that vision. During a time of possible uncertainty, such as changes in upper management, you should clarify the situation and help the team stay focused on the project.

- **Motivation.** This is needed to energize team members to achieve high levels of performance and to overcome barriers to change. During the times when the team is in a low-morale mode, you should be able to lift the team morale and thereby contribute to team development.

- **Negotiation and conflict management.** This is needed to work with team members to resolve their conflicts and facilitate negotiations when necessary in resolving conflicts or in assigning tasks. Depending on the nature of the conflict, you can take it as a team development opportunity. An effective resolution of a conflict contributes to team building.

- **Problem solving.** This ability is needed to define, analyze, and solve problems.

Team management is further discussed later in this chapter.

Ground rules. A very important management technique is to establish clear expectations at the beginning of a project. You can do this by establishing a set of ground rules. Early commitment to these guidelines will increase cooperation and productivity by decreasing misunderstandings.

Team-building activities. Team-building activities can range from indirect team-building activities, such as participating in constructing the WBS, to direct team-building activities, such as social gatherings where team members can get to know each other and start feeling comfortable with each other. While planning such activities, you should keep in mind that the team members might have different interests and different levels of tolerance for games and different icebreakers.

> Team-building activities can be direct or indirect.

The project kickoff meeting is another indirect method to start team development. This can be used as a formal way to introduce team members and other stakeholders and spell out the project goals for everyone at the same time. An ideal kickoff meeting is a combination of serious business and fun. The goal is to align the team with the project goals and to help the team members feel comfortable with each other.

In planning the kickoff meeting, you can assume that team members have the following questions in their heads that need to be answered before the end of the meeting:

> The main purpose of the kickoff meeting is to bring every team member onto the same page regarding the big picture of the project.

- Why am I here?
- Who are you and what are your expectations of me?
- What is this team going to do?
- How is the team going to do its work?
- How do I fit into all this?

Consider the following steps to make your kickoff meeting successful:

- **Agenda.** Putting the meeting agenda in the hands of the team members always helps to run the meeting more smoothly and effectively and keep it on the track.
- **Welcome.** Take immediate charge of the meeting by introducing yourself and welcoming the participants. Quickly walk through the agenda and set the stage for the rest of the meeting.

- **Project overview.** Define the project, its goals, and its deliverables. Introduce the project team members and briefly describe their roles. The goal is to provide a big picture and to help individual team members figure out how they fit into the big picture.

- **Expectations.** Many of the project team members might not already know you and your management style. You should take this opportunity to set expectations about how the team will function. For example, state that you expect all team members to attend the weekly status meetings. Remind the team to focus on the project goal, to do their part, and to look out for one another in a team spirit.

- **Guest speakers.** Depending upon the size and the visibility of the project, you might also invite relevant guest speakers, such as the project sponsor, the customer, or an executive stakeholder. Before the meeting, spend some time communicating with the guest speaker about the message to deliver.

- **Closure.** Ask for feedback and hold the question-and-answer session before closing the meeting.

Remember that the main purpose of the kickoff meeting is to bring every team member onto the same page regarding the big picture of the project. Don't get bogged down by discussing every item in detail.

The five stages of team development according to the Tuckman model are forming, storming, norming, performing, and adjourning.

You should know that team development is not an instant process. Generally speaking, when you form a team it goes through five stages of development (according to the Tuckman model), as shown in Figure 11.2 and explained in the following list.

1. **Forming.** This is the orientation stage, with high dependence on the leader (the project manager, in this case) for guidance and direction. Individual roles and responsibilities are unclear, and there is little agreement on the team goals other than those received from the leader. Processes are often ignored, and the team members test the tolerance of the system and the leader. It's time to establish the ground rules and clear expectations. The leader directs in this stage.

2. **Storming.** This stage represents the struggle for control and power as team members work to establish themselves relative to other team members. The clarity of team goals increases, but some uncertainties persist. Compromises might be required to make progress. Coaching and training can play effective roles during this stage.

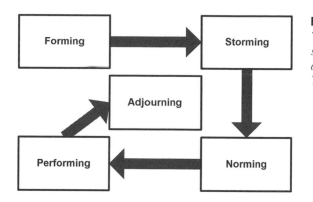

Figure 11.2
The five progressive stages of team development in the Tuckman model.

3. **Norming.** This is the routine stage during which consensus and agreement about team goals generally prevails among the team members. Roles and responsibilities are clear and accepted by the team members. Major decisions are made by group agreements, and minor decisions can be delegated to the appropriate team members. During this stage, the leader facilitates.

4. **Performing.** This is the productivity stage in which the team knows what it's doing and why. The team is functioning in a cohesive mode and working toward the common goal in a more autonomous fashion. Disagreements might arise, but they are resolved within the team in a constructive way. During this stage, the leader delegates and oversees.

5. **Adjourning.** This is the closure stage. When the mission for which the team was formed is accomplished (or cancelled), the team is adjourned to free the team members to move on to other things.

Being aware of these stages of team development will help you to better understand the behaviors of the team members and thereby develop your team more effectively.

Training. The goal of training is to improve the competencies of the project team members, which in turn helps in meeting the project objectives. It might be aimed at the individual members or at the team as a whole, depending upon the needs. The training might be scheduled in the staff management plan, or it might result from the observations, conversations, and project performance appraisals as the project progresses.

Following are examples of some training methods:

- Coaching
- Mentoring
- On-the-job training of a team member by another team member
- Online training
- Instructor-led classroom training

Co-location. This technique keeps all (or most) of the project team members in the same physical location to improve communication and to create a sense of community among the team members. In this age of virtual teams, this is not an increasingly popular technique, but when most of the team members are in the same location, this technique is a default choice. It can include a war room, which is a meeting room used for regular face-to-face meetings. Some organizations apply a hybrid approach—that is, a virtual team meeting face to face from time to time.

Recognition and rewards. The recognition and rewards strategy set up during the human resource planning process can be used to develop the project team. Remember the following rules in setting up a fair reward system:

- Only desirable behavior should be rewarded.
- Any member should be able to win the reward.
- Win-lose rewards, such as team member of the month, can hurt team cohesiveness.
- The cultural diversity of the team should be considered and respected.

The effects of the team development efforts are measured by the team performance assessment, which includes the following indicators:

- Improvement in individual skills that enables a team member to perform project activities more efficiently
- Improvement in team skills that help the team to improve overall performance and work more effectively as a group
- Reduced staff turnover rate

The project team needs to be managed throughout the project.

Study Checkpoint 11.1

Question: True or False: Project teams are temporary.

Answer: True, because by definition projects are temporary; therefore, a project team is temporary and is disbanded during the project closure.

Managing the Project Team

Managing the project team is aimed at improving the project performance by executing the following tasks:

- Tracking the performance of each team member
- Providing feedback to the team members
- Coordinating changes
- Resolving issues

Input to Managing the Project Team

The input to managing the project team comes from all other three components of human resource management: human resource planning, acquiring the project team, and developing the project team.

Human resource plan. The following output items from the human resource plan are useful in managing the project team:

- **Roles and responsibilities.** Used to monitor and evaluate performance.
- **Project organizational charts.** Used to find out the reporting relationships among project team members.
- **Staffing management plan.** Contains information such as training plans, compliance issues, and certification requirements, along with the time periods when the team members are expected to work.

Performance information. The following items regarding performance can be used in managing the project team:

- **Team performance assessment.** These assessments are generated while developing the project team.

- **Performance reports.** Performance reports prepared from the work performance data collected from directing and managing the project execution contain the progress of the project against the project baseline. They basically reflect how the project resources are being used to achieve the project objectives. The information from the performance reports helps determine future human resource requirements, updates to the staffing management plan, and recognitions and rewards.

Organizational process assets. The project management team can use the following organizational assets in managing the project team:

- The organization's policies, procedures, and system for rewarding the team members
- Other items that should be available to the project management team for use in managing the team, such as organizational recognition dinners, certificates of appreciation, bulletin boards, newsletters, and internal websites for information sharing

To manage the team effectively, you should be aware of the tools and techniques that can be used for that.

Tools and Techniques for Managing the Project Team

The tools and techniques used in managing the team include observation and conversation, conflict management, an issue log, and project performance appraisals.

Observation and conversation. Observations and conversations are both means to stay in touch with the work and attitudes of the project team members. The indicators to monitor these include the following:

- Progress toward completion of assigned activities and therefore project deliverables
- Distinguished accomplishments contributing to the project performance
- Interpersonal issues

Conflict management. The purpose of conflict management is to nourish the positive working relationships among the team members that result in increased productivity. The common sources for conflicts include the following:

- Scarce resources resulting in unsatisfied needs
- Scheduling priorities

- Personal work styles
- Perceptions, values, feelings, and emotions
- Power struggles

You can reduce the number of conflicts by setting ground rules, clearly defining roles and goals, and implementing solid project management practices.

Initially, the project team members who are parties to a conflict should be given the opportunity to resolve it themselves. If the team members fail to resolve the conflict and it becomes a negative factor for the project, you, the project manager, should facilitate the conflict resolution, usually in private and using a direct and collaborative approach. If the conflict continues, you might have no option other than to use formal procedures, such as disciplinary actions.

The first step in conflict management is analyzing the nature and type of conflict, which might involve asking questions. You can meet with (interview) the parties involved in the conflict. The next step is to determine the management strategy. Different management strategies are summarized here:

- **Avoidance.** In this strategy, at least one party to the conflict ignores (or withdraws) from the conflict and decides not to deal with the problem. This strategy can be used by the project manager as a cooling-off period, to collect more information, or when the issue is not critical. However, if the issue is critical, this is the worst resolution strategy and can give rise to lose/lose situations if both parties withdraw or yield/lose situations if one party withdraws. This strategy is also called withdrawal strategy.

- **Competition.** In this approach, one party uses any available means to get its way, often at the expense of the other party. This is a win/lose situation. It can be justified under some situations, such as when the basic rights of a party in conflict are at stake or when you want to set a precedent. However, if used unfairly from a power position (such as if it is a management style), it can be destructive for team development. This strategy can cause the conflict to escalate, and the loser party might attempt to retaliate. When used by a party in power, competition is also called forcing.

Differences of opinions should not be considered as sources of conflict. If managed properly, differences can be very healthy and can lead to better solutions and thereby increase productivity.

You should always look for how the different processes overlap and interact with each other. For example, conflict management is a technique for managing the team. However, the purpose of conflict management is to nourish the positive working relationships among the team members that result in increased productivity, so resolving a conflict can also be looked upon as a team development activity.

- **Compromising.** In this strategy, both parties gain something and give up something. This is a lose-win/lose-win strategy. You can use this strategy to achieve temporary solutions and to avoid a damaging power struggle when there is a time pressure. The downside of this approach is that both parties can look at the solution as a lose/lose situation and can be distracted from the merits of the issues involved. In this way, this short-term solution can hurt the long-term objectives of the project.

- **Accommodation.** This strategy is opposite of the competition strategy. One party attempts to meet the other party's needs at the expense of their own. This might be a justifiable strategy when the concerns of the accommodating party are less significant than the concerns of the other party in the context of the project. Sometimes it's used as a goodwill gesture. However, it is a lose/win approach (the accommodating party loses and the accommodated party wins), and the accommodating party runs the risk of losing credibility and influence in the future.

- **Collaboration.** This strategy is based on reaching consensus among the parties in the conflict. Both parties work together to explore several solutions and agree on the one that satisfies the needs and concerns of both parties. This is a win/win strategy and is generally considered the best of all the strategies because it helps build commitment and promotes goodwill between the parties involved.

- **Confronting.** Some experts consider this approach as a variation of collaboration. You confront the problem causing the conflict head on and then solve that problem through an open dialogue and by examining several alternatives. This approach is also called problem solving.

Issue log. Issues generally involve obstacles that can stop the project team from achieving the project objectives. A written log should be maintained that contains the list of team members responsible for resolving the issues by target dates. The purpose of the issue log is to monitor the issues until they are closed.

STUDY CHECKPOINT 11.1

Problem: As a project manager, you report to a program manager in your company named Rick. Rick asks you to perform an assignment in a certain fashion. You give all the reasons you can to convince him that the method is not very effective. At the end of this conversation, Rick says, "Just go and do it the way I told you."

What conflict resolution strategy did Rick apply?

Solution: Forcing—a form of competition strategy.

Project performance appraisals. Conducting project performance appraisals includes evaluating the performance of the project team members and providing them with feedback based on the evaluation. The evaluation is based on information collected from several people interacting with the team member. This method of collecting information is called the *360-degree feedback principle* because the information comes from several sources

The objectives for conducting performance appraisals include the following:

- Providing positive feedback to team members in a possibly hectic environment
- Clarifying roles and responsibilities
- Discovering new issues and reminding oneself of unresolved issues
- Discovering the needs of individual training plans
- Setting specific goals for the future

While you are managing the team using these techniques, you might recommend some actions as an output of the manage project team process.

Output of Managing the Project Team

The output from managing the project team includes recommended corrective and preventive actions, change requests, and updates to organization process assets and the project management plan.

> You might find that the project managers in your organization are not responsible for performance appraisals. The need for formal or informal performance appraisals depends on the organization's policy, the contract requirements, and the size and complexity of the project.

Recommended Actions

Managing the project team might generate recommendations for corrective and preventive actions, as discussed here:

- **Recommended corrective actions.** A corrective action is a direction for executing the project work to bring the future performance in line with what is expected in the project management plan. The corrective actions recommended during project team management might include the following:
  - Staffing changes, such as changing assignments of the team members, replacing team members (for example, the ones who leave), and outsourcing some work
  - Training for the team or for individual team members
  - Recognition and rewards based on the reward system
  - Disciplinary actions
- **Recommended preventive actions.** A preventive action is a direction to perform an activity to stop or reduce the probability of an anticipated event occurrence generally associated with a project risk. Preventive action can also be taken to reduce the anticipated impact of an event in case it happens. The preventive actions recommended during project team management might include the following:
  - Cross-training so that in the absence of a team member, another team member can take over the assignment
  - Role clarifications to ensure that all the responsibilities associated with the role are performed
  - Planning for overtime in anticipation of extra work that might be needed to meet project deadlines

Change Requests and Updates

Managing the project team can generate the change requests and updates discussed in the following subsections.

Change Requests

The team management activities can generate some change requests for the project management plan. For example, staffing changes can generate requests for extending the schedule, increasing the budget, or reducing the scope. The change requests should be processed through the integrated change control system.

Updates to Enterprise Environmental Factors and Organizational Process Assets

Here are some examples of updates in this these categories:

- **Performance appraisals.** The project staff member that interacts with a project team member in a significant way can offer input to the performance appraisal for that team member.

- **Lessons-learned database.** The lessons-learned database should be updated with the lessons learned during team management, which can come from different areas that include the following:

  - Issues and solutions in the issue log

  - Special skills and competencies discovered during the project work for the team members

  - Successful and unsuccessful ground rules, conflict management techniques, and recognition events

Updates to the Project Management Plan

Approved change requests and corrective actions can result in updates to the staffing management plan, which is a part of the project management plan. New role assignments, training plans, and reward decisions are some examples of updates.

Standardize This

Figure 11.3 illustrates the three standard processes used to build and manage the project team. All the items in this figure were discussed in this chapter.

Quick Success Mantras

- Implementation of the human resource plan is constituted by acquiring, developing, and managing the project team.

- Generally speaking, you do not acquire or hire a team. You hire the individuals and develop a high-performance team with them.

- Generally speaking, when you form a team, it goes through five stages of development: forming, storming, norming, performing, and adjourning.

Managing the project team is a complex task when the team members are accountable to both the project managers and the functional managers—for example, in a matrix organization. Effectively managing this dual relationship is critical to the success of the project and is therefore generally the responsibility of the project manager.

- A high-performance team has two essential components: competent team members and constructive interaction among them.

- The conflict resolution strategy, collaboration, is the most productive strategy in most conflict situations.

- Differences of opinion should not be considered as sources of conflict. If managed properly, differences can be very healthy and can lead to better solutions and thereby increase productivity.

- Successful conflict resolution also contributes to building a high-performance project team.

- The skills needed to develop a high-performance project team include leadership, negotiation, conflict resolution, and effective communication.

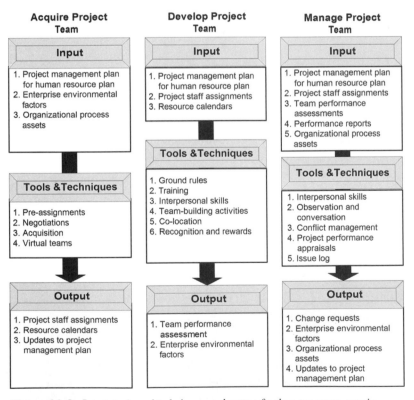

Figure 11.3 *Input, tools and techniques, and output for three processes: acquire project team, develop project team, and manage project team.*

Chapter 12

Managing the Stakes

- Stakeholder Management: Big Picture
- Distributing Information
- Standardize This
- Quick Success Mantras

Even if your project succeeded according to the project management plan, it can be deemed as a failure if you did not do one thing right, and that is to manage the project stakeholders. That is how important it is to manage project stakeholders effectively, which includes understanding and managing the influences and expectations of the stakeholders.

The core element of managing stakeholders is to manage their expectations to keep them in line with the project management plan. To accomplish that, you need to distribute the right information to the right stakeholders at the right time by using the right communication method. The right stakeholders can be identified from the stakeholder register developed during project initiation. Also, you should perform the management according to the stakeholder management strategy developed during the project initiation and communicate with the stakeholders according to the communication management plan developed during project planning.

So, the core question in this chapter is how to effectively manage stakeholders. In search of an answer, we will explore three avenues—the big picture of stakeholder management, managing stakeholder expectations, and distributing information.

In this chapter, you'll:

- Identify different aspects of managing stakeholders
- Learn how to manage stakeholder expectations
- Understand how to distribute information to the stakeholders effectively
- Understand how identifying stakeholders, managing stakeholder expectations, and distributing information are related to each other
- Identify the standard processes for managing stakeholder expectations and distributing information

Stakeholder Management: Big Picture

As shown in Figure 12.1, managing stakeholders includes the following processes:

- **Identify stakeholders.** This is the process of identifying all the stakeholders, positive and negative (defined in Chapter 3), during the project initiation. In this process, you develop a stakeholder register and a stakeholder management strategy.

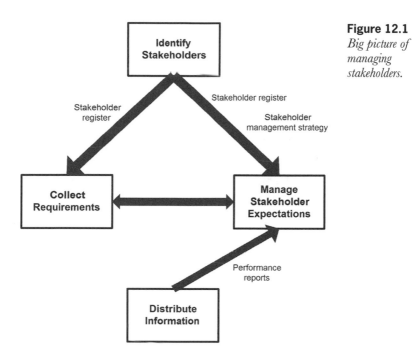

Figure 12.1
Big picture of managing stakeholders.

- **Collect requirements.** This is the process of collecting project and product requirements that will meet the stakeholders' needs and expectations. In this process you generate the stakeholder requirements document and the requirements management plan.

- **Manage stakeholder expectations.** This is the process of staying on the same page with the stakeholders regarding requirements by addressing their needs and issues.

- **Distribute information.** This is the process of distributing relevant information to the right stakeholders at the right time by using the right methods.

Identifying stakeholders, discussed in Chapter 4, is performed during project initiation, and collecting requirements, discussed in Chapter 5, is performed during project planning. In this chapter, we explore the other two components of stakeholder management: managing stakeholder expectations and distributing information.

Managing stakeholders includes identifying the stakeholders, collecting the requirements, managing the stakeholders' expectations, and distributing information.

Managing Stakeholder Expectations

Managing stakeholder expectations means communicating and working with the stakeholders to stay on the same page with them on the project requirements by addressing their needs and issues as they arise. This is a three-pronged task that includes:

The importance of resolving issues in a timely fashion cannot be overstated. An unresolved issue can grow into a major source of conflict and delay in the completion of project activities.

- **Containment.** Monitor and keep the expectations of the stakeholders within the project scope and project management plan through active communication.

- **Concerns.** Address the stakeholder concerns that have not become issues yet—for example, anticipation of problems in the near future. Addressing such concerns may uncover some potential risks that will need to be addressed.

- **Issues.** Understand, clarify, and resolve issues raised by the stakeholders. Some of the resolutions can give rise to change requests; other issues may be postponed to the next project or the next phase.

You can see that managing stakeholders' expectations will keep them on the same page with you by ensuring that they understand the internal dynamics and realities of the project, such as risks and interdependencies. Keeping stakeholders in touch with the project reality and on the same page with you will increase the probability of project success.

> ### SUCCESS SHOT: ALIGNING YOUR SUCCESS WITH THEIR SUCCESS
> Managing stakeholders' expectations is crucial for project success because it keeps their expectations in line with the project goals, objectives, and requirements in the project management plan. Otherwise, their definition of success will be different from your definition of success, and the project will fail in their eyes even if it succeeds according to the project management plan.

There are three dimensions to managing the stakeholders' expectations:

- **Manage stakeholders according to a strategy.** This strategy is documented in the stakeholder management strategy that you developed in the stakeholder identification process during project initiation.

- **Identify the right stakeholders to communicate with.** A list of stakeholders and information about them is in the stakeholder register that you created during the initiation stage when you were identifying the stakeholders.

- **Communicate with the stakeholders according to the communication management plan.** This plan was developed during project planning. That would mean you are communicating the right information at the right time to the right stakeholders by using the right methods.

You can use the issue log, also called the *action item log*, to open the issue, monitor it, resolve it, and close it. Issues should be clearly stated, categorized, and prioritized. An action item (or issue) log is a tool used to document and monitor the actions that need to be taken or the issues that need to be resolved. This is an important tool to ensure that important items do not fall through the cracks of communication.

Similarly, you can maintain a change log to document the changes that are requested, have occurred, or are implemented during the project lifecycle.

The organizational process assets that can affect managing stakeholders' expectations include the following:

- **Organizational change control procedures.** These are important because some change requests may arise in the process of managing stakeholder expectations.

- **Issue management procedures.** You should comply with these procedures while managing stakeholder issues.

- **Organizational communication requirements.** These requirements must be met while communicating with the stakeholders.

- **Information from previous projects.** It's always useful to learn from the experience in order to do better.

The tools and techniques that you can use in managing stakeholder expectations include the following:

- **Management skills, including interpersonal skills.** You will need these skills to manage change, resolve conflicts, and build trust. These skills include presentation skills, writing skills, and public speaking.

- **Communication methods.** You will use the appropriate communication methods as described in the communication management plan.

As a result of managing stakeholder expectations, some changes can occur. For example, you may need to make some changes to the stakeholder management strategy in order to accommodate

Rarely does an issue grow to become a project or a project activity. It is your responsibility to resolve issues in a timely fashion in order to maintain a constructive relationship with the stakeholders. However, the resolution may cause change requests for the project, which should go through the proper evaluation and approval process before they are implemented.

unexpected situations and needs. Furthermore, you may find a communication method ineffective, and perhaps you would like to replace it with a more effective method, but this will cause an update to the communication management plan. You may end up identifying a new stakeholder, and that will require a change in the stakeholder register, and so on. The point here is that when a change occurs, you should think through it and update all the documents and plans that need to be updated to ensure consistency after the change has been accommodated.

STUDY CHECKPOINT 12.1

Question: True or False: A stakeholder is proposing something that is not within the planned scope of the project. The appropriate response to this proposal is to oppose it.

Answer: False. A project manager is not a *de facto* opponent to change; instead, you should be an agent for change. Your response should be to evaluate the change for its effects on the project and then put it through the approval process, where it may either be rejected or selected.

You should also document your experience of managing stakeholder expectations, which includes causes of issues, how the issues were resolved, lessons learned, and so on. This will add to the organizational process assets and will be useful for upcoming projects and as a record through the lifecycle of the current project.

To stay on the same page with the stakeholders, it's important to distribute the relevant information at the right time.

Distributing Information

Throughout the project lifecycle, you need to continually distribute relevant information to the right stakeholders at the right time by using appropriate methods. The information is distributed according to the communication management plan developed during the planning stage.

Input to Information Distribution

The information distribution process is used to distribute the information according to the communication management plan.

Therefore, the information to be distributed and the communication management plan are the obvious input items to the information distribution process. These and other input items are discussed here.

The distributed information includes performance reports, which contain items such as the following:

- Performance information, including cost and schedule
- Status information
- Results from risk analysis and risk monitoring
- Any other useful information
- Current forecasts

In addition to the communication management plan and performance reports, the following organizational process assets can affect the information distribution process:

- Information and lessons learned from the past projects
- Organizational policies, procedures, and guidelines for distributing information
- Templates to facilitate information distribution

With this input in place, you use some tools, such as communication technology, to generate the output of this process—that is, to distribute the information.

Tools and Techniques for Information Distribution

Communication skills are a necessary condition for successful information distribution. This and other tools and techniques for information distribution are discussed in the following list.

Communication skills. Because communication is the exchange of information, communication skills are a necessary requirement for information distribution. Communication skills, an essential part of general management skills, are used to ensure that:

The success of information distribution depends on the sender and the receiver.

- The right stakeholders get the right information at the right time.
- The communication requirements and expectations of stakeholders are properly managed.

As discussed in Chapter 8, the communication line has two ends. There is a sender on one end and a receiver on the other. Both the sender and the receiver need to have communication skills. The sender has the following responsibilities:

- Ensure that the information is clear and complete.
- Confirm that the information is received and properly understood.

The receiver has the following responsibilities:

- Ensure that the information is received in its entirety.
- Confirm that the information is correctly understood.

So, the success of information distribution depends on both the sender and the receiver. The communication has two flavors in each of the following dimensions:

- **Media.** Writing and speaking on the sender end, and reading and listening on the receiver end.
- **Place.** Internal to the project—that is, within the project—and external—that is, communicating to the entities external to the project, such as customers, the media, and the public.
- **Format.** Formal, such as reports and briefings, and informal, such as memos and ad hoc conversation.
- **Hierarchy.** Horizontal means communication among the peers, and vertical means communication between different levels of organizational hierarchy—for example, a manager communicating with the team that reports to the manager.

The information that needs to be communicated also needs to be gathered, stored, and retrieved.

Information can be distributed synchronously or asynchronously.

Information distribution methods. The information can be distributed in a number of ways that fall into the following two categories:

- **Synchronous.** Both the sender and the receiver have to be present at the same time for this method; examples include face-to-face project meetings and teleconferencing.
- **Asynchronous.** The sender and receiver don't have to be present at the same time for this method; examples include written papers or electronic documents, online bulletin boards, email, and the World Wide Web in general.

The communication methods and models are discussed in Chapter 8.

Information distribution tools. You can use one or more appropriate tools to distribute information. These sets of tools include the following:

* **Document format.** Could be hard copy or electronic.
* **Messages.** Email, fax, voicemail, Internet bulletin board, blog.
* **Meetings.** Face-to-face meetings, video conferences, and tele-conferences.
* **Management tools.** Project scheduling tools.

Information can be distributed via documents, messages, meetings, or management tools.

You use these tools and techniques to generate the output of the information distribution process.

Output of Information Distribution

The output of the information distribution process is, well, the distribution of information. This distribution (or communication) of information falls into two categories:

* **Formal distribution.** This distribution refers to communication of the information as planned—for example, regular status and progress information at scheduled times, such as once a week every Wednesday.
* **Informal distribution.** This refers to the communication of information on an as-needed basis. For example, the project sponsor can ask you for information that is not part of the regular schedule of distributing information.

Some of the distributed information can be added as a record to the organizational process assets. Here are some examples:

* Performance and status reports
* Notifications about resolved issues and approved changes
* Project presentations
* Project records, such as memos, meeting minutes, and project files, such as plans and schedules
* Feedback from stakeholders
* Lessons learned

Standardize This

Figure 12.2 illustrates the two standard processes used to manage stakeholder expectations and distribute information. All the items in these figures were discussed in this chapter.

Figure 12.2
Input, tools and techniques, and output for two processes: manage stakeholder expectations and distribute information.

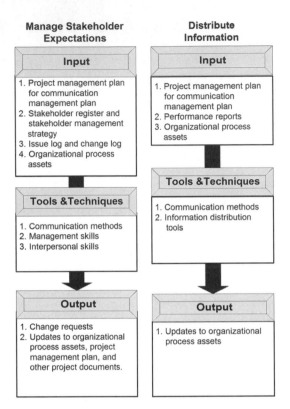

Manage Stakeholder Expectations

Input
1. Project management plan for communication management plan
2. Stakeholder register and stakeholder management strategy
3. Issue log and change log
4. Organizational process assets

Tools &Techniques
1. Communication methods
2. Management skills
3. Interpersonal skills

Output
1. Change requests
2. Updates to organizational process assets, project management plan, and other project documents.

Distribute Information

Input
1. Project management plan for communication management plan
2. Performance reports
3. Organizational process assets

Tools &Techniques
1. Communication methods
2. Information distribution tools

Output
1. Updates to organizational process assets

Quick Success Mantras

- Managing stakeholders includes identifying stakeholders, collecting requirements from the stakeholders, managing stakeholder expectations, and distributing information to the stakeholders.

- Managing stakeholder expectations is crucial for the success of the project by keeping these expectations in line with the project management plan.

- Resolving issues in a timely fashion helps with maintaining constructive relationships with the stakeholders.

- Unresolved issues can grow to become a source of conflict.

- Distributing the right information to the right stakeholders at the right time by using the right communication method helps with managing the stakeholder expectations.

PART IV

Monitoring and Controlling the Project

You need to continually monitor and control your project. In general, monitoring means watching the course, and controlling means taking action to either stay the course or change the wrong course. Applied to project management, you monitor the project by activities such as making performance measurements to ensure that it is on the track set by the project management plan, and you control the project to keep it on the track and to bring it back on track if it falls off. The core of monitoring and controlling the project includes collecting the work performance data from the project execution and comparing it to the accepted performance baseline that consists of the scope baseline, schedule baseline, and cost baseline. This comparison generates the performance measurements, which may generate some change requests. The change requests must be processed through an integrated change control system for approval, and only the approved changes should be implemented. The performance measurements may also expose some previously undetected risks.

Chapter 13

Monitoring and Controlling the Project Work

- Monitoring and Controlling the Project: Big Picture
- Controlling Changes in an Integrated Way
- Controlling Quality
- Standardize This
- Quick Success Mantras

Success is not a sudden event that happens instantaneously; you have to work your way to it. While you are managing the execution of your project, how do you know it's on the track to success? There is a two-word answer to this question: monitor and control. All the hard project work may lead to failure if you do not continually monitor and control it to keep the project on the right track as determined by the project management plan. However, this does not mean that no changes can be made to the project. You should evaluate all the requested changes, estimate their impact across the project, process them, and ensure that only the approved changes are implemented—a process called *integrated change control*. The approved changes, of course, will modify the original (existing) project management plan, and the right track will be determined by the modified plan. Nevertheless, at a given point in time there is one right track for the project determined by the project management plan at that time. That is your path to success.

Quality is an integrated part of any project. Therefore, monitoring and controlling the project work includes controlling the quality. You also need to ensure that the procurement part of your project is being properly administered. So, the core question in this chapter is how to monitor and control the project work. In search of an answer, we will explore three avenues—performing integrated change control, performing quality control, and administering procurements.

In this chapter you will:

- Understand the big picture of monitoring and controlling a project
- Understand how the project changes are monitored and controlled
- Identify the seven tools of quality control
- Know what's involved in administering procurements
- Identify the standard processes for monitoring and controlling project work, changes, quality, and procurements

Monitoring and Controlling the Project: Big Picture

You monitor and control your project by monitoring and controlling the project performance, changes, and risks. Monitoring includes measuring the project performance, collecting and distributing information about the project performance, and evaluating the performance information to see the trends. Continuous monitoring helps the project management team identify the areas that need to be controlled closely by, for example, taking preventive or even corrective actions. Some of the major tasks involved in monitoring and controlling the project are the following:

> Monitoring and controlling does not start only after the project starts execution. Rather, the project needs to be monitored and controlled all the way from initiation through closing.

- Monitoring project performance by measuring it against the project management plan in terms of parameters such as cost, schedule, and scope

- Monitoring various aspects of the project by collecting information to support status reporting, progress measurement, and predictions, and then distributing this information among the stakeholders

- Evaluating performance to determine whether it needs to be controlled by taking corrective or preventive actions

- Monitoring risks by tracking and analyzing the already identified project risks and by identifying new risks

- Controlling risks by managing the execution of risk response plans when the risks occur

- Maintaining an accurate and timely information base regarding the project as it progresses

- Monitoring and controlling changes and monitoring the implementation of approved changes

As shown in Figure 13.1, monitoring and controlling the project is composed of two high-level tasks: monitoring and controlling the project work and controlling the changes. Monitoring and controlling project work is performed by executing more specific tasks, such as controlling cost, schedule, and scope.

The change requests arising from monitoring and controlling the project or originating from any other source, such as the stakeholders, must be processed through the integrated change control process.

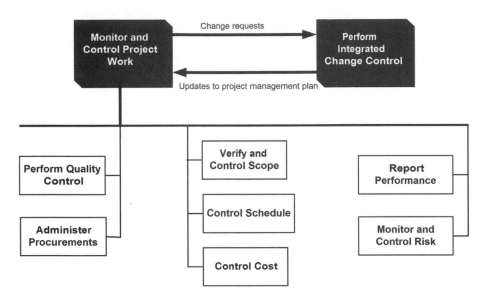

Figure 13.1 *Big picture of monitoring and controlling the project.*

Controlling Changes in an Integrated Way

You need to manage changes to the project from project initiation through project closure. A project rarely runs exactly according to the project management plan, and therefore changes will inevitably appear. The change requests can come from evaluating the project performance to bring the project in line with the project management plan, or they can come from other sources, such as the stakeholders. Regardless of where they originate from, all changes need to be managed (monitored and controlled), which includes getting the changes rejected or approved, seeing the approved changes implemented, and changing the affected plans accordingly. You, the project manager, must manage changes proactively, which includes the following activities:

- Identifying a change that has occurred and receiving a change request.
- Getting the requested changes approved or rejected. Depending on the project and the performing organization, the authority to determine whether a change is eventually rejected or approved might lie with the project manager, a customer, a sponsor, or a committee.

- Monitoring and controlling the flow of approved changes, which includes:
  - Making sure they are implemented.
  - Maintaining the integrity of the project baseline (cost, schedule, and scope) by updating it to incorporate the approved changes.
  - Coordinating changes and their impact across the project and updating the affected documentation. For example, an approved schedule change might impact cost, quality, risk, and staffing.
- Controlling project quality—for example, through defect repairs and recommended corrective and preventive actions.
- Making sure that only the approved changes are implemented.

SUCCESS SHOT

Especially in a startup organization, you will notice quite often the changes making their way through the back door—for example, a product manager talking to an engineer directly and introducing changes. Do not consider yourself an opponent of changes by default, but you do need to manage changes and make sure each change goes through the integrated change control process. So, when it comes to changes, the keyword is *control*, and not necessarily *oppose*.

Incoming Stream of Change Requests

As a change agent, you monitor the incoming stream of change requests. Each requested change and recommended action must be processed through the integrated change control process. The approved changes have their effects on the project management plan, and therefore the plan needs to be updated accordingly. You may find the following items in the incoming stream of change requests:

- **Requested changes.** A change to any aspect of the project, such as schedule, scope, or cost.
- **Recommended items.** Theses can include:
  - Recommended corrective actions
  - Recommended preventive actions
  - Recommended defect repairs

These recommendations might arise from performance evaluations, and they are the output of various processes discussed in this chapter.

The following items in the organizational process assets can influence the change control process:

Organizational process assets including organizational procedures, measurements, project files, and the configuration management system can also influence the change control process.

- **Organizational procedures.** Your organization may have proper procedures related to change control—for example, how to modify documents, such as plans, and how to process (evaluate and approve or reject) changes.

- **Measurements database.** A database of process measurements in the past can greatly help you in controlling changes. Also, the process measurements data in the current project can be stored into this database.

- **Project files.** Project files from previous projects may be a useful input to the change control process in order to learn from the past.

- **Configuration management system.** This system can be used to monitor and control the changes, and it may have a knowledge base that can also be used.

Tools and Techniques for Integrated Change Control

The tools and techniques used in controlling changes include the project management information system, meetings, and expert judgment.

The tools and techniques used in controlling changes can vary by the size and complexity of the project and the performing organization. It may include the items discussed in the following list.

Project management information system. This is a collection of tools and techniques (manual and automated) used to gather, integrate, and disseminate the output of project management processes. This system is used to facilitate processes from the initiation stage all the way to the closing stage. Microsoft Project, a product that lets you create a project schedule, is an example of such a tool. Another example of the components of the project management information system could be a document management system to create, review, change, and approve the documents to facilitate the change control procedure.

The project management information system might also have tools that can help the project management team implement the integrated change control process.

Meetings. Meetings are an effective tool that the change control body, such as the change control board, can use to evaluate a change in order to reject or approve it.

Expert judgment. The project management team can use the experts on the change control board to make approval or rejection decisions about change requests. The rejection or approval of the change request is an obvious output of the integrated change control process.

Output from Integrated Change Control

The changes that are processed through the integrated change control process will be either rejected or approved. As a result of the approved changes, the project management plan might need to be updated. Accordingly, following are the output items of the integrated change control process:

Output items of the integrated change control process are change request status updates and document updates.

Change request status updates. The items processed through the integrated change control process will ultimately be either approved or rejected. In the meantime, each change request must have some status that could be reported. Here are some examples of status:

- Being processed
- Approved
- Rejected
- Implemented
- Implementation validated

Document updates. As a result of approved changes, items such as the project management plan and the project scope statement might need to be updated.

So, the requested changes are either rejected or approved in the integrated change control process.

SUCCESS SHOT

You deal with both kinds of changes: changes that have occurred and changes that need to occur. You identify and process them promptly to minimize their negative effect and maximize their positive effect. The first response to a change identification is almost always to understand it and evaluate its impact across the project. For example, a proposed change in schedule may affect cost, quality, risk, and staffing.

Some changes may originate from how the project is performing. Project performance, a factor that you monitor and control, is closely related to quality, which is the degree to which the projects requirements are fulfilled. For example, a good-quality project is a project that is completed within its planned cost, scope, and schedule. Any variations from the planned cost, schedule, and scope performance indicate the degradation of project quality. So, controlling the performance correlates strongly to controlling the quality.

Controlling Quality

Quality control (QC) can be performed by the QA department or by the QC department if the performing organization has one. Nevertheless, the project management team should have a working knowledge of statistical aspects of quality control, such as sampling and probability. This will help evaluate the QC output.

Controlling quality involves monitoring specific results to determine whether they comply with the planned quality standards, which include project processes and product goals, and controlling the results by taking actions to eliminate unsatisfactory performance. Performing quality control includes monitoring and controlling quality by accomplishing the following goals:

- Monitoring specific project results, such as cost performance and schedule performance, to determine whether they comply with the planned quality standards, which include project processes and product goals and requirements.

- Identifying ways to eliminate the causes of unsatisfactory performance and recommending changes or actions accordingly.

The results under scrutiny include both deliverables by the project team and performance measurements by the project management team. Quality control is performed throughout the project.

Talking the Quality Talk

In project management, as in any other field, talking the talk is as important as walking the walk: Confusing talk will adversely affect the walk. While dealing with quality control, you must be able to distinguish the two terms in each of the following pairs from each other:

- Prevention and inspection
  - Prevention is a direction to perform an activity that will keep an error from entering the product and the process.
  - Inspection is a technique to examine whether an activity, component, product, result, or service complies with planned requirements. The goal of inspection is to ensure that errors do not reach the customer.

- Attribute sampling and variable sampling
  - Attribute sampling is a technique to determine whether a result conforms to the specified standard.
  - Variable sampling is a technique to rate a result on a continuous scale that measures the degree of conformity.
- Common cause and special cause
  - Common cause is a source of variation that is inherent to the system and is predictable. Such variations are also called normal variations, and the common causes for them are also called random causes.
  - Special cause is a source of variation that is not inherent to the system and is removable. It can be assigned to a defect in the system.
- Control limits and tolerances
  - Control limits describes the area occupied by three standard deviations on either side of the central line or the mean of a normal distribution of data plotted on a control chart that reflects the expected variation of the data. If the results fall within the control limits, they are within the quality control.
  - Tolerance is the range within which a result is acceptable if it falls within those limits.
- Precision and accuracy
  - Precision refers to the consistency among several measurements in the same experiment by the same apparatus. A set of measurements with a narrow spread (all values are close to each other) is more precise than another set of values with a wide spread.
  - Accuracy refers to how close the measured value is to the true value. The closer the measured value is to the true value, the more accurate the measurement is.

It is possible for a set of values to be more accurate and less precise or to be less accurate and more precise. For example, the accepted true value for the molecular weight of table salt is 58 g. A set of measurements with the values 70.0 g, 70.5g, and 71.0g is more precise and less accurate than the set of measurements with the values 56.0 g, 58.5 g, and 60.5 g.

Input to Quality Control

As mentioned earlier, the goal of quality control is to ensure that the performance from the project execution meets the planned quality standards. Therefore, the outputs from the project execution and the quality planning are the obvious inputs to performing quality control.

These and other input items are discussed in the following list.

- **Quality planning output.** The following items from the output of quality planning, discussed in Chapter 9, are the input to the perform quality control process:
  - The quality management plan lets you know how the quality standards are supposed to be implemented.
  - Quality metrics specify which quality features to monitor and how to measure them.
  - Quality checklists show which quality steps need to be performed.
- **Output from directing and managing project execution.** The following items from the output of the direct and manage project execution process, discussed in Chapter 10, are input into performing quality control:
  - A list of deliverables from the project execution to ensure that all the required deliverables are produced before the project completion.
  - Work performance measurements (data) to monitor performance. From this data, you may develop metrics, such as planned versus actual schedule performance and planned versus actual cost performance.
- **Approved change requests.** You need this list to ensure that all the approved changes are implemented in a timely fashion. The list of approved change requests also includes modifications, such as revised work methods and a revised schedule.
- **Organizational process assets.** These include quality policies and procedures, change control procedures, quality-related historical data, and issue opening and defect reporting procedures.

Quality control is a very involved process and has a plethora of tools and techniques, discussed next.

Tools and Techniques for Quality Control

The tools and techniques used for quality control include inspection, defect repair reviews, and the so-called seven basic tools of quality.

Seven Basic Tools of Quality

Table 13.1 shows the seven kinds of charts used in quality control, also known as the seven basic tools of quality. These tools are described in the following sections, too.

Table 13.1 Seven Basic Tools of Quality

Chart	Purpose
Flowchart	To anticipate what and where the quality problems might occur
Run chart	To perform trend analysis: predict the future results based on the past performance
Scatter diagram	To find the relationship between two variables, such as cause and effect, or two causes
Histogram	To display the relative importance of different variables
Pareto diagram	To identify and rank the errors based on the frequency of defects caused by them
Control chart	To monitor whether the variance of a specified variable is within the acceptable limits dictated by quality control
Cause and effect diagram	To explore all the potential causes of a problem, not just the obvious ones

Flowcharts

A flowchart is a diagram that depicts inputs, actions, and outputs of one or more processes in a system. Flowcharts, commonly used in many disciplines, show the activities, decision points, and order of processing. They help to understand how a problem occurs. You can also use flowcharts to anticipate what quality problems might be, where they might occur, and how you might deal with them.

You can use flowcharts to anticipate how you might deal with the quality problems that may occur.

Run Charts

Run charts are used to perform trend analysis, which is the science of predicting future performance based on past results. In quality control, trend analysis can be used to predict such things as the number of defects and the cost to repair them. You can use the results of trend analysis to recommend preventive actions if needed.

Scatter Diagrams

A scatter diagram is used to show the pattern of the relationship between two variables—an independent variable and another variable that depends on the independent variable. The dependent variable is plotted corresponding to the independent variable. For example, a variable representing a cause can be the independent variable, and a variable representing the effect can be a dependent variable. The closer the data points are to a diagonal line, the stronger the relationship (called the *correlation*) is between the two variables.

Histograms

A histogram is a bar chart that shows a distribution of variables. Each bar can represent an attribute, such as defects due to a specific cause, and its height can represent the frequency of the attribute, such as the number of defects. This tool helps to identify and rate the causes of defects.

You might wonder how the defects can be repaired efficiently. Pareto diagrams, which are examples of histograms, have the answer for you.

Pareto Diagrams

Pareto's Law states that 80 percent of project defects are caused by 20 percent of errors (or types of errors).

Pareto's Law, in its original form, was presented as an economic theory by Vilfredo Pareto, a 19th-century Italian economist, and it states that 80 percent of income is earned by 20 percent of the population. Since then, it has been applied to other fields, such as project management.

A Pareto diagram is used to rank the importance of each error (problem) based on the frequency of its occurrence over time in the form of defects. A defect is an imperfection or deficiency that keeps a component from meeting its requirements or specifications. A defect is caused by an error (problem) and can be repaired by fixing the error. An error in a product can give rise to multiple defects, and by fixing the error, you repair all the defects caused by that error.

However, all errors are not equal. Some errors cause more defects than others. According to Pareto's Law, which is also known as the *80/20 rule*, 80 percent of project defects are caused by 20 percent of errors (or types of errors). Qualitatively, it means that most defects are caused by a small set of errors. The Pareto diagram lets you rank errors based on the frequency of defects they cause. You begin by having the error that causes most of the defects fixed and make your way to other errors that cause smaller numbers of defects. This way, the efforts of the project team are optimized: You get the maximum number of defects repaired with minimal effort.

The advantages of a Pareto diagram are twofold:

- It ranks errors according to the frequency of defects they cause.
- It optimizes efforts to repair the defects by working on the errors that cause most of the defects.

As an example, Table 13.2 presents data on the frequency of defects caused by certain errors. The data is displayed in Figure 13.2 in the form of a Pareto diagram. In this example, 200 defects are caused by 7 errors, and Error A alone causes 75 defects, which

Table 13.2 Frequency of Defects Corresponding to Errors Causing the Defects

Error Causing the Defects	Number of Defects	Percentage of Defects Caused by This Error	Cumulative Percentage
A	75	37.5	37.5
B	50	25.0	62.5
C	30	15.0	77.5
D	20	10.0	87.5
E	15	7.50	95.0
F	7	3.5	98.5
G	3	1.5	100.0

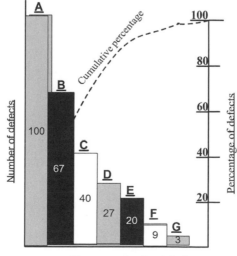

Figure 13.2
An example of a Pareto diagram.

is 37.5 percent of all the defects. Similarly, you can understand the impact of other errors by looking at Table 13.2 and Figure 13.2. The Pareto diagram tells you that you should address Error A first, Error B second, and so on.

You might ask: How many defects are acceptable? To find an answer to this question, you need to understand another tool, called the *control chart*.

Control Charts

Control charts are used to monitor whether the variance of a specified variable is within the acceptable limits dictated by quality control. A variance is a measurable deviation in the value of a project variable, such as cost from a known baseline or expected value. This is a way to monitor the deviations and determine whether the corresponding variable is in or out of control. The values are taken at different times to measure the behavior of a variable over time. The mean value in the control chart represents the expected value, and a predetermined spread from the mean value (usually $\pm 3\ \sigma$) is used to define the limits within which an acceptable value can fall.

Control charts can be used to monitor the values of any type of output variables. To illustrate their main features, consider the example of a control chart shown in Figure 13.3. In this example, assume that a manufacturer produces 100 units of a product each day, and it is expected that 95 out of 100 units should have no defect—that is, the expected number of defective units is equal to five. The control limits are set to ± 3. In other words, 95 units

Figure 13.3
An example of a control chart.

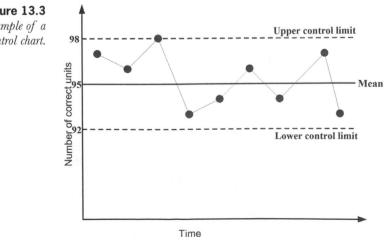

out of 100 must be correct, give or take three. That puts the lower limit at 92 and the upper limit at 98. Crossing the lower limits is not acceptable to the customer, and crossing the upper limits might require an unjustifiable cost.

Controlling quality includes dealing with defects and the problems that cause them. So, studying the causes of a problem is critical to quality control.

Cause and Effect Diagrams

A cause and effect diagram is used to explore all the potential causes (inputs) that result in a single effect (output), such as a problem or a defect. This type of diagram is the brainchild of Kaoru Ishikawa, who pioneered quality management processes in the Kawasaki shipyards, and therefore these diagrams are also called *Ishikawa diagrams*. Due to the shape of these diagrams, they are also known as *fishbone diagrams*. To construct and use cause and effect diagrams effectively, perform the following simple steps:

> Cause and effect diagrams are also known as Ishikawa diagrams and fishbone diagrams.

1. **Identify the problem.** Write down the problem in the box drawn on the right side of a large sheet of paper. This represents the head of the fish. Starting from the box draw a horizontal line across the paper. This represents the spine of the fish.

2. **Identify the possible areas of causes.** Identify the areas or factors from where the potential causes of the problem might come. Environment, people, materials, measurements, and methods are some examples of areas (factors) of causes. For each factor relevant to the problem under study, draw a line off the spine and label it with the name of the factor. These lines represent the fish bones.

> While constructing the cause and effect diagram, you can use the brainstorming method to identify the potential factors of causes and the potential causes for each factor.

3. **Identify the possible causes.** For each factor, identify possible causes. Represent each possible cause with a line coming off the bone that represents the corresponding factor.

4. **Analyze the diagram.** Analyzing the diagram includes narrowing down the most likely causes and investigating them further.

Figure 13.4 shows an example of a cause and effect diagram. The problem in this example is the delay in the release of a website. The factors considered are environment, methods, people, and time. Of course, the diagram is incomplete in the sense that more factors and related causes can be explored, and causes for each factor can be explored further. But you get the point.

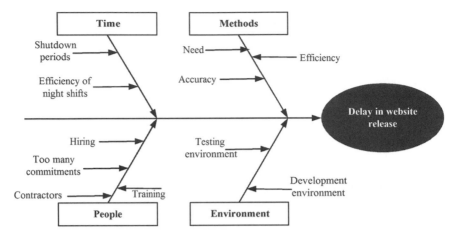

Figure 13.4 *An example of a cause and effect diagram: Explore the causes for a delay in a website release.*

A cause and effect diagram offers a structured way to think through all possible causes of a problem. You can use these diagrams to carry out a thorough analysis of a problematic situation. This kind of analysis is useful in complex situations when, to discover the real causes, you need to explore all the potential causes and not just the obvious ones.

In addition to the seven quality tools we have discussed, there are some other tools that you can use for quality control.

Other Quality Control Tools

In addition to the seven basic tools of quality, you can also use statistical sampling, inspection, and defect repair review to control quality.

In addition to the seven quality tools, the following tools can also be used for controlling quality:

- **Statistical sampling.** Statistical sampling involves randomly selecting a part of the population for study. In quality control, you can select a subset of features for inspection. This can save a substantial amount of resources.

- **Inspection.** This is a technique to examine whether an activity, component, product, service, or result conforms to specific requirements. Inspections can be conducted at various levels of project execution. For example, you can inspect the results of a single activity, or you can inspect the final product of the project. Nevertheless, inspection generally includes measurements. There are various forms of inspections, such as reviews, peer reviews, audits, and walkthroughs.

- **Defect repair review.** This review is conducted by the QC department or body to ensure that the defects are repaired to bring the defective product, service, or results in conformance with the specified requirements.

These tools can be used to make quality control measurements, which in turn can be used to recommend preventive and corrective actions: the output of quality control.

What Comes Out of Quality Control

The quality control measurements and the recommendations based on those measurements are the obvious output items of the quality control process. These and other output items are discussed in the following list.

Quality control measurements. These are the results of the QC activities and are fed back to the QA process. They are also used to make recommendations for corrective and preventive actions.

Recommended items. The quality control process can generate the following kinds of recommendations:

- **Recommended corrective actions.** These actions are recommended as a result of the QC process to meet the established quality goals.
- **Recommended preventive actions.** These actions are recommended as a result of the QC process to avoid future failure to meet the established quality goals.
- **Recommended defect repairs.** A defect is an imperfection or deficiency that keeps a component from meeting its requirements or specifications. Such a component needs to be repaired or replaced.

Validated items. These are the items that have been validated through the QC process:

- **Validated defect repairs and changes.** The implementation of approved changes and recommendations needs to be validated. For example, once a component has been repaired from a defect, it needs to be inspected so the repair will be accepted or rejected. The rejected items might need to be repaired again. The accepted repair is a validated defect repair.
- **Validated deliverables.** This refers to verifying the correctness of project deliverables. A deliverable accepted through a QC process is a validated deliverable.

> The quality control process can generate several kinds of recommendations, including recommended corrective actions, recommended preventive actions, recommended defect repairs, and requested changes.

Updates. The quality control process might generate updates to the following items:

- **Organizational process assets.** The completed checklists become part of the project record. Furthermore, you can update the lessons-learned database and documentation. These might include the causes of variances, the reasons for corrective and preventive actions, and the actions that worked and those that did not.
- **Project management plan.** The project management plan should be updated to reflect the changes to the quality management plan resulting from the QC process.
- **Quality baseline.** The quality baseline might need to be updated to reflect the changes to the quality plan resulting from the QC process.

High-quality projects deliver the promised product, service, or result within the planned cost, schedule, and scope. Therefore, it is necessary to monitor and control changes to these three parameters: cost, schedule, and scope.

Administering Procurements

Administering procurements is the process of monitoring and controlling the procurement part of the project. It's a three-pronged process:

1. Manage procurement-specific relationships.
2. Monitor the performance of the procurement part of the project.
3. Monitor and control the procurement-related changes.

Administering procurements has a two-pronged goal: the seller's performance should meet the procurement requirements, and the buyer should meet its agreed-upon contractual obligations. The project management processes that can be used for administering procurements include direct and manage project execution, perform quality control, perform integrated change control, report performance, and monitor and control risks. The tools and techniques used in administering procurements include contract change control system, payment system, claims administration, and inspections and audits.

Depending on the size and complexity of the project and the structure of the performing organization, procurement administration may be treated by a group outside of the project organization. But you will still need to integrate this function with the project and act as a communicator and coordinator to ensure that this function is performed smoothly, without adversely affecting the other aspects of the project.

Standardize This

The three standard processes to monitor and control project work, changes, and quality are illustrated in Figure 13.5, and the process to administer procurements is presented in Figure 13.6. All the items in these figures were discussed in this chapter.

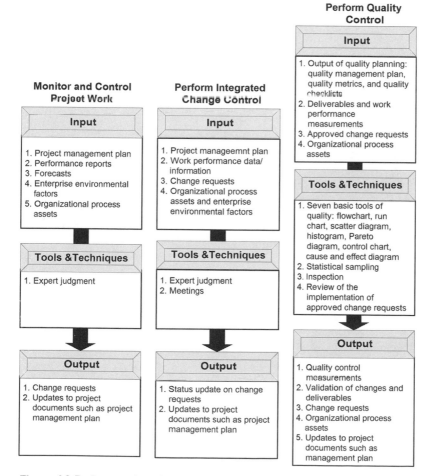

Figure 13.5 *Input, tools and techniques, and output for three processes: monitor and control project work, perform integrated change control, and perform quality control.*

Administer Procurements

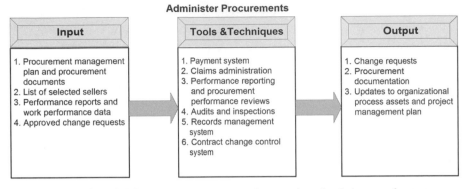

Input	Tools &Techniques	Output
1. Procurement management plan and procurement documents 2. List of selected sellers 3. Performance reports and work performance data 4. Approved change requests	1. Payment system 2. Claims administration 3. Performance reporting and procurement performance reviews 4. Audits and inspections 5. Records management system 6. Contract change control system	1. Change requests 2. Procurement documentation 3. Updates to organizational process assets and project management plan

Figure 13.6 *The administer procurements process: input, tools and techniques, and output.*

Quick Success Mantras

- You must monitor and control your project to keep it on the right track in order to lead it to success.

- At a given point in time, the path to success for your project is determined by the project management plan at that time. You work the way to success by executing that plan.

- All requested changes must be evaluated and processed, and only approved changes should be implemented. The project management plan must be modified to reflect the approved changes.

- Quality control is the process of monitoring and controlling specific project results to ensure the implementation of the quality plan and recommending changes or actions in case of poor implementation.

- Administering procurements is a high-level process that can be executed by performing multiple project management processes, such as quality control and integrated change control.

Chapter 14

Monitoring and Controlling the Golden Triangle

- Monitoring and Controlling the Golden Triangle: The Big Picture
- Controlling Schedule
- Controlling Scope
- Measuring Performance
- Standardize This
- Quick Success Mantras

Igh-quality projects deliver the promised product, service, or result within the planned budget, schedule, and scope. This is also a very important and basic criterion of success: Complete the project with complete scope, on schedule, and within budget. Cost and time are the underlying fundamental parameters that determine budget and schedule, respectively. So, the three fundamental parameters that we are talking about here are scope, time, and cost. You will see in this chapter that these three project parameters are intrinsically connected by a triangular relationship. Because the success of the project depends highly on how you manage this triangle, we call it the *golden triangle*.

So, the core issue in this chapter is how to monitor and control the golden triangle. In search of an answer, we will explore three avenues: control scope, control schedule, and control cost.

In this chapter you will:

- Understand the triangular relationship among scope, schedule, and cost
- Know how to monitor and control the project scope
- Understand how to monitor and control the project schedule
- Learn how to monitor and control the project cost
- Identify the standard processes for monitoring and controlling scope, schedule, and cost

Monitoring and Controlling the Golden Triangle: The Big Picture

If the scope, cost, or time of a project changes, at least one of the other two parameters must change as well.

The nutshell of running a project is delivering the scope according to some schedule, and it's going to cost someone. Completing a project successfully includes delivering the planned scope according to the planned schedule and within the planned budget. The fundamental parameters for budget and schedule are cost and time, respectively: Budget is the cost with a timeline, and schedule is determined from the time estimates for completing the schedule activities. So scope, time, and cost make the heart of any project. These three project parameters comprise a triple constraint that is a framework for evaluating competing demands. A triple constraint is often depicted as a triangle, with each side representing one of these three parameters. Figure 14.1 shows the triple constraint for the scope, time, and cost. This means if one of these parameters changes, at least one of the other two must change as well.

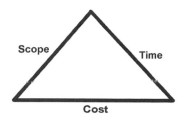

Figure 14.1
Triple constraint: scope, time, and cost. You cannot change one side of the triangle without changing at least one of the other two sides.

For example, assume you are being interviewed by a functional manager for a project manager position. Don't be surprised if you are asked a question based on the following situation:

1. The project is way behind the schedule.
2. No extra resources, such as money or project team members to perform activities, are available.
3. You have to implement all the planned features.

The question is, what will you do to meet the deadline that is approaching within a week? From a project management viewpoint, this situation is a good example of the triple constraint. The project is behind schedule, which means there is a schedule change (or a change in time available to finish the remaining project). Therefore, at least one of the other two parameters must change. If you want to meet the deadline, either you should be allotted more funds to hire more human resources, or the scope of the project should be changed, which means some of the features would be left out. Depending upon the knowledge level of the functional manager about project management, this answer might not get you the job, but as a project manager, you must stand your ground. Project management is not magic; it involves dealing with cold, hard reality in a realistic way, thereby establishing clear and achievable objectives.

The scope-time-cost constraint is also interchangeably called *scope-schedule-cost*, so don't be confused. While considering the scope-schedule-cost constraint, you should also remember the schedule compression techniques, such as crashing and fast tracking, discussed in Chapter 6. Also remember that those techniques do not guarantee that no additional cost (or resources) will be required.

You can see the relationship of the golden triangle (triple constraint) with quality by recalling that a high-quality project delivers the required product on time and within planned scope and budget. Therefore, while balancing between these three constraints, the quality (and as a result, customer satisfaction) might be affected. The triple constraint is also a good example of how one change can give rise to other changes across the project. This highlights the importance of monitoring and controlling changes.

Because scope, schedule, and cost are highly correlated, it's not a surprise that monitoring and controlling these three parameters share a common set of input and output items, as shown in Figure 14.2.

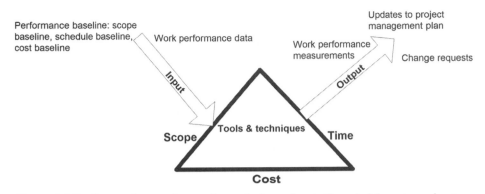

Figure 14.2 *Common input and output for monitoring and controlling schedule, scope, and cost.*

Controlling Schedule

Controlling schedule has a two-pronged goal—to ensure that the project is progressing on time as planned, and to monitor any changes to this progress. As a project manager, you should be out in front of the project, performing the following tasks on a regular basis:

- Determine the current status of the project schedule.
- Influence the factors that generate schedule changes.
- Determine whether the project schedule has changed—for example, if some activities are running late.
- Manage the changes as they occur.

You detect a schedule change by comparing the execution time against the time in the schedule baseline, which is a major input item into the schedule control process.

Input to Schedule Control

To control the project schedule, you need to know what the schedule baseline (that is, the expectation) is, how the project is performing from the perspective of the schedule, and what the plans are to monitor the schedule. Accordingly, the input items to the schedule control process are the following:

- **Project management plan.** The following two items in the project management plan are needed to control the schedule:
  - **The schedule management plan.** This plan specifies how to monitor and control the project at hand.
  - **Schedule baseline.** This is the approved version of the schedule, against which the schedule performance of the project will be measured.

- **Work performance information.** Work performance data related to the schedule should be looked at while controlling the schedule. Performance reports can also be useful because they provide information on the schedule performance of the project, such as missed and met planned dates.

- **Organizational process assets.** Organization process assets that can be helpful in controlling the schedule include cost- and budget-related organizational policies and procedures, schedule management tools, and schedule monitoring and reporting methods.

Tools and Techniques for Schedule Control

The schedule is monitored by measuring schedule performance and reporting progress and is controlled by using the change control or schedule change control system. These and other tools and techniques are discussed in this section.

Progress reporting. Progress reports and current schedule status are key items to monitor the schedule. They can include the finished activities, the percentage of in-progress activities that has been completed, and remaining durations for unfinished activities.

A schedule variance does not necessarily mean that a schedule change is required. For example, a delay on a schedule activity that is not on the critical path might not trigger any schedule change.

Schedule change control system. This is the system you use to receive, evaluate, and process schedule changes. It can include forms, procedures, approval committees, and tracking systems. It's part of the integrated change control system discussed in Chapter 13.

Performance measurement and analysis. The following tools and techniques can be used to measure and analyze the schedule performance of the project:

- **Performance measurement techniques.** These techniques are used to calculate the schedule variance and schedule performance index and are discussed in the "Measuring Performance" section later in this chapter. The schedule variance discussed there is in terms of cost, but you can also perform a barebones schedule variance analysis based on the start and end dates of the schedule activities.

- **Variance analysis.** Performing a barebones schedule variance analysis is crucial to schedule monitoring because it reveals the deviation of the actual start and finish dates from the planned start and finish dates of schedule activities. It might suggest corrective actions to be taken to keep the project on the track.

- **Schedule comparison bar charts.** Bar charts can be used to facilitate the schedule variance analysis. You can draw two bars corresponding to one schedule activity—one bar shows the actual progress, and the other bar shows the expected progress according to the baseline. This is a great tool to visually display where the schedule has progressed as planned and where it has slipped.

Project management software. You can use project management software for scheduling the project and for controlling the schedule—for example, to track planned start/finish dates versus actual dates for schedule activities. This software also enables you to predict the effects of project schedule changes. These are important pieces of information for monitoring and controlling the schedule.

Output of Schedule Control

Schedule performance measurements and recommendations for actions based on the measurements and progress reports are the important output items of the schedule control process.

Remember that corrective actions are not about going back and fixing past mistakes. Rather, they're about ensuring that future results match with the plan. You can do this by influencing the future results, such as expediting the execution, or by changing the plan.

Performance measurements. You use the work performance data and the project baselines to make the schedule performance measurements. The results from schedule performance measurements, such as the schedule variance (SV) and schedule performance index (SPI), should be documented and communicated to the stakeholders. These measurements might trigger recommendations for corrective actions and change requests.

Change requests. The schedule performance analysis and progress report review can result in requests for changes to the project schedule baseline. These changes must be processed through the integrated change control process for approval. As with any other change, you must think through whether a change to the schedule baseline has any other effect across the project. If it does, you might need to update the corresponding component of the project management plan accordingly.

The change requests might include recommendations for corrective actions. The goal of schedule-related corrective actions is to bring the future schedule performance in line with the schedule baseline—that is, the approved version of the planned schedule. To that end, you can take the following actions:

- Expedite the execution to ensure that schedule activities are completed on time or with minimal delay.
- Perform a root cause analysis to identify the causes of the schedule variance.
- Make plans to recover from the schedule delay.

Updates. The following updates can result from the schedule control process:

- **Schedule updates.** Schedule changes can happen at the activity level (the start/end date of an activity has changed) or at the project level (the start/end date of the project has changed). A schedule change at the project level is called a *schedule revision*. For example, when the schedule scope is expanded, the project end date might have to be changed to allow the extra work. All significant schedule changes must be reported to the stakeholders.
- **Activity updates.** The schedule changes and the project progress will cause changes in the activity list and in the list of activity attributes. These changes must be documented.
- **Project management plan updates.** The schedule management plan, a component of the project management plan, is updated to reflect the changes that occur during the schedule control process. The schedule updates may require an update to the schedule baseline. Any changes to resources and application of schedule compression techniques may require updates to scope and cost baselines.
- **Organizational process assets.** The lessons learned from the schedule control process can be documented to the historical database. Following are some examples:
  - The causes of schedule variance
  - The reasons for choosing the corrective actions that were taken
  - The effectiveness of the corrective actions
  Future projects can make use of this information.

The project schedule is there to execute the project work within the scope of the project. So, the project scope must be controlled as well.

Controlling Scope

Controlling the project scope includes influencing factors that create changes to the scope, as well as managing change requests and controlling their impact when the change actually occurs. While controlling the scope, you focus on the following tasks:

- Watching out for scope creep. Determine whether it has happened and correct the situation. Scope creep refers to scope changes applied without processing them though the change control process.

- Processing the scope change requests through the integrated change control process for approval.

- Managing the implementation of scope changes after approval, as well as their impact across the project.

TIP

In real life, scope creeps occur for various reasons. For example, perhaps a development engineer thought something was a cool feature to implement, or the customer spoke directly to the engineer to make a request for a minor additional feature, or maybe one of various other similar situations occurred. If a scope creep has gotten your project off track, you need to take corrective actions to get the project back on the track. You should also investigate how the scope creep happened and take steps to prevent it in the future—for example, by educating team members about the proper scope change process.

The obvious input items to the scope control process are the elements that define the scope, such as the project scope statement, the scope baseline, the WBS, the WBS dictionary, and a scope management plan that describes how to manage the scope. The performance reports might help to detect a scope change, and some change requests in other areas can result in scope change, as well.

The main output of the scope control process is the update to scope-related input elements, such as the project scope statement, the WBS, the WBS dictionary, and the scope baseline. The components of the project management plan affected by these changes might also need to be updated. Change requests and recommendations for corrective actions are other obvious output items from the scope control process.

The main tools used in the scope control process are the change control system and the project performance analysis, including the scope variance and the schedule variance. Schedule variance can have an effect on the scope if you want to finish the project on time and there are no additional resources available. The change control system of an organization is a collection of formal documented procedures that specify how the project deliverables and documents will be changed, controlled, and approved.

You monitor the project by watching its progress, which is a measure of its performance. Therefore, performance measurement and analysis are an important category of tools and techniques in monitoring and controlling the project.

Measuring Performance

Project performance is measured by comparing the work performance data from the project execution against the performance measurement baseline, which is an approved integrated plan for scope, schedule, and cost for the project, as explained here:

- **Cost baseline.** This is the planned budget for the project over a time period, used as a basis against which to measure, monitor, and control the cost performance of the project. The cost performance is measured by comparing the actual cost with the planned cost over a time period.

- **Schedule baseline.** This is a specific version of the project schedule developed from the schedule network analysis and the schedule model data, discussed in Chapter 6. This is the approved version of the schedule with a start date and an end date, and it is used as a basis against which the project schedule performance is measured.

- **Scope baseline.** This is the approved project scope that includes the approved project scope statement, the WBS based on the approved project scope statement, and the corresponding WBS dictionary.

The elaborate nature of the performance measurement analysis can be seen in the cost control process.

Performance Measurement Analysis for Cost Control

Cost control includes influencing the factors that can create changes to the cost baseline. But to detect the arising changes, you need to detect and understand variances from the cost baseline by monitoring cost performance.

In general, variance is a measurable deviation in the value of a project variable (or parameter), such as cost or schedule, from a known baseline or expected value. Variance analysis is a technique used to assess the magnitude of variation in the value of a variable, such as cost from the baseline or expected value, determine the cause of the variance, and decide whether a corrective action is required. A common technique to assess the cost variance is called the *earned value technique (EVT)*; in this technique, you calculate the cumulative value of the budgeted cost of work performed in terms of the originally allocated budgeted amount and compare it to the following:

1. Budgeted cost of work scheduled—that is, planned

2. Actual cost of work performed

Don't worry about it if these terms sound confusing right now; I will go through an example soon. However, as you will see, the greatest difficulty in understanding EVT stems from the coupling of cost and schedule. You must realize that the project cost and the project schedule are inherently related to each other. Schedule relates to performing certain work over a certain time period, whereas cost refers to the money spent to perform the work on a project (or a project activity) over a certain period of time. The relationship between cost and schedule can be realized by understanding that it costs money to perform a schedule activity. The "time is money" principle is at work here. For example, a project activity can be looked upon in terms of an amount of work that will be needed to complete it or in terms of its monetary value, which will include the cost of the work that needs to be performed to complete the activity.

The EVT involves calculating some variables where you will see the interplay of schedule (work) and cost. I will work through an example to help you understand the variables. Assume you are a project manager for the construction of a 16-mile road. Further assume that the work is uniformly distributed over 12 weeks. The total approved budget for this project is $600,000. At the end of first four weeks of work, $125,000 has been spent, and four miles of road have been completed.

I will use this example to perform the cost performance analysis and the schedule performance analysis in terms of cost.

Cost Performance

Cost performance refers to how efficiently you are spending money on the project work, measured against the expectations set in the project management plan—that is, the cost baselines. The total cost approved in the baseline is called the *budget at completion (BAC)*.

> The variables discussed in this section, such as BAC, EV, and AC, can be calculated either for the whole project or for a part of the project, such as a project activity.

Budget at completion (BAC). This is the total budget authorized for performing the project work (or a project activity), also called the *planned budget*. In other words, it is the cost originally estimated in the project management plan. You use this variable in defining almost all the following variables. In our example, the value of BAC is $600,000.

Earned value (EV) or budgeted cost of work performed (BCWP). This is the value of the actually performed work expressed in terms of the approved budget for a project or a project activity for a given time period. In this variable, you see the relationship of schedule (work) and cost in action. BAC represents the total value of the project. But when you perform some work on the project, you have earned some of that value, and the earned value is proportional to the fraction of the total work performed, as shown by the formula here:

$$EV = BAC \times (\text{work completed} / \text{total work required})$$

So, in our example, EV can be calculated as:

$$EV = \$600,000 \times (4 \text{ miles} / 16 \text{ miles}) = \$150,000$$

This is the earned value of the work, which may or may not be equal to the actual money that you spent to perform this work.

Actual cost (AC) or actual cost of work performed (ACWP). This is the total cost actually incurred until a specific point on the timescale in performing the work for a project. In our running example, $125,000 has already been used up to this point. So the actual cost at this point in time is $125,000. This cost is to be compared with the earned value to calculate the cost variance and cost performance.

Cost variance (CV). This is a measure of cost performance in terms of deviation of reality from the plan, and it is obtained by subtracting the actual cost (AC) from the earned value (EV), as shown in the formula here:

$$CV = EV - AC$$

So, in our example, CV can be calculated as shown here:

$$CV = \$150,000 - \$125,000 = \$25,000$$

The expected value of CV is zero because we expect the earned value to be equal to the actual cost. The positive result indicates better cost performance than expected, whereas a negative result indicates worse cost performance than expected. Deviation is one way of comparison, and ratio is another.

Variables that will help you determine cost performance include BAC (budget at completion), EV (earned value), AC (actual cost), CV (cost variance), and CPI (cost performance index).

Cost performance index (CPI). Earned value represents the portion of the work completed, and actual cost represents the money spent. So, the CPI indicates whether you are getting a fair value for your money. This is a measure of the cost efficiency of a project calculated by dividing earned value (EV) by the actual cost (AC), as shown in the formula here:

$$CPI = EV / AC$$

So, the CPI for our example can be calculated as:

$$CPI = \$150,000 / \$125,000 = 1.2$$

This means you are getting $1.20 worth of performance for every dollar spent. A value of CPI greater than one indicates good performance, whereas a value less than one indicates bad performance. The expected value of CPI is one.

So both the CV and the CPI indicate that you are getting more value for each dollar spent. Hold back a little before opening the champagne, though. If you read the text of our example again, note that four out of 12 weeks have already passed, and only four out of 16 miles of road have been built. That means that only one-fourth of the work has been accomplished in one-third of the total scheduled time. This means we are lagging behind in our schedule. Although cost performance is good, schedule performance needs to be investigated, too.

Schedule Performance in Terms of Cost

Schedule performance refers to how efficiently you are executing your project schedule as measured against the expectations set in the project management plan. It can be measured by comparing the earned value to the planned value, just like cost performance is measured by comparing the earned value to the actual cost. Planned value refers to the value that we planned to create in the time spent so far.

Planned value (PV) or budgeted cost for the work scheduled (BCWS). This is the authorized cost for the scheduled work on the project or a project activity up to a given point on the timescale. The planned value is also called the *budgeted cost for the work scheduled (BCWS)*. PV is basically how much you were authorized to spend in the fraction of schedule time spent so far, as shown in the formula here:

$$PV = BAC \times (\text{time passed} / \text{total schedule time})$$

Therefore, the planned value for the project in our example at the end of the first four weeks is calculated as shown here:

$$PV = \$600,000 \times (4 \text{ weeks} / 12 \text{ weeks}) = \$200,000$$

So, PV represents the planned schedule in terms of cost. You can calculate the schedule performance by comparing the planned schedule to the performed schedule in terms of cost.

Schedule variance (SV). This is the deviation of the performed schedule from the planned schedule in terms of cost. No confusion is allowed here because you already know that the schedule can be translated to cost. SV is calculated as the difference between EV and PV, as shown in the formula here:

$$SV = EV - PV$$

So, the SV in our example can be calculated as:

$$SV = \$150,000 - \$200,000 = -\$50,000$$

The negative value means we are behind schedule. Deviation represented by schedule variance is one way of comparison, and ratio represented by schedule performance index is another.

Schedule performance index (SPI). Earned value represents the portion of work completed in terms of cost, and planned value represents how much work was planned by this point in time in terms of cost. So, the SPI indicates how the performed work compared to the planned work. This is a measure of the schedule efficiency of a project calculated by dividing earned value (EV) by planned value (PV), as shown in the formula here:

$$SPI = EV / PV$$

So, the SPI for our example can be calculated as shown here:

$$SPI = \$150,000 / \$200,000 = 0.75$$

This indicates that the project is progressing at 75% of the planned pace—not good.

You should note that all these performance variables except the BAC are calculated at a given point in time. The value of the BAC does not change with time because it is the cost at completion time. Further note that given the BAC, the PV can be calculated at any point in time, even before the project execution starts. EV and EC are accumulated as the project execution continues.

By using the variables discussed so far, you can monitor the project performance as time progresses. Not only that, you can also make predictions about future performance based on the past performance.

Forecasting Techniques

Forecasting refers to predicting some information about the project in the future based on the performance in the past. The forecasting is regularly updated as the project progresses and more data of the past performance becomes available.

Estimate to complete (ETC). This is the prediction about the expected cost to complete the remaining work for the project or for a project activity. This is basically how much value remains to be earned in terms of the BAC. Therefore, the value of the ETC is obtained by subtracting the earned value (EV) from the budget at completion (BAC), as shown in the formula here:

$$ETC = BAC - EV$$

So, in our example, the value of ETC can be calculated as:

$$ETC = \$600,000 - \$150,000 = \$450,000$$

The next question that can be asked about the future is how much it will cost to complete the whole project.

Estimate at completion (EAC). This is the estimate made at the current point in time for how much it will cost to complete the project or a project activity. The value of the EAC is obtained by adding the value of ETC to AC, as shown in the formula here:

EAC = ETC + AC

Accordingly, the value of EAC for our example can be calculated as:

EAC = $450,000 + $125,000 = $575,000

Another useful prediction to be made is how much performance you need in the future to complete the remaining work within budget.

To complete performance index (TCPI). This is the variable to predict the future performance needed to finish the work within budget. It is calculated as the ratio of the remaining work to the remaining budget, as shown in the formula here:

TCPI = Remaining work / Remaining funds = (BAC − BCWP) / (BAC − ACWP) = (BAC − EV) / (BAC − AC)

Therefore, the value of TCPI in our example can be calculated as:

TCPI = ($600,000 − $150,000) / ($600,000 − $125,000) = 450,000 / 475,000 = 0.95 = 95%.

Table 14.1 summarizes all these performance variables.

The variables used in forecasting include ETC (estimate to complete), EAC (estimate at completion), and TCPI (to complete performance index).

Table 14.1 Performance Variables Used in the Earned Value Technique Analysis

Variable	Abbreviation	Description	Formula
Budget at completion	BAC	Total planned cost.	None
Earned value or budgeted cost of work performed	EV or BCWP	Fraction of the completed work in terms of the planned budget at a given point in time.	EV = BAC × (work completed % total work required)
Actual cost	AC or ACWP	The money spent on the work until a given point in time.	The sum of all the costs until a given point in time.

Table 14.1 (Continued)

Variable	Abbreviation	Description	Formula
Cost variance	CV	The difference between what you planned to spend and what is actually spent until a given point in time.	CV = EV − AC
Cost performance index	CPI	The work performed per actual cost.	CPI = EV % AC
Planned value or budgeted cost of work scheduled	PV or BCWS	The fraction of work planned to be completed at a given point in time.	PV = BAC × (time passed % total schedule time)
Schedule variance	SV	The difference between work actually completed and the work planned to be completed at a given point in time.	SV = EV − PV
Schedule performance index	SPI	The actual work performed per planned work performed in terms of cost.	SPI = EV % PV
Estimate to complete	ETC	Estimate of what will be spent on the remaining project (or a project activity) based on the performance so far and the planned cost.	ETC = BAC − EV
Estimate at completion	EAC	Estimate of what will be spent on the whole project (or a project activity) based on the performance so far and the planned cost.	EAC = ETC + AC
To complete performance index	TCPI	Calculates the efficiency: remaining work per remaining funds.	(BAC − EV) % (BAC − AC)

Standardize This

Figure 14.3 illustrates the three standard processes to monitor and control project scope, schedule, and cost. All the items in these figures were discussed in this chapter.

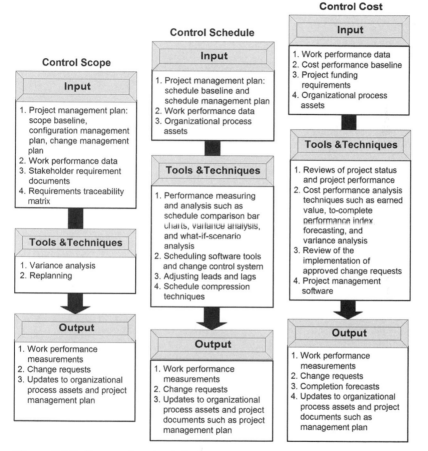

Figure 14.3 *Input, tools and techniques, and output for three processes: control scope, control schedule, and control cost.*

Quick Success Mantras

- The golden triangle in project management refers to the triple constraint among scope, schedule, and cost.
- Triple constraint means that if any of the three items—that is, scope, schedule, or cost—changes, at least one of the other two items must change as well.

- Performance baselines and work performance data are the common inputs to monitoring and controlling the golden triangle, and work performance measurements and change requests are the common output.
- Project performance is measured by comparing the work performance data from the project execution against the performance measurement baseline: scope baseline, schedule baseline, and cost baseline.

Chapter 15

Monitoring and Controlling Reporting and Risks

- Performance Reporting and Risk Controlling: Big Picture
- Performance Reporting
- Monitoring and Controlling Risks
- Standardize This
- Quick Success Mantras

At any given point in time, the project is in a certain state called the *project status*, and the difference between two states in time is called the *project progress*. Your success as a project manager is directly proportional to successfully communicating the project performance, including the project status and the progress to the right stakeholders at the right time by using the right methods. It is not a matter of chance that I used the words *communicating* and *performance* in the same sentence; they are intimately connected and highly correlated concepts in project management. Communicating performance to the right stakeholders at the right time by using the right methods is called *performance reporting*, or *reporting* for brevity. Effective reporting is the oxygen for a project. Among many other benefits, reporting helps you control project risks—the enemies within.

So, the core question in this chapter is how to use reporting and risk control to keep the project on the right track. In search of an answer, we will explore three avenues: reporting performance, controlling risks, and using standard processes for reporting performance and controlling risks.

In this chapter, you'll:

- Understand performance reporting and risk controlling in the context of other project management processes
- Know what's involved in performance reporting
- Understand how to control risks
- Identify the standards process for reporting performance and controlling risks

Performance Reporting and Risk Controlling: Big Picture

Figure 15.1 puts performance reporting and risk controlling in context of the other project management processes. Directing and managing project execution generates work performance data, which is the raw data for making work performance measurements in the process of controlling scope, schedule, and cost. These work performance measurements are used in preparing reports during the report performance process, which in turn are used in controlling risks and in some other processes, such as administering procurements and distributing information.

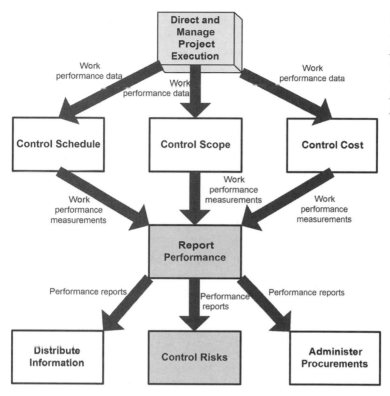

Figure 15.1
*Reporting
performance and
controlling risks in
the context of other
project management
processes.*

Performance Reporting

While you are directing and managing the project execution, the work results and the progress toward creating the project results are generated. Just producing the results is no guarantee of success. The success is determined by the performance with which the results are being produced. You need to know the performance to keep the project on the right track. Furthermore, the stakeholders need to know with what rate, efficiency, and work quality the resources are being used to deliver the project output. For this, you need to collect the project performance data and use this data to make performance measurements while controlling the scope, schedule, and cost. You use these data and performance measurements to prepare performance reports, which in turn are used for distributing information and controlling risks.

Ongoing project success is determined by the performance with which results are produced.

Performance reporting is the process of collecting performance information, putting it into the distribution format, and distributing it. Performance reporting, for brevity, is also called *reporting*, and it is focused on the following components:

- **Project status.** The current state of the project.
- **Project progress.** The progress made with some previous state as a reference.
- **Forecast.** The prediction of the progress in the future based on the progress in the past.

> **TIP**
> Do not confuse the report performance process with the distribute information process discussed in Chapter 12, even though you must recognize the overlap. Distributing information means distributing all the relevant information, whereas performance reporting focuses on the performance part of the information. You can use the information distribution system to report performance.

What Goes into Performance Reporting

As input to the performance reporting process, you need performance measurements, work performance data, the project management plan, and organizational process assets.

The core of performance reporting is using the performance measurements to prepare performance reports. To serve this core, following are the items you need as input to the performance reporting process:

Performance measurements. These measurements are mostly made in other monitoring and controlling processes, such as control scope, control schedule, and control cost. However, you may need to make some measurements during the performance reporting process.

Work performance data. To make performance measurements and to put them in the right perspective, you need the work performance data you collected during monitoring and controlling project execution.

Project management plan. This plan has project baselines, such as the scope baseline, schedule baseline, and cost baseline. The work performance data is compared to these baselines to make performance measurements.

Organizational process assets. The organizational process assets that may be handy in preparing the performance reports include report templates, measurement guidelines, and variance limits accepted in the organization.

SUCCESS SHOT

Performance reporting is a rare display of the intimacy of science and art. Realizing that measuring performance is an act of science, whereas reporting performance is an art, can improve your effectiveness in measuring and reporting performance.

Tools and Techniques for Performance Reporting

Tools and techniques used in performance reporting include communication methods, variance analysis, forecasting techniques, and reporting systems. Communication methods were discussed in Chapters 8 and 12, and variance analysis was discussed in Chapter 14. Forecasting techniques include the following:

- **Earned value forecasting techniques.** Forecasting techniques based on earned value analysis were discussed in Chapter 14.

- **Extrapolation techniques.** Extrapolation is a scientific method to predict future results based on past data. It makes use of concepts such as trend, growth, and decay. These techniques are also called *time series methods.*

- **Causal methods.** These techniques are based on predicting the behavior of a variable by identifying the underlying causes of that behavior. Regression analysis is an example of such a method.

- **Judgment techniques.** These techniques use intuitive judgment in making predictions and can also use other methods, such as analogy and the Delphi technique.

A reporting system is used to collect, store, maintain, and distribute information. Modern reporting systems often include software tools. There can be specialized reporting systems to support performance reporting, including the following:

- **Cost reporting system.** This system can store and report the cost expended on the project and on its different activities and aspects.

- **Time reporting system.** This system can store and report how much time has been expended on the project and on its different activities and aspects.

These tools and techniques can be used to generate the output of performance reporting.

What Comes Out of Performance Reporting

Performance reports are an obvious output of performance reporting. This and other output items are discussed in the following list.

Performance reports may contain a summary of work performance information, the current status of the project, and the project progress.

Project performance reports. Performance reports present the relevant information from the work performance data and the performance measurements in a suitable format. The relevancy and the suitability depend on the audience, the stakeholders that are the consumers of these reports. The report format may include presentation elements, such as tables, bar charts, and histograms, in order to make the information easy to understand. The performance reports can contain the following:

Performance reporting yields project performance reports, forecasts, change requests, and updates to organizational process assets.

- **Summary of work performance information.** These are the results from the comparison of the actual work results to the planned performance—that is, the performance baseline.
- **The current status.** This is the current state in which the project is right now.
- **The progress.** Progress made from some reference point in the past. The status refers to where things are right now, and the progress refers to what has been accomplished since a previous status.

Forecasts. Performance reporting includes making forecasts based on past performance. These forecasts include estimates, such as what will be the total cost incurred at the project completion—called *estimate at completion (EAC)*—and how much cost will be incurred to complete the remaining project—called *estimate to complete (ETC)*. These forecasts can be updated as more performance information comes in.

Change requests. Measuring and communicating performance may generate change requests, which must be processed through integrated change control before implementation. For example, performance reporting may expose that certain aspects of the project are not on the right track or the project is not performing as expected by the stakeholders. The forecasting may expose danger ahead. All this can generate recommendations for corrective and preventive actions.

Updates to organizational process assets. During performance reporting, there will be lots of revelations by performance measurements and feedback from the stakeholders. This will result in updating the organizational process assets, such as lessons learned.

Performance reports generated during performance reporting are an important input to the process of monitoring and controlling risks.

Monitoring and Controlling Risks

The project management plan contains the list of risks you identified during risk planning and the responses you will execute if the risks occur. You must actively monitor the identified risks and identify and respond to the new risks as they appear. Risk monitoring and controlling includes the following:

- Tracking identified risks
- Monitoring residual risks—the risks that remain after risk responses have been implemented
- Identifying new risks and preparing responses for them
- Executing the risk plan and evaluating its effectiveness

To monitor and control risks, you must have a list of identified risks, a plan to deal with the risks, and the signs of risk occurrence. You also need work performance data and performance reports to determine the changing status of existing risks and to identify new risks. Accordingly, the input items to risk monitoring and controlling are the risk management plan, the risk register, work performance data, and performance reports.

Tools and Techniques for Risk Monitoring and Controlling

There are some tools and techniques available to detect risk triggers, to respond effectively to risks that have occurred, and to identify new risks.

Risk audits. A risk audit is conducted to examine the following:

- Root causes of the identified risks
- Effectiveness of responses to the identified risks
- Effectiveness of the risk management processes

Risk reassessment. The risks should be continually reassessed as the project progresses. For example, a risk on the watch list may become important enough that you need to prepare a response plan for it.

Tools and techniques for risk monitoring and controlling include risk audits, risk reassessment, risk analyses, technical performance measurements, and status meetings.

Risk analyses. Risk analyses are necessary to effectively respond to risks that have occurred, to detect risk triggers, and to identify new risks. The following two kinds of analyses are appropriate for risk monitoring:

- **Variance and trend analysis.** Trends in the project performance should be reviewed on a regular basis as the project execution progresses. These trends can be determined by analyzing the performance data based on various performance control techniques, such as variance and earned value analysis, discussed earlier in this chapter. This analysis can help in detecting new risks.

- **Reserve analysis.** Recall that the contingency reserve is the amount of funds or time (in schedule) in addition to the planned budget reserved to keep the impact of risks at an acceptable level when the project is executing. The risks occurring during the project execution may have positive or negative effects on the contingency reserve. You perform the reserve analysis at a given time to compare the remaining reserve amount to the remaining risk to determine whether the remaining reserve amount is adequate.

Technical performance measurements. Technical performance measurements compare actual versus planned parameters related to the overall technical progress of the project. The deviation determines the degree to which system requirements are met in terms of performance, cost, schedule, and progress in implementing risk handling. The parameters chosen to measure technical performance could be any parameters that represent something important related to the project objectives and requirements: Software performance, human resource performance, and system test performance are some examples.

Status meetings. You should always put risk management as an agenda item at project status meetings. The time spent on this item will depend on the number of identified risks, their priorities, and the complexity of the responses planned for them. Nevertheless, keeping risks on your agenda and discussing them with the team on regular basis helps make risk management smoother and more effective.

These tools and techniques are used to monitor the risks that may generate recommendations for actions, which are parts of the output of the risk monitoring and controlling process.

Output from Risk Monitoring and Controlling

The output of monitoring risks includes recommendations for actions and requests for changes to control the risks. These and other output items are discussed in this list.

> The output from risk monitoring and controlling includes recommendations for preventive and corrective actions; requests for changes to control the risks; and updates to the risk register, project management plan, and/or organizational process assets.

Updates. The risk monitoring and controlling process may require updates to the following items:

- **Risk register.** You may need to include the following updates to the risk register:
  - Outcome of the risk reassessments, reviews, and audits
  - Outcome of risks and responses to risks
- **Project management plan.** The project management plan may need to be updated as a result of risk monitoring and controlling. For example, the change requests may change the risk management processes, which in turn will change the project management plan.
- **Organizational process assets**. As a result of the risk monitoring and controlling process, some organizational process assets may need to be updated, such as templates for the project management plan, the historical information database (such as actual costs and durations of project activities), the lessons-learned knowledge database, and checklists.

Change requests. There are two kinds of actions that can be recommended as a result of risk monitoring: corrective actions and preventive actions. Corrective actions include contingency plans and workaround plans. A workaround is a response to a negative risk that has occurred. It is based on a quick solution and is not planned in advance of the risk occurrence event. Preventive actions are recommended to bring the project into compliance with the project management plan. Recommended corrective and preventive actions are input to the integrated change control process.

You may need to make some change requests as a result of risk monitoring and controlling. For example, the recommended actions, such as contingency plans and workarounds, may result in requirements to change some elements of the project management plan to respond to certain risks. Of course, the change requests will need to go through the integrated change control process for approval, and the approved change requests will become the input to the direct and manage project execution process for implementation.

Standardize This

Figure 15.2 illustrates the two standard processes for performance reporting and monitoring and controlling risks. All the items in this figure were discussed in this chapter.

Figure 15.2

Input, tools and techniques, and output for two processes: report performance and monitor and control risks.

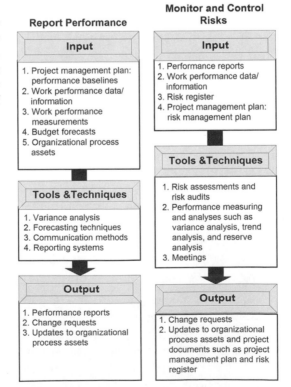

Report Performance

Input
1. Project management plan: performance baselines
2. Work performance data/information
3. Work performance measurements
4. Budget forecasts
5. Organizational process assets

Tools &Techniques
1. Variance analysis
2. Forecasting techniques
3. Communication methods
4. Reporting systems

Output
1. Performance reports
2. Change requests
3. Updates to organizational process assets

Monitor and Control Risks

Input
1. Performance reports
2. Work performance data/information
3. Risk register
4. Project management plan: risk management plan

Tools &Techniques
1. Risk assessments and risk audits
2. Performance measuring and analyses such as variance analysis, trend analysis, and reserve analysis
3. Meetings

Output
1. Change requests
2. Updates to organizational process assets and project documents such as project management plan and risk register

Quick Success Mantras

- Performance, reporting, and risk controlling are highly correlated concepts.

- Performance reporting requires the science of measuring performance and the art of reporting those measurements.

- Work performance measurements made during monitoring and controlling scope, schedule, and cost are the raw data for performance reporting.

- The core of performance reporting is to prepare and distribute the performance reports to the right stakeholders at the right time by using the right methods and formats.

- Performance reports can be used to determine the changing status of existing risks and to identify new risks.

PART V

Finishing the Project

To most of us it may be common sense that every start has a finish. A project that has been started will have a finish. As we discussed in Chapter 1, people have been doing projects even when there was no field of project management. The underlying philosophy of project management is to perform projects deliberately—that is, to plan them and monitor and control them. Finishing a project deliberately means finishing it in a controlled way—not just letting it finish—even when it's cancelled.

There are three main elements of a successful project closure: verification of the project deliverables by the project team, verification and acceptance of the deliverables that were procured, and acceptance of project deliverables by the appropriate party, such as the customer or the sponsor.

Chapter 16

Closing the Project: Reaching the Finish Line

- Closing the Project: Big Picture
- Verifying the Scope of Project Deliverables
- Performing Project Closure
- Performing Procurement Closure
- The Finishing Touch
- Standardize This
- Quick Success Mantras

Completing the project work and producing the planned output does not complete the project. You need to formally close the project. This involves finalizing all the project and project management activities and giving them a proper closure. You should do this even when the project is being terminated before the planned finish line.

First, you need to verify that the project deliverables produced in house by the project team meet the scope—in other words, what was planned to be done has actually been done. The project deliverables that were procured must also be verified before they go for the customer acceptance. After all the planned deliverables have been verified, the project should be closed with the acceptance of the deliverables by the appropriate person or group and by archiving the appropriate documents.

So the core issue in this chapter is how to properly close a project. In search of an answer, we will explore three avenues: verifying the scope of project deliverables, closing procurements, and closing the project.

In this chapter, you'll learn:

- Why you should learn project management
- Project management in terms of timely implementation of knowledge

Closing the Project: Big Picture

Completed projects have met their completion criteria; terminated projects were terminated before their completion for any of various reasons.

Project closure refers to a set of tasks that are required to formally end the project. There are two kinds of projects that you need to close formally:

- **Completed projects.** A project that has met its completion criteria falls into this category.
- **Terminated projects.** A project that was terminated before its completion falls into this category. A project can be terminated at various stages for various reasons. Following are some examples:
  - The project management plan is not approved for whatever reason.
  - The project has been executing, but you have run out of resources, and no more resources are available.

- The project has been cancelled because it was going nowhere.
- The project has been indefinitely postponed because there is not a large enough market for the product it would produce.

> The processes of the closing process group can be used to close a project, as well as to close a phase of a project.

A project, in general, may have in-house activities—that is, project activities being performed within the performing organization—and procurement activities. Accordingly, there are two aspects of project closure:

- Close the in-house activities of the project.
- Close the procurement part of the project.

Project closure includes the following activities:

- Activities to verify that all deliverables have been provided and accepted.
- Activities to confirm that all the project requirements, including stakeholder requirements, have been met.
- Activities to verify that the completion or exit criteria have been met.
- Activities to ensure that the project product is transferred to the right individual or group.
- Activities to review the project for lessons learned and to archive the project records.

Figure 16.1 presents the big picture of project closure in a nutshell:

1. Verify the scope of the project deliverables developed in house.
2. Accept the procured deliverables through the procurement closure process.
3. Get the deliverables from Steps 1 and 2 and get them accepted by the customer or sponsor to actually close the project.
4. Archive the project documents.

In the following sections, we will discuss details of these steps.

Figure 16.1
Closing a project: big picture.

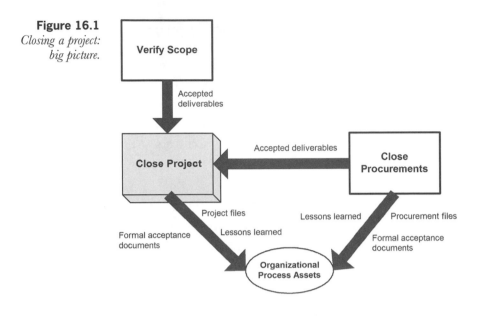

Verifying the Scope of Project Deliverables

You should perform the scope verification process even if the project is terminated—that is, ended before completion. In that case you would verify and document the level and extent of the project and product scope that was completed.

Depending on the organization, the scope verification activity might be called an audit, inspection, product review, or walkthrough.

Before you hand over the project deliverables to the appropriate party mentioned in the project management plan, such as the customer or the sponsor, you need to verify that these deliverables actually meet the planned scope. So, verifying the scope of the project deliverables includes reviewing deliverables to ensure that all of them are completed as planned and therefore as expected.

To verify the scope of deliverables, you need to pull out the project management plan and look at the sections related to the planned scope: project scope statement, WBS, and WBS dictionary. The project scope statement includes the list of deliverables, the product scope description, and the product acceptance criteria. You'll find more scope-related details in the WBS, which defines the decomposition of each deliverable into work packages. You'll find further details, such as descriptions of each WBS component, the related statement of work, and technical requirements, in the WBS dictionary.

The product requirements should be considered part of the scope and can be found in two documents: the stakeholder requirements document and the requirement traceability matrix that you prepared in the process of collecting requirements during the planning stage of the project. Finally, before you go through the process of scope verification, you should get all the deliverables validated through the quality control process.

The actual scope verification activity has different names in different organizations, such as audit, inspection, product review, and walkthrough. The output of this activity is documentation of two kinds:

- A document discussing which deliverables have been accepted—that is, verified.

- A document discussing those deliverables that have not passed verification and therefore are not accepted. Also, the document may describe the reasons why they failed the verification.

The scope verification process may also give rise to change requests, such as requests for defect repairs.

SUCCESS SHOT

Do not confuse scope verification with quality control. Quality control is primarily focused on checking the correctness of the deliverables and other quality requirements, whereas scope verification is primarily concerned with the overall acceptance of the project deliverables. Quality control is usually performed before scope verification, but they can be performed simultaneously.

The project deliverables that have been accepted through the scope verification process still need to go through final acceptance by the appropriate party, such as the customer or the sponsor.

Performing Project Closure

Closing the project means finalizing all activities across the project. You also need to determine and coordinate the procedures required for verifying and documenting the project deliverables. The items that describe what the project planned to deliver and what it has delivered would be the obvious inputs to the process of closing the project.

Input to the Close Project Process

You need a list of project deliverables that will go through the acceptance procedure. The project management plan contains guidelines on how to close the project. These and other input items are discussed in the following list:

- **Project management plan.** This defines how to close this project and will be useful in establishing the project closure procedure. The project management plan is also used in verifying and accepting the project deliverables because it explains what deliverables are expected.

- **Accepted deliverables.** These are the deliverables that have been verified through the scope verification process. That means these deliverables meet the scope requirements. It includes the deliverables from procurements that have been accepted through the procurement closure process.

- **Organizational process assets.** These can include project closure guidelines or requirements—for example, product validation and acceptance criteria, final project audits, and project evaluations. Also, you can learn from the historical information what kind of project documents you need to archive and in what detail you want to review the project to gather and store lessons learned.

These input items provide information about what the project was supposed to deliver and what it has delivered. You use this input and some tools and techniques to carry on the project closure.

For example, you can use the expert judgment in the various aspects of project closure, such as developing the closure procedures and ensuring that the closure procedures are performed, to meet the appropriate standards. You can also use the project management information system to perform closure activities, such as archiving the project documents.

You use these tools to carry on the project closure.

Output of the Close Project Process

The project closure accomplishes three main elements—completion of all the closing procedures; final acceptance of the project deliverables by the customer, including handing over the deliverables to the appropriate party; and archival of project-related documents. These elements are described in the following subsections.

Completing Closure Procedures

These procedures specify the step-by-step methodology for the administrative closure of the project, which includes specifying all the necessary activities, roles, and responsibilities of the project team members who will participate in the closure process. The activities defined by this procedure include the following:

- Activities to define the requirements for getting approval from the stakeholders, such as customers and the sponsor, on the project deliverables and the approved changes that were supposed to be implemented.

- Activities that are necessary to satisfy the project completion or exit criteria.

- Activities related to the project completion, such as:

  - Confirm that the project has met all requirements.

  - Verify that all deliverables have been provided and accepted.

  - Verify that the completion or exit criteria have been met.

Activities related to project completion include confirming that the project has met all requirements and verifying that all deliverables have been provided and accepted and that the completion/exit criteria have been met.

Formal Acceptance for the Final Product

This includes handing over the final product to the customer and getting formal acceptance for it—for example, in the form of a receipt that contains a formal statement to the effect that the requirements of the project have been met, including the terms of the contracts.

Updates to Organizational Process Assets

The closure process will add the following documents to the organizational process assets:

- **Acceptance documentation.** This is the documentation that proves that the fulfillment of the project requirements have been confirmed, completion of the project has been verified, and the product has been formally accepted by the customer. In the case of a project termination, of course, the documentation should show that the exit criteria have been met.

- **Project closure documentation.** In addition to the acceptance documentation, you should also archive the other project closure documents, such as the closure procedure and the handing-over of project deliverables to an operation group.

The closure process adds to the organizational process assets acceptance documentation, project closure documentation, project files archives, and updates to the lessons-learned database.

If the project was terminated, then the formal documentation indicating why the project was terminated should be included in the archive.

- **Project files archive.** This includes the documents from the project's lifecycle, such as the project management plan, risk registers, planned risk responses, and baselines for cost, schedule, scope, and quality.

- **Lessons-learned database.** The documentation on lessons learned should be saved in the organization's knowledge database so that future projects can benefit from it.

The deliverables that are processed through the project closure include the deliverables from the procurements that are accepted through the procurement closure process. Therefore, in order to complete the project closure, you need to perform the procurement closure.

Performing Procurement Closure

A project might include work that was procured. Performing procurement closure means completing each procurement and giving it a proper closure. Project closure is not complete without procurement closure.

All the procurement contracts are closed at the end of a project or a phase by using the contract closure procedure. Procurement closure accomplishes the following two major goals:

- Close all the contracts applicable to the project.
- Receive verification (if you are a seller) or issue verification (if you are a buyer) that all the procured deliverables were received and accepted. In this respect, the contract closure process supports the administrative closure of the project.

If the project terminates without completion, you still need to go through the contract closure procedure if there is a contract. Usually a contract contains a contract termination clause, which contains the terms of the project termination, including the rights and responsibilities of the parties in case of the project's early termination.

Input to Closing Procurements

The input items to the contract closure process are what you need to close the contract. They are discussed in the following list:

- **Procurement management plan.** This is needed to check whether the procurement requirements are met; it might have some procedures that you need to follow during closure.

- **Procurement documentation.** You need all the procurement documentation at this time for two purposes: You want to close the procurements according to the requirements in the procurement documents, and you want to archive the documentation.

The procurement management plan may contain a contract closure procedure developed to formally close all contracts associated with the project. It specifies a step-by-step methodology to execute activities needed to close the contracts. The roles and responsibilities of the team members who will be involved in the closure process are also specified.

You implement the contract closure procedure by using the available tools and techniques, discussed in the next section.

> A procedure and a process are not the same thing. For example, the administrative closure procedure and the contract closure procedure are two of several output items of the close project process.

Tools and Techniques for Closing Procurements

The tools and techniques for the contract closure process are the items you need to facilitate the contract closure. They are discussed in the following list.

Procurement audits. This is a structured review of the procurement process with the purpose of identifying successes and failures from the planning through the executing stages of the project. The lessons learned from the audit can be applied to other phases of the same project (if it is a phase closeout) or to other projects within the same performing organization.

Settlement negotiations. Negotiations are a tool, technique, and skill that become very useful during the procurement closure process. Negotiations are used to give a proper closure through settlements to all outstanding claims, issues, and disputes. If direct negotiations fail, you should explore the option of some kind of mediation or arbitration. Obviously, the legal department of your organization should be involved here.

> To facilitate contract closure, you need procurement audits, settlement negotiations, and the records management system.

Records management system. This is a part of the project management information system and can be used to manage contract documentation and records. For example, you can use this system to archive documents, maintain an index of contract and communication documents, and retrieve documents.

Output of Closing Procurements

The obvious output of closing procurements is the closed procurements. This and other output items are discussed here.

Closed procurements. A closed procurement means the procured work is completed with all its requirements and is accepted. Generally, it is accomplished by a formal notice from the buyer to the seller, which might come, for example, through the buyer's authorized administrator. The requirements for the formal contract closure are usually defined in the terms of the contract and are included in the procurement management plan.

Updates to organizational process assets. The following items should be added to the organizational process assets:

- **Procurement documentation.** This includes all the procurement documents, including the procurement management plan, closed contracts, and the procurement closure notice.

- **Acceptance notice.** This notice formally acknowledges the acceptance of deliverables through a notice from the buyer to the seller, notifying that the procurement deliverables have been accepted. This is an important document and should be preserved.

- **Lessons learned.** The procurement experience for this project should be analyzed, and the lessons learned should be gathered, recorded, and archived so that the future projects can benefit from them.

Some important elements that are usually part of the details of a project closure are discussed in more detail in the next section.

The Finishing Touch

Reviewing the project, releasing the project resources, and turning over the project deliverables to another group are the elements of the administrative closure that need to be explored further.

Reviewing the Project

Part of project closure is analyzing project success or failure. You can accomplish this by collecting and generating the project evaluation information, such as what went well and what did not. Some of this information already exists in the work performance reports. However, you can gather the final information in various ways, such as a post-project review meeting with the team or a questionnaire. The most important output (and the whole purpose) of the review are the lessons learned. The review should be comprehensive and should cover the following:

The purpose of the post-project review, also called the *post-project assessment*, is to learn lessons that can be applied to future projects to run them more effectively. Do not let the review turn into a finger-pointing show.

- Both the technical and nontechnical components

- Both positive and negative aspects—that is, the things that went well and the things that did not go well

- All stages and phases of the project

As part of the project review, you should also measure customer satisfaction from the customer feedback collected by using techniques such as interviews and surveys. This will help the organization establish and maintain a long-term relationship with the customer.

The findings of the review should be recorded in a document that might have different names in different organizations, such as the *post-project review report* or the *project assessment report*. Your organization might even have a template or standard for such a report. Depending upon the size of the project, the review report might be a part of the project closure report or a separate report. The report will be distributed among the stakeholders and will be added to the project archive. The project closure report can also include the final project performance as compared to the baselines, as well as a description of the final project product.

Releasing the Resources

For the effective and efficient use of the organization's resources, it is imperative that they be released in an efficient and proper manner. The release procedure might be included in the resource planning—for example, the staff management plan should address the issue of releasing the human resources. Well-planned release or transfer of team members reflects managerial professionalism, which requires that employees be treated with respect and dignity. By ensuring a well-planned release and a smooth transition to other projects, you are helping the employees focus wholeheartedly on the project toward the very end, rather than worrying about the next assignment. This will obviously improve the productivity of the team members and the efficiency of the project. Following are some suggestions to consider for properly releasing human resources:

- Although it is possible that different team members will be released at different times, at the project closure you should organize some closure event to honor and thank the project team members, including the contractors, for their contributions. However, you must check your company policy regarding including the contractors in company-sponsored events and giving them rewards.

- Plan ahead, and do not wait until the last minute. Communicate with the functional manager ahead of time about when a staff member is going to be released.

- Work closely with your organization's human resources department, which might have some guidelines or a procedure that you need to follow.

- Write (or offer to write) recommendation letters for team members who have made outstanding contributions to the project.

Once all the closure tasks are completed and the documents are finalized, the project might need to be turned over to another group in the organization—for example, to the maintenance or operations group.

Saying Goodbye: The Project Turnover

Depending upon the project, you might need to coordinate the turnover of the project deliverables to the customer or to another group in your organization, such as the maintenance or operations group. The turnover requirements, such as training the help-desk employees, should have been included in the project management plan.

Standardize This

Figure 16.2 illustrates the three standard processes that can be used to close a project. All the items in these figures were discussed in this chapter.

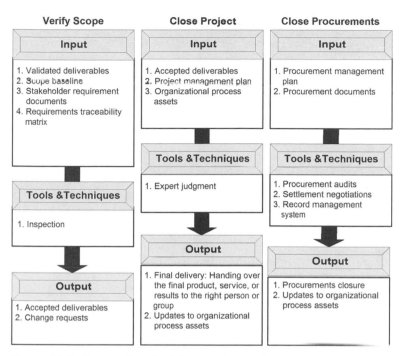

Figure 16.2 *Input, tools and techniques, and output for three processes: verify scope, close project, and close procurements.*

For logistical purpose, we have covered the verify scope process in this chapter. According to PMI, the verify scope process belongs to the monitoring and controlling process group, although in my opinion it should be part of the closing process group.

Quick Success Mantras

- Before the project closure begins, the scope of the project deliverables must be verified.

- The deliverables that were procured should be accepted through the procurement closure process.

- The project deliverables that have been accepted through the scope verification and procurement closure processes still need to go through final acceptance by the appropriate party, such as the customer or the sponsor.

- Not only the completed project, but the terminated project must also be closed formally.

Although the standard project processes are the same for each organization, the details and the manners in which they are implemented might be different for different organizations. Each organization can develop its own implementation details, which consist of items such as detailed steps for how to carry on the project processes, templates, meetings, and procedures.

- The processes of the closing process group can be used to close a completed project, a terminated project, or a project phase.
- The major results of a successful project closure are the acceptance of the project deliverables by the appropriate party and archiving the project documents, such as lessons learned and other project files.

Chapter 17

Project Management for Success

- The Big Picture of Project Management
- The Art and Science of Project Management
- The Top 10 Rules of Success in Project Management
- Quick Success Mantra

T he previous chapters of this book presented an introduction to the body of knowledge in the field of project management. Project management is the implementation of this body of knowledge. To become a successful project manager, you need to implement the appropriate parts of this knowledge to the project efforts at appropriate times.

Remember, project management is both an art and a science.

The first requirement for successful implementation of knowledge is to have the knowledge. The essential requirement for success is that all the pieces at the end should fall at the right places to generate the planned outcome of the project. For this to happen, you must have the big picture of project management in mind while paying attention to the details in implementing the pieces. One thing that helps in performing project management successfully is to realize that project management is both an art and a science. Throughout this book, I have offered tips and success shots to help you kick start your successful career in project management. In this chapter, I offer the top 10 rules of success in project management.

So, the central issue in this chapter is: Given the project management body of knowledge, how you can become a successful project manager. In search of an answer, we will explore three avenues: the big picture of project management, the art and science of project management, and the top 10 rules of success in project management.

In this chapter, you will:

- Understand the big picture of project management
- Understand how project management is both an art and a science
- Identify the top 10 rules of success in project management

The Big Picture of Project Management

Figure 17.1 presents the big picture of project management in a nutshell. As the name suggests, project management is about managing projects and therefore consists of two elements: a project and management. A project by definition is a definite effort that generates a unique product. The term *definite effort* means an effort that has a beginning and an end. This duration with a

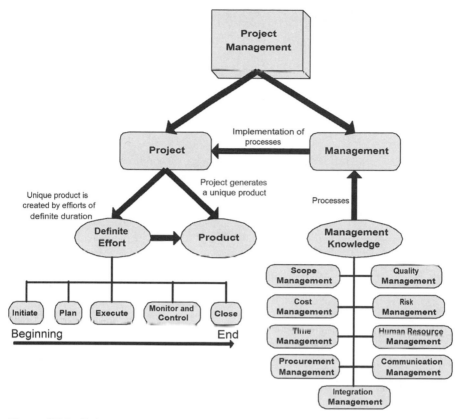

Figure 17.1 *Project management in a nutshell.*

beginning and an end holds five types, or stages, of efforts: initiate, plan, execute, monitor and control, and close.

This effort is managed by implementing the project management processes, which fall into nine knowledge areas: scope management, cost management, time management, procurement management, quality management, risk management, communication management, human resource management, and integration management.

So, project management is an implementation of processes from nine knowledge areas to the definite work effort being made to produce a unique product. Project management has two sides to it: art and science.

The Art and Science of Project Management

It will greatly help you to succeed if you understand that project management is both an art and a science. The science part is the whole framework of project management: five process groups, nine knowledge areas, and the relationships among them. The art part is to act—that is, to manage the effort by implementing the processes from the knowledge areas. This is called *implementation* of processes or project management knowledge. The science part of project management is to know, and the art part is to implement.

As Figure 17.2 illustrates, you can only implement if you know. Correct implementation will produce success, and wrong implementation will produce failure.

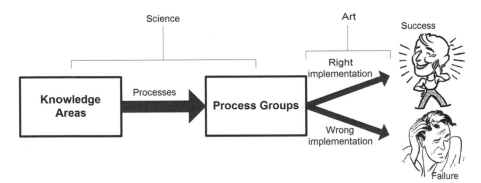

Figure 17.2 *Correct implementation equals success; incorrect implementation equals failure.*

The Top 10 Rules of Success in Project Management

As we discussed in Chapter 1, projects happen in your life all the time, regardless of whether you manage them. A managed project has a much better chance for success. Therefore, project management is an open secret to the success of projects. However, project management by itself does not guarantee the success of the projects. But successful (or effective) project management greatly enhances the chances for the success of a project.

Following are 10 important rules of successful project management:

1. **Initiate.** Initiate your project properly. The foundations for the success of a project are laid in the project definition. A poorly defined project is destined to fail. Initiation tells you where you are going.

2. **Plan.** Plan your project thoroughly. Without a plan you do not know whether your current path is leading to success or failure. Planning further defines where you are going, and it determines how to get there.

3. **Execute.** You can do all the planning in the world, but you will not get anything until you execute your plan—I'm stating the obvious here. Put together the best team you can to execute the plan.

4. **Monitor and control.** Even the best team in the world executing the best plan cannot succeed if you do not monitor and control the project. Only by monitoring and controlling will all the pieces come together to generate the planned output.

5. **Close.** Close the project properly. There is no success without completion, and there is no completion without a proper closure.

6. **Golden triangle.** Manage the triangle of scope, cost, and time very closely and carefully. If ignored, interdependencies can be detrimental to the success of your project, but they can be exploited to achieve success if they are properly managed. The greatest interdependency in project management is the triple constraint: scope, cost, and time.

7. **Critical path.** On your schedule, watch closely the critical paths. The delay in any activity on a critical path will delay the whole project.

8. **Scope creep.** Scope your project thoroughly. A loosely scoped project leaves a lot of room for scope creep. These projects can linger on forever, suck up all of your resources, and ultimately end in a failure.

9. **Comfort zone.** Your comfort zone is your greatest enemy. If you do not continuously push the boundaries drawn around your capabilities by the comfort zone, your listening

Effective project management itself doesn't guarantee the success of a project; however, it greatly increases your chances to achieve success.

capabilities (and therefore your communication skills) will be impaired, you will miss out on better ideas, you will hire less capable employees because a better employee may be outside of your comfort zone, and so on.

10. **Communication.** Communication is the thread that runs through the whole project lifetime.

Quick Success Mantra

The mother of all success mantras is: There is no substitute for experience. Take what you've learned in this and other books and apply it to perform project management. Learn from your experience, both successes and failures. In the long run, a failure can be turned into a success if you learn from it.

Happy and successful project management.

Go for it!

Index

procurement closure, 336–338
project assessment report, 339
project file archives, 336
releasing the resources, 339–340
reviewing the project, 339
standards, 340–341
success mantras, 341–342
terminated projects, 330
turnover requirements, 340
project communication management, 28–29
project control, 278–279
project cost management, 26
project definition document, 66–67
project execution
change requests, 229–230
components, 224–225
deliverables, 228–229
directing and managing, 226–231
goals of, 224
work performance data, 230–231
project integration management, 28
project management
advantages of, 19
functional management and, 19
implementation, 346
importance of, 6–7
management skills of, 41–42
overall efforts, 344–345
poorly managed projects, 5–6
process, 33
process illustration, 8
process mapping, 29–31
standards, 9–10
success mantras, 11, 34
successful project techniques, 346–348
timely implementation of knowledge concept, 7
what is, 18–20
why you should learn, 4–7
Project Management Body of Knowledge (PMBOK), 10–11

project management information system, 282
Project Management Institute (PMI), 10
Project Management Professional (PMP), 10
project management team, 57
project manager
challenges, 37
change agent, 38
change manager, 38
as coach, 41
excelling in project environment, 49
expectations and success factors, 46–47
as facilitator, 40
interpersonal skills of, 44–46
knowing your stakeholders, 47
as leader, 40–41
as mentor, 41
as navigator, 46
as organizer/planner, 40
as point person, 40
project charter, 69
roles of, 37–39
as stakeholder, 56
sub-roles, 40–41
success mantras, 59
project performance baseline, 186–187
project procurement management, 26
project progress, 316
project quality management, 27–28
project schedule network diagrams, 114–115
project scope
determining the scope, 94
identification of alternatives, 94
project charter, 68
project planning, 86–89
project scope statement, 95–98
stakeholder analysis, 94
project scope control, 304–305